THE

BLOOD COVENANT

A PRIMITIVE RITE

AND ITS BEARINGS ON SCRIPTURE

BY

H. CLAY TRUMBULL

The Blood Covenant, by H.Clay Trumbull
ISBN #0-89228-029-8

Copyright ©, 1975
  by Impact Books, Inc,
now **Impact Christian Books, Inc.**
332 Leffingwell Ave., Suite 101,
Kirkwood, MO 63122
314-822-3309

1975 First Printing
1981 Second Printing
1986 Third Printing
1991 Fourth Printing
1994 Fifth Printing
1998 Sixth Printing
2003 Seventh Printing

Printed in the United States of America

PREFACE TO THE FIRST EDITION.

It was while engaged in the preparation of a book —still unfinished—on the Sway of Friendship in the World's Forces,[1] that I came upon facts concerning the primitive rite of covenanting by the inter-trans-fusion of blood, which induced me to turn aside from my other studies, in order to pursue investigations in this direction.

Having an engagement to deliver a series of lectures before the Summer School of Hebrew, under Professor W. R. Harper, of Chicago, at the buildings of the Episcopal Divinity School, in Philadelphia, I decided to make this rite and its linkings the theme of that series; and I delivered three lectures, accordingly, June 16–18, 1885.

The interest manifested in the subject by those who heard the Lectures, as well as the importance of the theme itself, has seemed sufficient to warrant its presentation to a larger public. In this publishing, the form of the original Lectures has, for convenience' sake, been adhered to; although some considerable

---

[1] Since published, with the title of "Friendship the Master-Passion."

additions to the text, in the way of illustrative facts,
have been made since the delivery of the Lectures;
while other similar material is given in an Appendix.

From the very freshness of the subject itself, there
was added difficulty in gathering the material for its
illustration and exposition.   So far as I could learn,
no one had gone over the ground before me in this
particular line of research ; hence the various items
essential to a fair statement of the case must be
searched for through many diverse volumes of travel
and of history and of archæological compilation, with
only here and there an incidental disclosure in return.
Yet, each new discovery opened the way for other
discoveries beyond; and even after the Lectures, in
their present form, were already in type, I gained
many fresh facts, which I wish had been earlier available to me.   Indeed, I may say that no portion of the
volume is of more importance than the Appendix;
where are added facts and reasonings bearing directly
on well-nigh every main point of the original Lectures.

There is cause for just surprise that the chief facts
of this entire subject have been so generally overlooked, in the theological discussions, and in the
physio-sociological researches, of the earlier and the
later times.   Yet this only furnishes another illustration of the inevitably cramping influence of a preconceived fixed theory,—to which all the ascertained

facts must be conformed,—in any attempt at thorough and impartial scientific investigation. It would seem to be because of such cramping, that no one of the modern students of myth and folk-lore, of primitive ideas and customs, and of man's origin and history, has brought into their true prominence, if, indeed, he has even noticed them in passing, the universally dominating primitive convictions: that the blood is the life; that the heart, as the blood-fountain, is the very soul of every personality; that blood-transfer is soul-transfer; that blood-sharing, human, or divine-human, secures an inter-union of natures; and that a union of the human nature with the divine is the highest ultimate attainment reached out after by the most primitive, as well as by the most enlightened, mind of humanity.

Certainly, the collation of facts comprised in this volume grew out of no preconceived theory on the part of its author. Whatever theory shows itself in their present arrangement, is simply that which the facts themselves have seemed to enforce and establish, in their consecutive disclosure.

I should have been glad to take much more time for the study of this theme, and for the rearranging of its material, before its presentation to the public; but, with the pressure of other work upon me, the choice was between hurrying it out in its present shape, and postponing it indefinitely. All things considered, I chose the former alternative.

In the prosecution of my investigations, I acknowledge kindly aid from Professor Dr. Georg Ebers, Principal Sir William Muir, Dr. Yung Wing, Dean E. T. Bartlett, Professors Doctors John P. Peters and J. G. Lansing, the Rev. Dr. M. H. Bixby, Drs. D. G. Brinton and Charles W. Dulles, the Rev. Messrs. R. M. Luther and Chester Holcombe, and Mr. E. A. Barber; in addition to constant and valuable assistance from Mr. John T. Napier, to whom I am particularly indebted for the philological comparisons in the Oriental field, including the Egyptian, the Arabic, and the Hebrew.

At the best, my work in this volume is only tentative and suggestive. Its chief value is likely to be in its stimulating of others to fuller and more satisfactory research in the field here brought to notice. Sufficient, however, is certainly shown, to indicate that the realm of true biblical theology is as yet by no means thoroughly explored.

H. Clay Trumbull.

Philadelphia,
August 14, 1885.

PREFACE TO THE SECOND EDITION.

THE first edition of this work was soon exhausted, and a second was called for. But further investigations of mine in the same general field had revealed a new line of facts, which I desired to present in a supplement to a second edition. 1 wished, also, to give fuller proofs in the direction of specific exceptions taken by eminent critics to certain positions in the original work. Therefore I delayed the issue of a new edition.

Circumstances quite beyond my control have hindered me in the execution of my purpose until the present time. I now send out a new edition, with a Supplement containing important facts in the line of the original investigation. But much of the matter that I have discovered in other lines is reserved for a new work in the field of primitive covenants, including the Name Covenant, the Covenant of Salt, and the Threshold Covenant. This new work I hope to have ready at an early day.

The reception accorded to The Blood Covenant by scientists and theologians on both sides of the ocean was gratifying beyond my highest anticipations. From various directions I am hearing of the restatement of religious dogmas by prominent and influential Christian teachers, in the light newly thrown on the terminology of Scripture by the disclosures of this volume, and it is with pleasure that I respond to calls from all sides for a fresh edition of it.

In my careful revision of the work I am indebted for valuable aid to Professor Dr. Hermann V. Hilprecht, the eminent Assyriologist.

H. CLAY TRUMBULL.

PHILADELPHIA,
January 30, 1893.

CONTENTS.

LECTURE I.

THE PRIMITIVE RITE ITSELF.

LECTURE II.

SUGGESTIONS AND PERVERSIONS OF THE RITE.

ix

LECTURE III.

INDICATIONS OF THE RITE IN THE BIBLE.

APPENDIX.

SUPPLEMENT TO SECOND EDITION.

INDEXES.

LECTURE I.

THE PRIMITIVE RITE ITSELF

I.

THE PRIMITIVE RITE ITSELF.

THOSE who are most familiar with the Bible, and who have already given most time to its study, have largest desire and largest expectation of more knowledge through its farther study. And, more and more, Bible study has come to include very much that is outside of the Bible.

For a long time, the outside study of the Bible was directed chiefly to the languages in which the Bible was written, and to the archæology and the manners and customs of what are commonly known as the Lands of the Bible. Nor are these well-worked fields, by any means, yet exhausted. More still remains to be gleaned from them, each and all, than has been gathered thence by all searchers in their varied lore. But, latterly, it has been realized, that, while the Bible is an Oriental book, written primarily for Orientals, and therefore to be understood only through an

3

understanding of Oriental modes of thought and speech, it is also a record of God's revelation to the whole human race; hence its inspired pages are to receive illumination from all disclosures of the primitive characteristics and customs of that race, everywhere. Not alone those who insist on the belief that there was a gradual development of the race from a barbarous beginning, but those also who believe that man started on a higher plane, and in his degradation retained perverted vestiges of God's original revelation to him, are finding profit in the study of primitive myths, and of aboriginal religious rites and ceremonies, all the world over. Here, also, what has been already gained, is but an earnest of what will yet be compassed in the realm of truest biblical research.

2. AN ANCIENT SEMITIC RITE.

One of these primitive rites, which is deserving of more attention than it has yet received, as throwing light on many important phases of Bible teaching, is the rite of blood-covenanting: a form of mutual covenanting, by which two persons enter into the closest, the most enduring, and the most sacred of compacts, as friends and brothers, or as more than brothers, through the inter-commingling of their blood, by means of its mutual tasting, or of its inter-

transfusion. This rite is still observed in the un-
changing East; and there are historic traces of it,
from time immemorial, in every quarter of the globe;
yet it has been strangely overlooked by biblical
critics and biblical commentators generally, in these
later centuries.

In bringing this rite of the covenant of blood into
new prominence, it may be well for me to tell of it as
it was described to me by an intelligent native Syrian,
who saw it consummated in a village at the base of
the mountains of Lebanon; and then to add evidences
of its wide-spread existence in the East and elsewhere,
in earlier and in later times.

It was two young men, who were to enter into this
covenant. They had known each other, and had been
intimate, for years; but now they were to become
brother-friends, in the covenant of blood. Their relatives and neighbors were called together, in the open
place before the village fountain, to witness the sealing
compact. The young men publicly announced their
purpose, and their reasons for it. Their declarations
were written down, in duplicate,—one paper for each
friend,—and signed by themselves and by several witnesses. One of the friends took a sharp lancet, and
opened a vein in the other's arm. Into the opening
thus made, he inserted a quill, through which he
sucked the living blood. The lancet-blade was care-

fully wiped on one of the duplicate covenant-papers, and then it was taken by the other friend, who made a like incision in its first user's arm, and drank his blood through the quill, wiping the blade on the duplicate covenant-record. The two friends declared together: "We are brothers in a covenant made before God: who deceiveth the other, him will God deceive." Each blood-marked covenant-record was then folded carefully, to be sewed up in a small leathern case, or amulet, about an inch square; to be worn thenceforward by one of the covenant-brothers, suspended about the neck, or bound upon the arm, in token of the indissoluble relation.

The compact thus made, is called *M'âhadat ed-Dam* (معاهدة الدم), the "Covenant of Blood." The two persons thus conjoined, are *Akhwat el-M'âhadah* (اخوة المعاهدة), "Brothers of the Covenant." The rite itself is recognized, in Syria, as one of the very old customs of the land, as *'âdah qadeemeh* (عادة قديمة) "a primitive rite." There are many forms of covenanting in Syria, but this is the extremest and most sacred of them all. As it is the inter-commingling of very lives, nothing can transcend it. It forms a tie, or a union, which cannot be dissolved. In marriage, divorce is a possibility: not so in the covenant of blood. Although now comparatively rare, in view of its responsibilities and of its indissolubleness, this covenant is sometimes entered into by confidential partners in business, or by fellow-travelers; again, by robbers on the road—who would themselves rest fearlessly on its obligations, and who could be rested on within its limits, however untrustworthy they or their fellows might be in any other compact. Yet, again, it is the chosen compact of loving friends; of those who are drawn to it only by mutual love and trust.

This covenant is commonly between two persons of the same religion—Muhammadans, Druzes, or Nazarenes; yet it has been known between two persons of different religions;[1] and in such a case it would be held as a closer tie than that of birth[2] or sect. He who has entered into this compact with another, counts himself the possessor of a double life; for his friend, whose blood he has shared, is ready to lay down his life with him, or for him.[3] Hence the leathern case, or *Bayt hejâb* (بيت حجاب), "House of the amulet,"[4]

---

[1] Of the possibility of a covenant between those of different religions, Lane says (*Arab.-Eng. Lexicon*, s. v. *'Ahd*): "Hence ذو عهد (*dho 'ahd*), an appellation given to a Christian and a Jew (and a Sabean, who is a subject of a Muslim government), meaning one between whom and the Muslims a compact, or covenant, exists, whereby the latter are responsible for his security and freedom and toleration as long as he lives agreeably to the compact." And the Blood Covenant is more sacred and more binding than any other compact.

[2] Prov. 18 : 24.   [3] John 15 : 13.

[4] See Lane's *Lex.* s. v. "Hejâb."

containing the record of the covenant ('*uhdah*, عهدة), is counted a proud badge of honor by one who possesses it; and he has an added sense of security, because he will not be alone when he falleth.[1]

I have received personal testimony from native Syrians, concerning the observance of this rite in Damascus, in Aleppo, in Hâsbayya, in Abayh, along the road between Tyre and Sidon, and among the Koords resident in Salehayyah. All the Syrians who have been my informants, are at one concerning the traditional extreme antiquity of this rite, and its exceptional force and sacredness.

In view of the Oriental method of evidencing the closest possible affection and confidence by the sucking of the loved one's blood, there would seem to be more than a coincidence in the fact, that the Arabic words for friendship, for affection, for blood, and for leech, or blood-sucker, are but variations from a common root.[2] '*Alaqa* (علق) means "to love," "to adhere," "to feed." '*Alaq* (علق), in the singular, means "love," "friendship," "attachment," "blood." As the plural of '*alaqa* (علقة), '*alaq* means "leeches," or "blood-suckers." The truest friend clings like a leech, and draws blood in order to the sharing thereby of his friend's life and nature.

A native Syrian, who had traveled extensively in

---

[1] Eccl. 4:9, 10.   [2] See Freytag, and Catafago, s. v.

the East, and who was familiar with the covenant of
blood in its more common form, as already described,
told me of a practice somewhat akin to it, whereby a
bandit-chieftain would pledge his men to implicit and
unqualified life-surrendering fidelity to himself; or,
whereby a conspirator against the government would
bind, in advance, to his plans, his fellow conspirators,—
by a ceremony known as *Sharb el-'ahd* (شرب العهد),
" Drinking the covenant." The methods of such covenanting are various ; but they are all of the nature of
tests of obedience and of endurance. They sometimes include licking a heated iron with the tongue,
or gashing the tongue, or swallowing pounded glass or
other dangerous potions ; but, in all cases, the idea
seems to be, that the life of the one covenanting is, by
this covenant, devoted—surrendered as it were—to
the one with whom he covenants ; and the rite is
uniformly accompanied with a solemn and an imprecatory appeal to God as witnessing and guarding
the compact.

Dr. J. G. Wetzstein, a German scholar, diplomat,
and traveler, who has given much study to the peoples
east of the Jordan, makes reference to the binding
force and the profound obligation of the covenants of
brotherhood in that portion of the East; although
he gives no description of the methods of the covenant-rite. Speaking of two Bed'ween—Habbâs and

Hosayn—who had been "brothered" (*verbrüdert*), he explains by saying: "We must by this [term] understand the Covenant of Brotherhood (*Chuwwat el-Ahĕd* [خوة العهد]),[1] which is in use to-day not only among the Hadari [the Villagers], but also among the Bed'ween; and is indeed of pre-Muhammadan origin. The brother [in such a covenant] must guard the [other] brother from treachery, and [must] succor him in peril. So far as may be necessary, the one must provide for the wants of the other; and the survivor has weighty obligations in behalf of the family of the one deceased." Then, as showing how completely the idea of a common life in the lives of two friends thus covenanted—if, indeed, they have become sharers of the same blood—sways the Oriental mind, Wetzstein adds: "The marriage of a man and woman between whom this covenant exists, is held to be *incest*."[2]

There are, indeed, various evidences that the tie of blood-covenanting is reckoned, in the East, even a closer tie than that of natural descent; that a "friend" by this tie is nearer and is dearer, "sticketh closer," than a "brother" by birth. We, in the West, are accustomed to say that "blood is thicker than water"; but the Arabs have the idea that blood is thicker than milk,

---

[1] See "Brothers of the Covenant," p. 6, *supra.*

[2] *Sprachliches aus den Zeltlagern der syrischen Wüste*, p. 37.

than a mother's milk.   With them, any two children
nourished at the same breast are called " milk-brothers," [1] or " sucking brothers " ; [2] and the tie between
such is very strong.   A boy and a girl in this relation
cannot marry, even though by birth they had no family
relationship.   Among even the more bigoted of the
Druzes, a Druze girl who is a " sucking sister " of a
Nazarene boy is allowed a sister's privileges with him.
He can see her uncovered face, even to the time of
her marriage.   But the Arabs hold that brothers in
the covenant of blood are closer than brothers at a
common breast;   that those who have tasted each
other's blood are in a surer covenant than those who
have tasted the same milk together ; that " blood-lickers," [3] as the blood-brothers are sometimes called, are
more truly one than " milk-brothers," or " sucking
brothers " ; that, indeed, blood is thicker than milk, as
well as thicker than water.

   This distinction it is which seems to be referred to
in a citation from the Arabic poet El-A'asha, by the
Arabic lexicographer Qamus, which has been a puzzle to Lane, and Freytag, and others.[4]   Lane's transla-

   [1] See Redhouse's Turkish and English Dictionary, s. vv. *sood* and *soot*.
   [2] See Lane, and Freytag, s. vv. *rada 'a*, and *thady*.
   [3] See reference to Ibn Hishâm, 125, in Prof. W. Robertson Smith's
Old Test. in Jewish Church, Notes to Lect. XII. See, also, p. 59, *infra*.
   [4] See Lane, and Freytag, s. v. *sahama;* also Smith's *Old Test. in
Jewish Church*, Notes to Lect. XII.

tion of the passage is: " Two foster-brothers by the
sucking of the breast of one mother, swore together
by dark blood, into which they dipped their hands,
that they should not ever become separated." In other
words, two milk-brothers became blood-brothers by
interlocking their hands under their own blood in the
covenant of blood-friendship. They had been closely
inter-linked before; now they were as one; for blood is
thicker than milk. The oneness of nature which comes
of sharing the same blood, by its inter-transfusion, is
rightly deemed, by the Arabs, completer than the oneness of nature which comes of sharing the same milk;
or even than that which comes through having blood
from a common source, by natural descent.

3. THE PRIMITIVE RITE IN AFRICA.

Travelers in the heart of Africa, also, report the
covenant of "blood-brotherhood," or of "strong-friend-
ship," as in vogue among various African tribes, although naturally retaining less of primitive sacredness
there than among Semites. The rite is, in some cases,
observed after the manner of the Syrians, by the contracting parties tasting each other's blood; while, in
other cases, it is performed by the inter-transfusion of
blood between the two.

The first mention which I find of it, in the writings
of modern travelers in Africa, is by the lamented hero-

missionary, Dr. Livingstone. He calls the rite *Kasendi*. It was in the region of Lake Dilolo, at the watershed between the Indian Ocean and the Atlantic, in July, 1854, that he made blood-friendship, vicariously, with Queen Manenko, of the Balonda tribes.[1] She was represented, in this ceremony, by her husband, the ebony "Prince Consort"; while Livingstone's representative was one of his Makololo attendants. Woman's right to rule—when she has the right—seems to be as clearly recognized in Central Africa, to-day, as it was in Ethiopia in the days of Candace, or in Sheba in the days of Balkees.

Describing the ceremony, Livingstone says:[2] "It is accomplished thus: The hands of the parties are joined (in this case Pitsane and Sambanza were the parties engaged). Small incisions are made on the clasped hands, on the pits of the stomach of each, and on the right cheeks and foreheads. A small quantity of blood is taken off from these points, in both parties, by means of a stalk of grass. The blood from one person is put into a pot of beer, and that of the second into another; each then drinks the other's blood, and they are supposed to become perpetual friends, or relations. During the drinking of the beer, some of the party continue beat-

---

[1] See Livingstone's *Travels and Res. in So. Africa*, pp. 290–296.

[2] *Ibid.*, p. 525.

2

ing the ground with short clubs, and utter sentences
by way of ratifying the treaty. The men belonging
to each [principal's party], then finish the beer. The
principals in the performance of 'Kasendi' are henceforth considered blood-relations, and are bound to dis-
close to each other any impending evil. If Sekeletu
[chief of Pitsane's tribe—the Makololo—] should re-
solve to attack the Balonda [Sambanza's—or, more
properly, Manenko's—people], Pitsane would be under
obligation to give Sambanza warning to escape; and so
on the other side. [The ceremony concluded in this
case] they now presented each other with the most
valuable presents they had to bestow. Sambanza
walked off with Pitsane's suit of green baize faced
with red, which had been made in Loanda; and Pitsane, besides abundant supplies of food, obtained two
shells [of as great value, in regions far from the sea,
'as the Lord Mayor's badge is in London,'] similar to
that [one, which] I had received from Shinte [the uncle
of Manenko]."[1]

Of the binding force of this covenant, Livingstone
says farther: "On one occasion I became blood-relation to a young woman by accident. She had a large
cartilaginous tumor between the bones of the fore-
arm, which, as it gradually enlarged, so distended the
muscles as to render her unable to work. She ap-

[1] See Livingstone's *Travels and Res. in So. Africa*, p. 324 f.

plied to me to excise it. I requested her to bring her husband, if he were willing to have the operation performed; and while removing the tumor, one of the small arteries squirted some blood into my eye. She remarked, when I was wiping the blood out of it, ' You were a friend before; now you are a blood-relation; and when you pass this way always send me word, that I may cook food for you.' " [1]

Of the influence of these inter-tribal blood-friendships, in Central Africa, Dr. Livingstone speaks most favorably. Their primitive character is made the more probable, in view of the fact that he first found them existing in a region where, in his opinion, the dress and household utensils of the people are identical with those which are represented on the monuments of ancient Egypt.[2] Although it is within our own generation that this mode of covenanting in the region referred to has been made familiar to us, the rite itself is of old, elsewhere if not, indeed, there; as other travelers following in the track of Livingstone have noted and reported.

Commander Cameron, who, while in charge of the Livingstone Search Expedition, was the first European traveler to cross the whole breadth of the African continent in its central latitudes, gives several illustra-

---

[1] See Livingstone's *Travels and Res. in So. Africa,* p. 526.

[2] *Ibid.,* p. 213.

tions of the observance of this rite.   In June, 1874, at the westward of Lake Tanganyika, Syde, a guide of Cameron, entered into this covenant of blood with Pakwanya, a local chief.

"After a certain amount of palaver," says Cameron, "Syde and Pakwanya exchanged presents, much to the advantage of the former [for, in the East, the person of higher rank is supposed to give the more costly gifts in any such exchange] ; more especially [in this case] as he [Syde] borrowed the beads of me and afterward forgot to repay me. Pakwanya then performed a tune on his harmonium, or whatever the instrument [which he had] might be called, and the business of fraternizing was proceeded with. Pakwanya's head man acted as his sponsor, and one of my askari assumed the like office for Syde.

"The first operation consisted of making an incision on each of their right wrists, just sufficient to draw blood ; a little of which was scraped off and smeared on the other's cut; after which gunpowder was rubbed in [thereby securing a permanent token on the arm]. The concluding part of the ceremony was performed by Pakwanya's sponsor holding a sword resting on his shoulder, while he who acted [as sponsor] for Syde went through the motions of sharpening a knife upon it. Both sponsors meanwhile made a speech, calling down imprecations on Pakwanya and all his

relations, past, present, and future, and prayed that
their graves might be defiled by pigs if he broke the
brotherhood in word, thought, or deed. The same
form having been gone through with, [with] respect
to Syde, the sponsors changing duties, the brother-
making was complete."[1]

Concerning the origin of this rite, in this region,
Cameron says: "This custom of ' making brothers,'
I believe to be really of Semitic origin, and to have
been introduced into Africa by the heathen Arabs
before the days of Mohammed; and this idea is
strengthened by the fact that when the first traders
from Zanzibar crossed the Tanganyika, the ceremony
was unknown [so far as those traders knew] to the
westward of that lake."[2] Cameron was, of course,
unaware of the world-wide prevalence of this rite;
but his suggestion that its particular form just here
had a Semitic origin, receives support in a peculiar
difference noted between the Asiatic and the African
ceremonies.

It will be remembered, that, among the Syrians, the
blood of the covenant is taken into the mouth, and
the record of the covenant is bound upon the arm.
The Africans, not fully appreciating the force of a
written record, are in the habit of reversing this order,
according to Cameron's account. Describing the rite

[1] Cameron's *Across Africa*, I., 333.   [2] *Ibid.*, I., 333 f.

2*

as observed between his men and the natives, on the Luama River, he says: "The brotherhood business having been completed [by putting the blood from one party on to the arm of the other], some pen and ink marks were made on a piece of paper, which, together with a charge of powder, was put into a kettleful of water. All hands then drank of the decoction, the natives being told that it was a very great medicine."[1] That was "drinking the covenant"[2] with a vengeance; nor is it difficult to see how this idea originated.

The gallant and adventurous Henry M. Stanley also reports this rite of "blood-brotherhood," or of "strong friendship," in the story of his romantic experiences in the wilds of Africa. On numerous occasions the observance of this rite was a means of protection and relief to Stanley. One of its more notable illustrations was in his compact with "Mirambo, the warrior chief of Western Unyamwezi;"[3] whose leadership in warfare Stanley compares to that of both Frederick the Great[4] and Napoleon.[5]

It was during his first journey in pursuit of Livingstone, in 1871, that Stanley first encountered the forces of Mirambo, and was worsted in the conflict.[6] Writing

---

[1] *Across Africa,* I., 369.   [2] See page 9, *supra.*

[3] *Through the Dark Continent,* I., 107, 130 f.   [4] *Ibid.,* I., 492.

[5] *Ibid.,* I., 52, 492.   [6] *How I found Livingstone,* pp. 267–304.

of him, after his second expedition, Stanley describes Mirambo, as "the 'Mars of Africa,' who since 1871 has made his name feared by both native and foreigner from Usui to Urori, and from Uvinza to Ugogo, a country embracing 90,000 square miles; who, from the village chieftainship over Uyoweh, has made for himself a . name as well known as that of Mtesa throughout the eastern half of Equatorial Africa; a household word from Nyangwé to Zanzibar, and the theme of many a song of the bards of Unyamwezi, Ukimbu, Ukonongo, Uzinja, and Uvinza."[1]   For a time, during his second exploring expedition, Stanley was inclined to avoid Mirambo, but becoming "impressed with his ubiquitous powers,"[2] he decided to meet him, and if possible make "strong friendship" with him. They came together, first, at Serombo, April 22, 1876. Mirambo "quite captivated" Stanley. "He was a thorough African *gentleman* in appearance. . . . A handsome, regular-featured, mild-voiced, soft-spoken man, with what one might call a 'meek' demeanor; very generous and open-handed;" his eyes having "the steady, calm gaze of a master."[3]

The African hero and the heroic American agreed to "make strong friendship" with each other. Stanley thus describes the ceremony: "Manwa Sera [Stanley's

[1] *Thro. Dark Cont.*, I., 489 f.   [2] *Ibid.*, I., 130.

[3] *Ibid.*, I., 487–492.

'chief captain'] was requested to seal our friendship by performing the ceremony of blood-brotherhood between Mirambo and myself. Having caused us to sit fronting each other on a straw-carpet, he made an incision in each of our right legs, from which he extracted blood, and inter-changing it, he exclaimed aloud : ' If either of you break this brotherhood now established between you, may the lion devour him, the serpent poison him, bitterness be in his food, his friends desert him, his gun burst in his hands and wound him, and everything that is bad do wrong to him until death.'" [1] The same blood now flowed in the veins of both Stanley and Mirambo. They were friends and brothers in a sacred covenant; life for life. At the conclusion of the covenant, they exchanged gifts; as the customary ratification, or accompaniment, of the compact. They even vied with each other in proofs of their unselfish fidelity, in this new covenant of friendship.[2]

Again and again, before and after this incident, Stanley entered into the covenant of blood-brotherhood with representative Africans; in some instances by the opening of his own veins; at other times by allowing one of his personal escort to bleed for him. In January, 1875, a "great magic doctor of Vinyata" came to Stanley's tent to pay a friendly visit, "bringing with him a fine, fat ox as a peace offering." After

[1] *Thro. Dark Cont.*, I., 493.   [2] *Ibid.*, I., 493 f.

an exchange of gifts, says Stanley, "he entreated me to go through the process of blood-brotherhood, which I underwent with all the ceremonious gravity of a pagan."[1]

Three months later, in April, 1875, when Stanley found himself and his party in the treacherous toils of Shekka, the King of Bumbireh, he made several vain attempts to "induce Shekka, with gifts, to go through the process of blood-brotherhood." Stanley's second captain, Safeni, was the adroit, but unsuccessful, agent in the negotiations. "Go frankly and smilingly, Safeni, up to Shekka, on the top of that hill," said Stanley, "and offer him these three fundo of beads, and ask him to exchange blood with you." But the wily king was not to be dissuaded from his warlike purposes in that way. "Safeni returned. Shekka had refused the pledge of peace."[2] His desire was to take blood, if at all, without any exchange.

After still another three months, in July, 1875, Stanley, at Refuge Island, reports better success in securing peace and friendship through blood-giving and blood-receiving. "Through the influence of young Lukanjah—the cousin of the King of Ukerewé"—he says, "the natives of the mainland had been induced to exchange their churlish disposition for one of cordial welcome; and the process of blood-brotherhood had

[1] *Thro. Dark Cont.*, I., 123.   [2] *Ibid.*, I., 227–237.

been formally gone through [with], between Manwa Sera, on my part, and Kijaju, King of Komeh, and the King of Itawagumba, on the other part." [1]

It was at " Kampunzu, in the district of Uvinza, where dwell the true aborigines of the forest country," —a people whom Stanley afterwards found to be cannibals—that this rite was once more observed between the explorers and the natives. " Blood-brotherhood being considered as a pledge of good-will and peace," says Stanley, " Frank Pocock [a young Englishman who was an attendant of Stanley] and the chief [of Kampunzu] went through the ordeal ; and we interchanged presents "—as is the custom in the observance of this rite. [2]

At the island of Mpika, on the Livingstone River, in December, 1876, there was another bright episode in Stanley's course of travel, through this mode of sealing friendship. Disease had been making sad havoc in Stanley's party. He had been compelled to fight his way along through a region of cannibals. While he was halting for a breakfast on the river bank over against Mpika, an attack on him was preparing by the excited inhabitants of the island. Just then his scouts captured a native trading party of men and women who were returning to Mpika, from inland ; and to them his interpreters made clear his pacific

[1] *Thro. Dark Cont.*, I., 268.   [2] *Ibid.*, II., 144–146.

intentions. "By means of these people," he says, "we succeeded in checking the warlike demonstrations of the islanders, and in finally persuading them to make blood-brotherhood; after which we invited canoes to come and receive [these hostages] their friends. As they hesitated to do so, we embarked them in our own boat, and conveyed them across to the island. The news then spread quickly along the whole length of the island that we were friends, and as we resumed our journey, crowds from the shore cried out to us, '*Mwende Ki-vuké-vuké*' ('Go in peace!')"[1]

Once more it was at the conclusion of a bloody conflict, in the district of Vinya-Njara, just below Mpika Island, that peace was sealed by blood. When practical victory was on Stanley's side, at the cost of four of his men killed, and thirteen more of them wounded, then he sought this means of amity. "With the aid of our interpreters," he says, "we communicated our terms, viz., that we would occupy Vinya-Njara, and retain all the canoes unless they made peace. We also informed them that we had one prisoner, who would be surrendered to them if they availed themselves of our offer of peace: that we had suffered heavily, and they had also suffered; that war was an evil which wise men avoided; that if they came with two canoes with their chiefs, two canoes

[1] *Thro. Dark Cont.*, II., 177 f.

with our chiefs should meet them in mid-stream, and make blood-brotherhood; and that on that condition some of their canoes should be restored, and we would purchase the rest." The natives took time for the considering of this proposition, and then accepted it. "On the 22nd of December, the ceremony of blood-brotherhood having been formally concluded, in mid-river, between Safeni and the chief of Vinya-Njara," continues Stanley, "our captive, and fifteen canoes, were returned, and twenty-three canoes were retained by us for a satisfactory equivalent; and thus our desperate struggle terminated." [1]

On the Livingstone, just below the Equator, in February, 1877, Stanley's party was facing starvation, having been for some time "unable to purchase food, or indeed [to] approach a settlement for any amicable purpose." The explorers came to look at "each other as fated victims of protracted famine, or [of] the rage of savages, like those of Mangala." "We continued our journey," goes on the record, "though grievously hungry, past Bwena and Inguba, doing our utmost to induce the staring fishermen to communicate with us; without any success. They became at once officiously busy with guns, and dangerously active. We arrived at Ikengo, and as we were almost despairing, we proceeded to a small island opposite this settlement, and

[1] *Thro. Dark Cont.*, II., 188.

prepared to encamp. Soon a canoe with seven men came dashing across, and we prepared our moneys for exhibition. They unhesitatingly advanced, and ran their canoe alongside of us. We were rapturously joyful, and returned them a most cordial welcome, as the act was a most auspicious sign of confidence. We were liberal, and the natives fearlessly accepted our presents; and from this giving of gifts we proceeded to seal this incipient friendship with our blood, with all due ceremony."[1] And by this transfusion of blood the starving were re-vivified, and the despairing were given hope.

Twice, again, within a few weeks after this experience, there was a call on Stanley of blood for blood, in friendship's compact. The people of Chumbiri welcomed the travelers. "They readily subscribed to all the requirements of friendship, blood-brotherhood, and an exchange of a few small gifts."[2] Itsi, the king of Ntamo, with several of his elders and a showy escort, came out to meet Stanley; and there was a friendly greeting on both sides. "They then broached the subject of blood-brotherhood. We were willing," says Stanley, "but they wished to defer the ceremony until they had first shown their friendly feelings to us." Thereupon gifts were exchanged, and the king indicated his preference for a "big goat" of Stanley's,

[1] *Thro. Dark Cont.*, II., 305 f.   [2] *Ibid.*, II., 315.

3

as his benefaction—which, after some parleying, was transferred to him. Then came the covenant-rite. "The treaty with Itsi," says Stanley, "was exceedingly ceremonious, and involved the exchange of charms. Itsi transferred to me for my protection through life, a small gourdful of a curious powder, which had rather a saline taste; and I delivered over to him, as the white man's charm against all evil, a half-ounce vial of magnesia; further, a small scratch in Frank's arm, and another in Itsi's arm, supplied blood sufficient to unite us in one, and [by an] indivisible bond of fraternity."[1]

Four years after this experience of blood-covenanting, by proxy, with young Itsi, Stanley found himself again at Ntamo, or across the river from it; this time in the interest of the International Association of the Congo. Being short of food, he had sent out a party of foragers, and was waiting their return with interest. "During the absence of the food-hunters," he says, "we heard the drums of Ntamo, and [we] followed with interested eyes the departure of two large canoes from the landing-place, their ascent to the place opposite, and their final crossing over towards us. Then we knew that Ngalyema of Ntamo had condescended to come and visit us. As soon as he arrived I recognized him as the Itsi with whom, in 1877, I

[1] *Thro. Dark Cont.*, II., 330–332.

had made blood-brotherhood [by proxy]. During
the four years that had elapsed, he had become a
great man. . . . He was now about thirty-four
years old, of well-built form, proud in his bearing,
covetous and grasping in disposition, and, like all
other lawless barbarians, prone to be cruel and sanguinary whenever he might safely vent his evil humor.
Superstition had found in him an apt and docile pupil,
and fetishism held him as one of its most abject
slaves. This was the man in whose hands the desti-
nies of the Association Internationale du Congo were
held, and upon whose graciousness depended our only
hope of being able to effect a peaceful lodgment on
the Upper Congo." A pagan African was an African
pagan, even while the blood-brother of a European
Christian. Yet, the tie of blood-covenanting was the
strongest tie known in Central Africa. Frank Pocock,
whose covenant-blood flowed in Itsi's veins, was
dead;[1] yet for his sake his master, Stanley, was welcomed by Itsi as a brother; and in true Eastern
fashion he was invited to prove anew his continuing
faith by a fresh series of love-showing gifts. " My
brother being the supreme lord of Ntamo, as well as
the deepest-voiced and most arrogant rogue among
the whole tribe," says Stanley, " first demanded the
two asses [which Stanley had with him], then a large

[1] *Thro. Dark Cont.*, II., 402–408.

mirror, which was succeeded by a splendid gold-em-
broidered coat, jewelry, glass clasps, long brass chains,
a figured table-cloth, fifteen other pieces of fine cloth,
and a japanned tin box with a 'Chubb' lock. Finally,
gratified by such liberality, Ngalyema surrendered to
me his sceptre, which consisted of a long staff, banded
profusely with brass, and decorated with coils of brass
wire, which was to be carried by me and shown to all
men that I was the brother of Ngalyema [or, Itsi] of
Ntamo!"[1] Some time after this, when trouble arose
between Stanley and Ngalyema, the former suggested
that perhaps it would be better to cancel their brotherhood. "'No, no, no,' cried Ngalyema, anxiously; 'our
brotherhood cannot be broken; our blood is now
one.'" Yet at this time Stanley's brotherhood with
Ngalyema was only by the blood of his deceased
retainer, Frank Pocock.

More commonly, the rite of blood-friendship among
the African tribes seems to be by the inter-transfusion
of blood; but the ancient Syrian method is by no
means unknown on that continent. Stanley tells of
one crisis of hunger, among the cannibals of Rubunga,
when the hostility of the natives on the river bank
was averted by a shrewd display of proffered trinkets
from the boats of the expedition. "We raised our
anchor," he says, "and with two strokes of the oars

[1] *The Congo*, I., 304-312.

had run our boat ashore; and, snatching a string or two of cowries [or shell-money], I sprang on land, followed by the coxswain Uledi, and in a second I had seized the skinny hand of the old chief, and was pressing it hard for joy. Warm-hearted Uledi, who the moment before was breathing furious hate of all savages, and of the procrastinating old chief in particular, embraced him with a filial warmth. Young Saywa, and Murabo, and Shumari, prompt as tinder upon all occasions, grasped the lesser chiefs' hands, and devoted themselves with smiles and jovial frank bearing to conquer the last remnants of savage sullenness, and succeeded so well that, in an incredible short time, the blood-brotherhood ceremony between the suddenly formed friends was solemnly entered into, and the irrevocable pact of peace and good will had been accomplished."[1]

Apparently unaware of the method of the ancient Semitic rite, here found in a degraded form, Stanley seems surprised at the mutual tasting of blood between the contracting friends, in this instance. He says: " Blood-brotherhood was a beastly cannibalistic ceremony with these people, yet much sought after,— whether for the satisfaction of their thirst for blood, or that it involved an interchange of gifts, of which they must needs reap the most benefit. After an incision

[1] *Thro. Dark Cont.*, II., 281–283.

3*

was made in each arm, both brothers bent their heads, and the aborigine was observed to suck with the greatest fervor; whether for love of blood or excess of friendship, it would be difficult to say."[1]

During his latest visit to Africa, in the Congo region, Stanley had many another occasion to enter into the covenant of blood with native chiefs, or to rest on that covenant as before consummated. His every description of the rite itself has its value, as illustrating the varying forms and the essential unity of the ceremony of blood-covenanting, the world over.

A reference has already been made[2] to Stanley's meeting, on this expedition, with Ngalyema, who, under the name of Itsi, had entered into blood-brotherhood with Frank Pocock, four years before. That brotherhood by proxy had several severe strains, in the progress of negotiations between Stanley and Ngalyema; and after some eight months of these varying experiences, it was urgently pressed on Stanley by the chiefs of Kintamo (which is another name for Ntamo), that he should personally covenant by blood with Ngalyema, and so put an end to all danger of conflict between them. To this Stanley assented, and the record of the transaction is given accordingly, under date of April 9, 1882: "Brotherhood with Ngalyema was performed. We crossed arms; an incision

---

[1] *Thro. Dark Cont.*, II., 286.   [2] See pages 26-28, *supra.*

was made in each arm; some salt was placed on the
wound, and then a mutual rubbing took place, while
the great fetish man of Kintamo pronounced an incon-
ceivable number of curses on my head if ever I proved
false.   Susi [Livingstone's head man, now with Stan-
ley], not to be outdone by him, solicited the gods to
visit unheard-of atrocious vengeances on Ngalyema if
he dared to make the slightest breach in the sacred
brotherhood which made him and Bula Matari[1] one
and indivisible for ever."[2]

In June, 1883, Stanley visited, by invitation, Mangombo, the chief of Irebu, on the Upper Congo, and
became his blood-brother.   Describing his landing at
this "Venice of the Congo," he says: "Mangombo,
with a curious long staff, a fathom and a half in length,
having a small spade of brass at one end, much resembling a baker's cake-spade, stood in front.   He was a
man probably sixty years old, but active and by no
means aged-looking, and he waited to greet me.
.   .   .   Generally the first day of acquaintance with
the Congo river tribes is devoted to chatting, sound-
ing one another's principles, and getting at one another's ideas.   The chief entertains his guest with gifts
of food, goats, beer, fish, &c.; then, on the next day,

---

[1] "Bula Matari," or "Rock Breaker," or Road Maker, was a name
given to Stanley by the natives.

[2] *The Congo*, I., 383–385.

commences business and reciprocal exchange of gifts.
So it was at Irebu.   Mangombo gave four hairy thin-
tailed sheep, ten glorious bunches of bananas, two
great pots of beer, and the usual accompaniments of
small stores.   The next day we made blood-brotherhood.   The fetish-man pricked each of our right arms,
pressed the blood out; then, with a pinch of scrapings
from my gun stock, a little salt, a few dusty scrapings
from a long pod, dropped over the wounded arms,
. . . the black and white arms were mutually rubbed
together [for the inter-transfusion of the flowing
blood].   The fetish-man took the long pod in his
hand, and slightly touched our necks, our heads, our
arms, and our legs, muttering rapidly his litany of
incantations.   What was left of the medicine Mangombo and I carefully folded in a banana leaf [Was
this the 'house of the amulet?'[1]], and we bore it
reverently between us to a banana grove close by, and
buried the dust out of sight.   Mangombo, now my
brother, by solemn interchange of blood,—consecrated
to my service, as I was devoted in the sacred fetish
bond to his service,—revealed his trouble, and im-
plored my aid."[2]

Yet again, Stanley "made friendship" with th.
Bakuti, at Wangata, "after the customary forms of
blood-brotherhood";[3] similarly with two chiefs, Iuka

[1] See page 7 f., *supra.*   [2] *The Congo*, II., 21-24.   [3] *Ibid.*, II., 38.

and Mungawa, at Lukolela ;[1] with Miyongo of Usindi ;[2] and with the chiefs of Bolombo ;[3] of Yambinga,[4]
of Mokulu,[5] of Irungu,[6] of Upoto,[7] of Uranga ;[8] and
so all along his course of travel. One of the fullest
and most picturesque of his descriptions of this
rite, is in connection with its observance with a son
of the great chief of the Bangala, at Iboko ; and the
main details of that description are worthy of repro-
duction here.

The Bangala, or "the Ashantees of the Livingstone
River," as Stanley characterizes them, are a strong
and a superior people, and they fought fiercely against
Stanley, when he was passing their country in 1877.[9]
" The senior chief, Mata Bwyki (lord of many guns),
was [now, in October, 1883,] an old grey-haired man,"
says Stanley, " of Herculean stature and breadth of
shoulder, with a large square face, and an altogether
massive head, out of which his solitary eye seemed to
glare with penetrative power. I should judge him to
be six feet, two inches, in height. He had a strong,
sonorous voice, which, when lifted to speak to his
tribe, was heard clearly several hundred yards off.
He was now probably between seventy-five and eighty

[1] *The Congo*, II., 48. [2] *Ibid.*, II., 68. [3] *Ibid.*, II., 79.
[4] *Ibid.*, II., 109. [5] *Ibid.*, II., 118. [6] *Ibid.*, II., 132.
[7] *Ibid.*, II., 171. [8] *Ibid.*, II., 177.
[9] *Thro. Dark Cont.*, II., 297–302.

years old. . . . He was not the tallest man, nor
the best looking, nor the sweetest-dispositioned man, I
had met in all Africa; but if the completeness and
perfection of the human figure, combining size with
strength, and proportion of body, limbs, and head,
with an expression of power in the face, be considered,
he must have been at one time the grandest type of
physical manhood to be found in Equatorial Africa.
As he stood before us on this day, we thought of him
as an ancient Milo, an aged Hercules, an old Samson—
a really grand looking old man. At his side were seven
tall sons, by different mothers, and although they were
stalwart men and boys, the whitened crown of Mata
Bwyki's head rose by a couple of inches above the
highest head."

Nearly two thousand persons assembled, at Iboko,
to witness the " palaver" that must precede a decision
to enter into "strong friendship." At the place of
meeting, "mats of split rattan were spread in a large
semicircle around a row of curved and box stools, for
the principal chiefs. In the centre of the line, opposite
this, was left a space for myself and people," continues
Stanley. "We had first to undergo the process of
steady and silent examination from nearly two thous-
and pairs of eyes. Then, after Yumbila, the guide, had
detailed in his own manner, who we were, and what was
our mission up the great river; how we had built towns

at many places, and made blood-brotherhood with the chiefs of great districts, such as Irebu, Ukuti, Usindi, Ngombé, Lukolela, Bolobo, Mswata, and Kintamo, he urged upon them the pleasure it would be to me to make a like compact, sealed with blood, with the great chiefs of populous Iboko. He pictured the benefits likely to accrue to Iboko, and Mata Bwyki in particular, if a bond of brotherhood was made between two chiefs like Mata Bwyki and Tandelay, [Stanley,] or as he was known, Bula Matari."

There was no prompt response to Stanley's request for strong friendship with the Bangala. There were prejudices to be removed, and old memories to be overborne; and Yumbila's eloquence and tact were put to their severest test, in the endeavor to bring about a state of feeling that would make the covenant of blood a possibility here. But the triumph was won. "A forked palm branch was brought," says Stanley. " Kokoro, the heir [of Mata Bwyki], came forward, seized it, and kneeled before me; as, drawing out his short falchion, he cried, ' Hold the other branch, Bula Matari!' I obeyed him, and lifting his hand he cleaved the branch in two. ' Thus,' he said, ' I declare my wish to be your brother.'

" Then a fetish-man came forward with his lancets, long pod, pinch of salt, and fresh green banana leaf. He held the staff of Kokoro's sword-bladed spear,

while one of my rifles was brought from the steamer.
The shaft of the spear and the stock of the rifle were
then scraped on the leaf, a pinch of salt was dropped
on the wood, and finally a little dust from the long
pod was scraped on the curious mixture. Then, our
arms were crossed,—the white arm over the brown
arm,—and an incision was made in each; and over the
blood was dropped a few grains of the dusty compound; and the white arm was rubbed over the brown
arm [in the intermingling of blood]."

"Now Mata Bwyki lifted his mighty form, and with
his long giant's staff drove back the compressed
crowd, clearing a wide circle, and then roaring out in
his most magnificent style, leonine in its lung-force,
kingly in its effect: 'People of Iboko! You by the
river side, and you of inland. Men of the Bangala,
listen to the words of Mata Bwyki. You see Tandelay before you. His other name is Bula Matari. He
is the man with the many canoes, and has brought
back strange smoke-boats. He has come to see Mata
Bwyki. He has asked Mata Bwyki to be his friend.
Mata Bwyki has taken him by the hand, and has become his blood-brother. Tandelay belongs to Iboko
now. He has become this day one of the Bangala.
O, Iboko! listen to the voice of Mata Bwyki.' (I
thought they must have been incurably deaf, not to
have heard that voice). 'Bula Matari and Mata Bwyki

are one to-day. We have joined hands. Hurt not
Bula Matari's people; steal not from them; offend
them not. Bring food and sell to him at a fair price,
gently, kindly, and in peace; for he is my brother.
Hear you, ye people of Iboko—you by the river
side, and you of the interior?'

"'We hear, Mata Bwyki!' shouted the multitude."[1]
And the ceremony was ended.

A little later than this, Stanley, or Tandelay, or
Bula Matari, as the natives called him, was at Bumba,
and there again he exchanged blood in friendship.
"Myombi, the chief," he says, "was easily persuaded
by Yumbila to make blood-brotherhood with me; and
for the fiftieth time my poor arm was scarified, and
my blood shed for the cause of civilization. Probably
one thousand people of both sexes looked on the
scene, wonderingly and strangely. A young branch
of a palm was cut, twisted, and a knot tied at each
end; the knots were dipped in wood ashes, and then
seized and held by each of us, while the medicine-
man practised his blood-letting art, and lanced us both,
until Myombi winced with pain; after which the
knotted branch was severed; and, in some incompre-
hensible manner, I had become united forever to my
fiftieth brother; to whom I was under the obligation
of defending [him] against all foes until death."[2]

[1] *The Congo*, II., 79–90.   [2] *Ibid.*, II., 104 f.

4

The blood of a fair proportion of all the first families of Equatorial Africa now courses in Stanley's
veins; and if ever there was an American citizen who
could appropriate to himself pre-eminently the national
motto, "E pluribus unum," Stanley is the man.

The root-idea of this rite of blood-friendship seems
to include the belief, that the blood is the life of a
living being; not merely that the blood is *essential* to
life, but that, in a peculiar sense, it *is* life; that it
actually vivifies by its presence; and that by its passing from one organism to another it carries and
imparts life. The inter-commingling of the blood of
two organisms is, therefore, according to this view,
equivalent to the inter-commingling of the lives, of the
personalities, of the natures, thus brought together;
so that there is, thereby and thenceforward, one life in
the two bodies, a common life between the two friends:
a thought which Aristotle recognizes in his citation of
the ancient " proverb " : " One soul [in two bodies]," [1]
a proverb which has not lost its currency in any of the
centuries.

That the blood can retain its vivifying power whether
passing into another by way of the lips or by way of the
veins, is, on the face of it, no less plausible, than that

[1] Aristotle's *Ethics*, IX., 8, 3. This is not made as an original statement, by Aristotle, but as the citation of one of the well-known
" proverbs " of friendship.

the administering of stimulants, tonics, nutriments, nervines, or anæsthetics, hypodermically, may be equally potent, in certain cases, with the more common and normal method of seeking assimilation by the process of digestion. That the blood of the living has a peculiar vivifying force, in its transference from one organism to another, is one of the clearly proven re-disclosures of modern medical science ; and this transference of blood has been made to advantage by way of the veins, of the stomach, of the intestines, of the tissue, and even of the lungs—through dry-spraying.[1]

4. TRACES OF THE RITE IN EUROPE.[2]

Different methods of observing this primitive rite of blood-covenanting are indicated in the legendary lore of the Norseland peoples ; and these methods, in all their variety, give added proof of the ever underlying idea of an inter-commingling of lives through an inter-commingling of blood. Odin was the beneficent god of light and knowledge, the promoter of heroism, and the protector of sacred covenants, in the mythology of the North. Lôké, or Lok, on the other hand, was the discordant and corrupting divinity ;

[1] See *Nouveau Dictionnaire de Médecine et de Chirurgie Pratiques,* (ed. 1884) s. v. " Transfusion."   [2] See Appendix, *infra.*

symbolizing, in his personality, " sin, shrewdness, deceitfulness, treachery, malice," and other phases of evil.[1] In the poetic myths of the Norseland, it is claimed that at the beginning Odin and Lôké were in close union instead of being at variance;[2] just as the Egyptian cosmogony made Osiris and Set in original accord, although in subsequent hostility;[3] and as the Zoroastrians claimed that Ormuzd and Ahriman were at one, before they were in conflict.[4] Odin and Lôké are, indeed, said to have been, at one time, in the close and sacred union of blood-friendship; having covenanted in that union by mingling their blood in a bowl, and drinking therefrom together.

The Elder Edda,[5] or the earliest collection of Scandinavian songs, makes reference to this confraternity of Odin and Lôké. At a banquet of the gods, Lôké, who had not been invited, found an entrance, and there reproached his fellow divinities for their hostility to him. Recalling the indissoluble tie of blood-friendship, he said:

[1] See Carlyle's *Heroes and Hero-Worship*, Lect. I.; also Anderson's *Norse Mythology*, pp. 215–220; 371–374.

[2] See Anderson's *Norse Mythol.*, pp. 372, 408 f.

[3] See Wilkinson's *Ancient Egyptians*, III., 142; Renouf's *The Religion of Ancient Egypt*, p. 118 f.; Ebers's *Picturesque Egypt*, I., 100 f.

[4] See De Wette's *Biblische Dogmatik*, § 79.

[5] See Carlyle's *Hero Worship*, Lect. I.

" Father of Slaughter,[1] Odin, say,
　　Rememberest not the former day,
　　When ruddy in the goblet stood,
　　For mutual drink, our blended blood?
　　Rememberest not, thou then didst swear,
　　The festive banquet ne'er to share,
　　Unless thy brother Lok was there?"

In citing this illustration of the ancient rite, a
modern historian of chivalry has said: "Among barbarous people [the barbarians of Eu.ope] the fraternity
of arms [the sacred brotherhood of heroes] was established by the horrid custom of the new brothers drinking each other's blood; but if this practice was barbarous, nothing was farther from barbarism than the
sentiment which inspired it."[2]

Another of the methods by which the rite of blood-
friendship was observed in the Norseland, was by
causing the blood of the two covenanting persons to
inter-flow from their pierced hands, while they lay
together underneath a lifted sod. The idea involved
seems to have been, the burial of the two individuals,
in their separate personal lives, and the intermingling
of those lives—by the intermingling of their blood—
while in their temporary grave; in order to their

---

[1] Odin "is the author of war." He is called "Valfather (Father of the
slain), because he chooses for his sons all who fall in combat." Anderson's *Norse Mythol.*, p. 215 f.

[2] Mills's *History of Chivalry*, chap. IV.

rising again with a common life[1]—one life, one soul, in two bodies. Thus it is told, in one of the Icelandic Sagas, of Thorstein, the heroic son of Viking, proffering "foster-brotherhood," or blood-friendship, to the valiant Angantyr, Jarl of the Orkneys. "Then this was resolved upon, and secured by firm pledges on both sides. They opened a vein in the hollow of their hands, crept beneath the sod, and there [with clasped hands inter-blood-flowing] they solemnly swore that each of them should avenge the other if any one of them should be slain by weapons." This was, in fact, a three-fold covenant of blood; for King Bele, who had just been in combat with Angantyr, was already in blood-friendship with Thorstein.[2]

The rite of blood-friendship, in one form and another, finds frequent mention in the Norseland Sagas. Thus, in the Saga of Fridthjof the Bold, the son of Thorstein:

"Champions twelve, too, had he—gray-haired, and princes in exploits,—
Comrades his father had loved, steel-breasted and scarred o'er the forehead.
Last on the champions' bench, equal-aged with Fridthjof, a stripling
Sat, like a rose among withered leaves; Bjorn called they the hero—
Glad as a child, but firm like a man, and yet wise as a graybeard;
Up with Fridthjof he'd grown; they had mingled blood with each other,
Foster-brothers in Northman wise; and they swore to continue
Steadfast in weal and woe, each other revenging in battle."[3]

[1] Rom. 6 : 4–6; Col. 2 : 12
[2] Anderson's *Viking Tales of the North*, p. 59.   [3] *Ibid.*, p. 191 f.

A vestige of this primitive rite, coming down to us through European channels, is found, as are so many other traces of primitive rites, in the inherited folk-lore of English-speaking children on both sides of the Atlantic. An American clergyman's wife said recently, on this point: "I remember, that while I was a school-girl, it was the custom, when one of our companions pricked her finger, so that the blood came, for one or another of us to say 'Oh, let me suck the blood; then we shall be friends.'" And that is but an illustration of the outreaching after this indissoluble bond, on the part of thirty generations of children of Norseland and Anglo-Saxon stock, since the days of Fridthjof and Bjorn; as that same yearning had been felt by those of a hundred generations before that time.

5. WORLD-WIDE SWEEP OF THE RITE.

Concerning traces of the rite of blood-covenanting in China, where there are to be found fewest resemblances to the primitive customs of the Asiatic Semites, Dr. Yung Wing, the eminent Chinese educationalist and diplomat, gives me the following illustration: "In the year 1674, when Kănhi was Emperor, of the present dynasty, we find that the Buddhist priests of Shanlin Monastery in Fuhkin Province had rebelled against the authorities on account of persecution. In their encounters with the troops, they fought against great odds, and were finally defeated and scattered in different provinces, where they organized centres of the Triad Society, which claims an antiquity dated as far back as the Freemasons of the West. Five of these priests fled to the province of Hakwong, and there, Chin Kinnan, a member of the Hanlin College, who was degraded from office by his enemies, joined them; and it is said that they drank blood, and took the oath of brotherhood, to stand by each other in life or death."

Along the southwestern border of the Chinese Empire, in Burmah, this rite of blood-friendship is still practiced; as may be seen from illustrations of it, which are given in the Appendix of this work.

In his History of Madagascar, the Rev. William Ellis, tells of this rite as he observed it in that island, and as he learned of it from Borneo. He says:

"Another popular engagement in use among the Malagasy is that of forming brotherhoods, which though not peculiar to them, is one of the most remarkable usages of the country. . . . Its object is to cement two individuals in the bonds of most sacred friendship. . . . More than two may thus associate, if they please; but the practice is usually limited to that number, and rarely embraces more than three or four individuals. It is called *fatridá, i. e.,* 'dead blood,' either because the oath is taken over the blood of a

fowl killed for the occasion, or because a small portion
of blood is drawn from each individual, when thus
pledging friendship, and drunk by those to whom
friendship is pledged, with execrations of vengeance
on each other in case of violating the sacred oath.
To obtain the blood, a slight incision is made in the
skin covering the centre of the bosom, significantly
called *ambavafo*, 'the mouth of the heart.' Allusion
is made to this, in the formula of this tragi-comical
ceremony.

"When two or more persons have agreed on forming this bond of fraternity, a suitable place and hour
are determined upon, and some gunpowder and a ball
are brought, together with a small quantity of ginger,
a spear, and two particular kinds of grass. A fowl also
is procured; its head is nearly cut off; and it is left in
this state to continue bleeding during the ceremony.[1]

"The parties then pronounce a long form of im-
precation, and [a] mutual vow, to this effect:—'Should
either of us prove disloyal to the sovereign, or unfaithful to each other,[2] then perish the day, and perish

---

[1] Apparently these articles form a "heap of witness," or are the aggre-
gated symbolic witnesses of the transaction; as something answering to
this usage is found in connection with the rite in various parts of the
world.

[2] He who would be true in friendship must be true in all things. The
good friend is a good citizen. See 1 Peter 2:17.

the night.[1] Awful is that, solemn is that, which we are
now both about to perform! O the mouth of the heart!
—this is to be cut, and we shall drink each other's
blood. O this ball! O this powder! O this ginger!
O this fowl weltering in its blood!—it shall be killed,
it shall be put to excruciating agonies,—it shall be
killed by us, it shall be speared at this corner of the
hearth (Alakaforo or Adimizam, S. W.) And whoever would seek to kill or injure us, to injure our
wives, or our children, to waste our money or our
property; or if either of us should seek to do what
would not be approved of by the king or by the
people; should one of us deceive the other by making
that which is unjust appear just; should one accuse
the other falsely; should either of us with our wives
and children be lost and reduced to slavery, (forbid
that such should be our lot!)—then, that good may
arise out of evil, we follow this custom of the people;
and we do it for the purpose of assisting one another
with our families, if lost in slavery, by whatever property either of us may possess; for our wives are as one
to us, and each other's children as his own,[2] and our
riches as common property. O the mouth of the heart!
O the ball! O the powder! O the ginger! O this
miserable fowl weltering in its blood!—thy liver do we

---

[1] See Job 3 : 2–9.

[2] Here is the idea of an absolute inter-merging of natures, by this rite.

eat, thy liver do we eat. And should either of us retract from the terms of this oath, let him instantly become a fool, let him instantly become blind, let this covenant prove a curse to him: let him not be a human being: let there be no heir to inherit after him, but let him be reduced, and float with the water never to see its source; let him never obtain; what is out of doors, may it never enter; and what is within may it never go out; the little obtained, may he be deprived of it;[1] and let him never obtain justice from the sovereign nor from the people! But if we keep and observe this covenant, let these things bear witness.[2]   O mouth of the heart! (repeating as before),—may this cause us to live long and happy with our wives and our children; may we be approved by the sovereign, and beloved by the people; may we get money, may we obtain property, cattle, &c.; may we marry wives, (*vady kely*); may we have good robes, and wear a good piece of cloth on our bodies;[3] since, amidst our toils and labor, these are the things we seek after.[4] And this we do that we may with all fidelity assist each other to the last.'

[1] See Matt. 13: 12; 25: 29.

[2] Here is an indication of the witness-bearing nature of these accessories of the rite.

[3] Compare these blessings and cursings with those under the Mosaic laws: Deut. 27: 9–26; 28: 1–68.

[4] See Matt. 6: 31, 32.

" The incision is then made, as already mentioned ; a small quantity of blood [is] extracted and drank by the covenanting parties respectively, [they] saying as they take it, ' These are our last words, We will be like rice and water ;[1] in town they do not separate, and in the fields they do not forsake one another ; we will be as the right and left hand of the body ; if one be injured, the other necessarily sympathizes and suffers with it." [2]

Speaking of the terms and the influence of this covenant, in Madagascar, Mr. Ellis says, that while absolute community of all worldly possessions is not a literal fact on the part of these blood-friends, " the engagement involves a sort of moral obligation for one to assist the other in every extremity." " However devoid of meaning," he adds, " some part of the ceremony of forming [this] brotherhood may appear, and whatever indications of barbarity of feeling may appear in others, it is less exceptionable than many [of the rites] that prevail among the people. . . . So far as those who have resided in the country have observed its effects, they appear almost invariably to have been safe

[1] " This is a natural, simple, and beautiful allusion in common use among the Malagasy, to denote an inseparable association. The rice is planted in water, grows in water, is boiled in water, and water is the universal beverage taken with it when eaten."

[2] Ellis's *Hist. of Madagascar*, I., 187–190.

to the community, and beneficial to the individuals by whom the compact was formed."

Yet again, this covenant of blood-friendship is found in different parts of Borneo. In the days of Mr. Ellis, the Rev. W. Medhurst, a missionary of the London Missionary Society, in Java, described it, in reporting a visit made to the Dayaks of Borneo, by one of his assistants, together with a missionary of the Rhenish Missionary Society.[1]

Telling of the kindly greeting given to these visitors at a place called Golong, he says that the natives wished "to establish a fraternal agreement with the missionaries, on condition that the latter should teach them the ways of God. The travelers replied, that if the Dayaks became the disciples of Christ, they would be constituted the brethren of Christ without any formal compact. The Dayaks, however, insisted that the travelers should enter into a compact [with them], according to the custom of the country, by means of blood. The missionaries were startled at this, thinking that the Dayaks meant to murder them, and committed themselves to their Heavenly Father, praying that, whether living or dying, they might lie at the feet of their Saviour. It appears, however, that it is the custom of the Dayaks, when they enter into a covenant, to draw a little blood from the arms of the

[1] Cited in Ellis's *Hist. of Mad.*, I., 191, note.

5

covenanting parties, and, having mixed it with water, each to drink, in this way, the blood of the other.

" Mr. Barenstein [one of the missionaries] having consented [for both] to the ceremony, they all took off their coats, and two officers came forward with small knives, to take a little blood out of the arm of each of them [the two missionaries and two Dayak chiefs]. This being mixed together in four glasses of water, they drank, severally, each from the glass of the other; after which they joined hands and kissed. The people then came forward, and made obeisance to the missionaries, as the friends of the Dayak King, crying out with loud voices, ' Let us be friends and brethren forever; and may God help the Dayaks to obtain the knowledge of God from the missionaries!' The two chiefs then said, ' Brethren, be not afraid to dwell with us; for we will do you no harm; and if others wish to hurt you, we will defend you with our life's blood, and die ourselves ere you be slain. God be witness, and this whole assembly be witness, that this is true.' Whereupon the whole company shouted, *Balaak!* or ' Good,' ' Be it so.' "

Yet another method of observing this rite, is reported from among the Kayans of Borneo—quite a different people from the Dayaks. Its description is from the narrative of Mr. Spenser St. John, as follows: " Siñgauding [a Kayan chief] sent on board to request

me to become his brother, by going through the
sacred custom of imbibing each other's blood. I say
imbibing, because it is either mixed with water and
drunk, or else is placed within a native cigar, and
drawn in with the smoke. I agreed to do so, and the
following day was fixed for the ceremony. It is called
Berbiang by the Kayans ; *Bersabibah*, by the Borneans
[the Dayaks]. I landed with our party of Malays, and
after a preliminary talk, to allow the population to
assemble, the affair commenced. . . . Stripping
my left arm, Kum Lia took a small piece of wood,
shaped like a knife-blade, and, slightly piercing the
skin, brought blood to the surface ; this he carefully
scraped off. Then one of my Malays drew blood in
the same way from Siṅgauding ; and, a small cigarette
being produced, the blood on the wooden blade was
spread on the tobacco. A chief then arose, and, walk-
ing to an open place, looked forth upon the river, and
invoked their god and all the spirits of good and evil to
be witness of this tie of brotherhood. The cigarette
[blood-stained] was then lighted, and each of us took
several puffs [receiving each other's blood by inhalation],
and the ceremony was over." [1] This is a new method of
smoking the "pipe of peace"—or, the cigarette of inter-
union ! Borneo, indeed, furnishes many illustrations
of primitive customs, both social and religious.

[1] St. John's *Life in the Forests of the Far East*, I., 116 f.

One of the latest and most venturesome explorers
of North Borneo was the gallant and lamented Frank
Hatton, a son of the widely known international jour-
nalist, Joseph Hatton. In a sketch of his son's life-
work, the father says[1]: " His was the first white foot
in many of the hitherto unknown villages of Borneo ;
in him many of the wild tribes saw the first white man.
. . . Speaking the language of the natives, and possess-
ing that special faculty of kindly firmness so necessary
to the efficient control of uncivilized peoples, he jour-
neyed through the strange land not only unmolested,
but frequently carrying away tokens of native affection. Several powerful chiefs made him their ' blood-
brother'; and here and there the tribes prayed to him
as if he were a god." It would seem from the description of Mr. Hatton, that, in some instances, in Borneo,
the blood-covenanting is by the substitute blood of a
fowl held by the two parties to the covenant, while its
head is cut off by a third person—without any drinking of each other's blood by those who enter into the
covenant. Yet, however this may be, the other method
still prevails there.

Another recent traveler in the Malay Archipelago,
who, also, is a trained and careful observer, tells of this
rite, as he found it in Timor, and other islands of that
region, among a people who represent the Malays,

[1] In "The Century Magazine " for July, 1885, p. 437.

the Papuan, and the Polynesian races. His description is: "The ceremony of blood-brotherhood, . . .
or the swearing of eternal friendship, is of an interesting nature, and is celebrated often by fearful orgies
[excesses of the communion idea], especially when
friendship is being made between families, or tribes, or
kingdoms. The ceremony is the same in substance
whether between two individuals, or [between] large
companies. The contracting parties slash their arms,
and collect the blood into a bamboo, into which *kanipa*
(coarse gin) or *laru* (palm wine) is poured. Having
provided themselves with a small fig-tree (*halik*) they
adjourn to some retired spot, taking with them the
sword and spear from the *Luli* chamber [the sacred
room] of their own houses if between private individuals, or from the *Uma-Luli* of their *suku* [the sacred
building of their village] if between large companies.
Planting there the fig-tree, flanked by the sacred sword
and spear, they hang on it a bamboo-receptacle, into
which—after pledging each other in a portion of the
mixed blood and gin—the remainder [of that mixture]
is poured. Then each swears, 'If I be false, and be not
a true friend, may my blood issue from my mouth, ears,
nose, as it does from this bamboo!'—the bottom of the
receptacle being pricked at the same moment, to allow
the blood and gin to escape. The [blood-stained] tree
remains and grows as a witness of their contract."

5*

Of the close and binding nature of this blood-compact, among the Timorese, the observer goes on to say : " It is one of their most sacred oaths, and [is] almost never, I am told, violated ; at least between individuals." As to its limitless force and scope, he adds: " One brother [one of these brother-friends in the covenant of blood] coming to another brother's house, is in every respect regarded as free [to do as he pleases], and [is] as much at home as its owner. Nothing is withheld from him ; even his friend's wife is not denied him, and a child born of such a union would be recognized by the husband as *his ;* [for are not—as *they* reason—these brother-friends of *one blood*—of one and the same life ?] " [1]

The covenant of blood-friendship has been noted also among the native races of both North and South America. A writer of three centuries ago, told of it as among the aborigines of Yucatan. " When the Indians of Pontonchan," he said, "receive new friends [covenant in a new friendship]. . . as a proof of [their] friendship, they [mutually, each], in the sight of the friend, draw some blood . . . from the tongue, hand, or arm, or from some other part [of the body]." [2]

[1] Forbes's *A Naturalist's Wanderings in the Eastern Archipelago,* p. 452.

[2] Peter Martyr's *De Rebus Oceanicis et Novo Orbe,* p. 338 ; cited in Spencer's *Des. Soc.* II., 34.

And this ceremony is said to have formed " a compact for life." [1]

In Brazil, the Indians were said to have a rite of brotherhood so close and sacred that, as in the case of the Bed'ween beyond the Jordan,[2] its covenanting parties were counted as of one blood; so that marriage between those thus linked would be deemed incestuous. " There was a word in their language to express a friend who was loved like a brother; it is written *Atourrassap* ['erroneously, beyond a doubt,' adds Southey, 'because their speech is without the *r*']. They who called each other by this name, had all things in common; the tie was held to be as sacred as that of consanguinity, and one could not marry the daughter or sister of the other." [3]

A similar tie of adopted brotherhood, or of close and sacred friendship, is recognized among the North American Indians. Writing of the Dakotas, or the Sioux, Dr. Riggs, the veteran missionary and scholar, says: " Where one Dakota takes another as his *koda*, i. e., god, or friend, [Think of that, for sacredness of union—' god, or friend '!] they become brothers in each other's families, and are, as such, of course unable to intermarry." [4] And Burton, the famous traveler, who

[1] See Bancroft's *Native Races of the Pacific Coast*, I., 741.

[2] See page 10, *supra*. [3] Southey's *Brazil*, I., 240.

[4] Lynd's *History of the Dakotas*, p. 73, note.

made this same tribe a study, says of the Dakotas: "They are fond of adoption, and of making brotherhoods like the Africans [Burton is familiar with the customs of African tribes]; and so strong is the tie that marriage with the sister of an adopted brother is within the prohibited degree."[1]

Among the people of the Society Islands, and perhaps also among those of other South Sea Islands, the term *tayo* is applied to an attached personal friend, in a peculiar relation of intimacy. The formal ceremony of brotherhood, whereby one becomes the tayo of another, in these islands, I have not found described; but the closeness and sacredness of the relation, as it is held by many of the natives, would seem to indicate the inter-mingling of blood in the covenanting, now or in former times. The early missionaries to those islands, speaking of the prevalent unchastity there, make this exception: " If a person is a tayo of the husband, he must indulge in no liberties with the sisters or the daughters, because they are considered as *his own* sisters or daughters; and incest is held in abhorrence by them; nor will any temptations engage them to violate this bond of purity. The wife, however, is excepted, and considered as common property for the tayo.[2] Lieutenant Corner [a still earlier voyager] also added, that a tayoship formed

---

[1] Burton's *City of the Saints*, p. 117.   [2] See page 54, *supra*.

between different sexes put the most solemn barrier against all personal liberties."[1] Here is evidenced that same view of the absolute oneness of nature through a oneness of blood, which shows itself among the Semites of Syria,[2] among the Malays of Timor,[3] and among the Indians of America.[4]

And so this close and sacred covenant relation, this rite of blood-friendship, this inter-oneness of life by an inter-oneness of blood, shows itself in the primitive East, and in the wild and pre-historic West; in the frozen North, as in the torrid South. Its traces are everywhere. It is of old, and it is of to-day; as universal and as full of meaning as life itself.

It will be observed that we have already noted proofs of the independent existence of this rite of blood-brotherhood, or blood-friendship, among the three great primitive divisions of the race—the Semitic, the Hamitic, and the Japhetic; and this in Asia, Africa, Europe, America, and the Islands of the Sea; again, among the five modern and more popular divisions of the human family: Caucasian, Mongolian, Ethiopian, Malay, and American. This fact in itself would seem to point to a common origin of its various manifestations, in the early Oriental home of the now scattered peoples of the world. Many references to

---

[1] *Miss. Voyage to So. Pacif. Ocean*, p. 360 f.

[2] See page 10, *supra*. [3] See page 54, *supra*. [4] See page 55 f., *supra*.

this rite, in the pages of classic literature, seem to have the same indicative bearing, as to its nature and primitive source.

6. LIGHT FROM THE CLASSICS.

Lucian, the bright Greek thinker, who was born and trained in the East, writing in the middle of the second century of our era, is explicit as to the nature and method of this covenant as then practised in the East. In his " Toxaris or Friendship,"[1] Mnesippus the Greek, and Toxaris the Scythian, are discussing friendship. Toxaris declares: "It can easily be shown that Scythian friends are much more faithful than Greek friends; and that friendship is esteemed more highly among us than among you." Then Toxaris goes on to say[2]: "But first I wish to tell you in what manner we [in Scythia] make friends; not in our drinking bouts as you do, nor simply because a man is of the same age [as ourselves], or because he is our neighbor. But, on the contrary, when we see a good man, and one capable of great deeds, to him we all hasten, and (as you do in the case of marrying, so we think it right to do in the case of our friends) we court him, and we [who would be friends] do all things together, so that we may not offend against friendship, or seem

[1] *Opera*, p. 545.　　　　　　[2] *Toxaris*, chap. 37.

worthy to be rejected. And whenever one decides to be a friend, we [who would join in the covenant] make the greatest of all oaths, to live with one another, and to die, if need be, the one for the other. And this is the manner of it: Thereupon, cutting our fingers, all simultaneously, we let the blood drop into a vessel, and having dipped the points of our swords into it, both [of us] holding them together,[1] we drink it. There is nothing which can loose us from one another after that."

Yet a little earlier than Lucian, Tacitus, foremost among Latin historians, gives record of this rite of blood-brotherhood as practised in the East. He is telling, in his Annals, of Rhadamistus, leader of the Iberians, who pretends to seek a covenant with Mithridates, King of the Armenians (yet farther east than Scythia), which should make firm the peace between the two nations, "*diis testibus*," "the gods being witnesses." Here Tacitus makes an explanation:[2] "It is the custom of [Oriental] kings, as often as they come together to make covenant, to join right hands, to tie the thumbs together, and to tighten them with a knot. Then, when the blood is [thus] pressed to the finger tips, they draw blood by a light stroke, and lick[3] it in turn.

---

[1] See references to arms as accessories to the rite, in Africa, and in Madagascar, and in Timor, at pages 16, 32, 35 f., 45 f., 53, *supra.*

[2] *Annales*, XII., 47.　　　　　[3] See page 11, *supra.*

This they regard as a divine[1] covenant, made sacred as it were, by mutual blood [or blended lives]."

There are several references, by classical writers, to this blood-friendship, or to this blood-covenanting, in connection with Catiline's conspiracy against the Roman Republic. Sallust, the historian of that conspiracy, says: " There were those at that time who said that Catiline, at this conference [with his accomplices] when he inducted them into the oath of partnership in crime, carried round in goblets human blood, mixed with wine; and that after all had tasted of it, with an imprecatory oath, as is men's wont in solemn rites [in " *Sharb el-'ahd*,"[2] as the Arabs would say] he opened to them his plans."[3] Florus, a later Latin historian, describing this conspiracy, says: " There was added the pledge of the league,— human blood,—which they drank as it was borne round to them in goblets."[4] And yet later, Tertullian suggests that it was their own blood, mingled with wine, of which the fellow-conspirators drank together. "Concerning the eating of blood and other such tragic dishes," he says, "you read (I do not know where), that blood drawn from the arms, and tasted by one another,

---

[1] *Arcanum ;* literally " mysterious,"—not in the sense of secret, or occult, but with reference to its sacred and supernatural origin and sanction.

[2] See p. 9, *supra.*   [3] *Catilina*, cap. XXII.   [4] *Historiæ*, IV., 1, 4.

was the method of making covenant among certain nations. I know not but that under Catiline such blood was tasted."[1]

In the Pitti Palace, in Florence, there is a famous painting of the conspiracy of Catiline, by Salvator Rosa; it is, indeed, Salvator Rosa's masterpiece, in the line of historical painting. This painting represents the covenanting by blood. Two conspirators stand face to face, their right hands clasped above a votive altar. The bared right arm of each is incised, a little below the elbow. The blood is streaming from the arm of one, into a cup which he holds, with his left hand, to receive it; while the dripping arm of the other conspirator shows that his blood has already flowed into the commingling cup.[2] The uplifted hand of the daysman between the conspirators seems to indicate the imprecatory vows which the two are assuming, in the presence of the gods, and of the witnesses who stand about the altar. This is a clear indication of the traditional form of covenanting between Catiline and his fellow conspirators.

As far back, even, as the fifth century before Christ, we find an explicit description of this Oriental rite of blood-covenanting, in the writings of "the Father of History." "Now the Scythians," says Herodotus,[3] "make covenants in the following manner, with whom-

---

[1] *Apologet.*, cap. IX. [2] See stamp on outside cover. [3] *Hist.*, IV., 70.

soever they make them.   Having poured out wine into
a great earthen drinking-bowl, they mingle with it the
blood of those cutting covenant, striking the body [of
each person having a part in it] with a small knife, or
cutting it slightly with a sword.   Thereafter, they dip
into the bowl, sword, arrows, axe, and javelin.[1]   But
while they are doing this, they utter many invokings
[of curse upon a breach of this covenant] ;[2] and, afterwards, not only those who make the covenant, but
those of their followers who are of the highest rank,
drink off [the wine mingled with blood] ."

Again Herodotus says of this custom, in his day[3]:
" Now the Arabians reverence in a very high degree
pledges between man and man.   They make these
pledges in the following way.   When they wish to
make pledges to one another, a third man, standing in
the midst of the two, cuts with a sharp stone the inside
of the hands along the thumbs of the two making
the pledges.   After that, plucking some woolen floss
from the garments of each of the two, he anoints with
the blood seven stones [as the " heap of witness "[4]]
which are set in the midst.   While he is doing this he

[1] See note, at page 59, *supra.*

[2] See the references to imprecatory invokings, in connection with the
observance of the rite in Syria, in Central Africa, in Madagascar, and in
Timor, at pages 9, 20, 31, 46 f., 53, *supra.*

[3] *Hist.,* III., 8.   [4] See page 45 *supra*, note.

invokes Dionysus and Urania. When this rite is completed, he that has made the pledges [to one from
without] introduces the [former] stranger to his
friends [1]—or the fellow citizen [to his fellows] if the
rite was performed with a fellow-citizen."

Thus it is clear, that the rite of blood-brotherhood,
or of blood-friendship, which is to-day a revered form
of sacred covenanting in the unchangeable East, was
recognized as an established custom among Oriental
peoples twenty-three centuries ago. Its beginning
must certainly have been prior to that time; if not
indeed long prior.

An indication of the extreme antiquity of this rite
would seem to be shown in a term employed in its
designation by the Romans, early in our Christian era;
when both the meaning and the origin of the term
itself were already lost in the dim past. Festus,[2] a
writer, of fifteen centuries or more ago, concerning
Latin antiquities, is reported[3] as saying, of this drink
of the covenant of blood: "A certain kind of drink,
of mingled wine and blood, was called *assiratum* by

[1] See references to the welcoming of new friends by the natives of Africa and of Borneo, at the celebration of this rite, at pages 36 f., 51, *supra*.

[2] Sextus Pompeius Festus, whose chief work, in the third or fourth
Christian century, was an epitome, with added notes and criticisms, of
an unpreserved work of M. Verrius Flaccus, on the Latin language and
antiquities.

[3] See Rosenmüller's *Scholia in Vet. Test.*, apud Psa. 16: 4.

the ancients; for the ancient Latins called blood, *assir*." Our modern lexicons give this isolated claim, made by Festus, of the existence of any such word as "assir" signifying "blood," in "the ancient Latin language;"[1] and some of them try to show the possibilities of its origin;[2] but no convincing proof of any such word and meaning in the Latin can be found.

Turning, however, to the languages of the East, where the binding vow of blood-friendship was pledged in the drink of wine and blood, or of blood alone, from time immemorial, we have no difficulty in finding the meaning of "assir." *Asar* (אָסַר) is a common Hebrew word, signifying "to bind together"—as in a mutual covenant. *Issar* (אִסָּר), again, is a vow of self-renunciation. Thus we have *Asar issar 'al nephesh* (אָסַר אִסָּר עַל נֶפֶשׁ) "To bind a self-devoting vow upon one's life"[3]—upon one's blood; "for the blood is the life."[4] In the Arabic, also, *asara* (اسر) means "to bind," or "to tie"; while *asar* (اسر) is "a covenant," or "a compact"; and *aswâr* (اسوار) is "a bracelet"; which in itself is "a band," and may be "a fetter."[5] So, again, in the Assyrian, the verb "to bind," and the noun for "a bracelet" or "a fetter,"

---

[1] See Scheller's, and Harpers', *Latin Dictionary*, s. v. "Assiratum."

[2] See Curtius's *Griechische Etymologie*, s. v., ἔαρ (*ear*).

[3] See Gesenius, and Fuerst, *s. vv.*   [4] Deut. 12: 23.

[5] See Lane, and Freytag. *s. vv.*

are from the same root.[1] The Syriac gives *esar*
(ܐܣܪ), "a bond," or "a belt."[2] All these, with
the root idea, "to bind"—as a covenant binds. In the
light of these facts, it is easy to see how the "issar" or
the "assar," when it was a covenant of blood, came to
be counted by the Latins the blood which was a covenant.

7. THE BOND OF THE COVENANT.

Just here it may be well to emphasize the fact, that,
from time immemorial, and the world over, the armlet,
the bracelet, and the ring, have been counted the symbols of a boundless bond between giver and receiver;
the tokens of a mutual, unending covenant. Possibly,
—probably, as I think,—this is in consequence of the
primitive custom of binding, as an amulet, the enclosed
record—enclosed in the "house of the amulet"[3]— of
the covenant of blood on the arm of either participant
in that rite; possibly, again, it is an outgrowth of the
common root idea of a covenant and a bracelet, as a
binding agency.

Blood-covenanting and bracelet-binding seem—as
already shown—to be intertwined in the *languages* of
the Oriental progenitors of the race. There are, likewise, indications of this intertwining in the *customs* of

---

[1] See, for example, Delitzsch's *Assyrische Lesestücke*, second edition,
p. 101, line 72.

[2] See Castell's *Lexicon Syriacum*, s. v.　　[3] See page 7, *supra*.

peoples, East and West. For example, in India, where blood-shedding is peculiarly objectionable, the gift and acceptance of a bracelet is an ancient covenant-tie, seemingly akin to blood-brotherhood. Of this custom, an Indian authority says: "Amongst the rajput races of India the women adopt a brother by the gift of a bracelet. The intrinsic value of such pledges is never looked to, nor is it necessary that it should be costly, though it varies with the means and rank of the donor, and may be of flock silk and spangles, or of gold chains and gems. The acceptance of the pledge is by the '*katchli*,' or corset, of simple silk or satin, or gold brocade and pearls. Colonel Tod was the *Rakhi-bund Bhai* [the Bracelet-bound Brother] of the three queens of Oodipur, Bundi, and Kotch; as also of Chund-Bai, the maiden sister of the Rana, and of many ladies of the chieftains of rank. Though the bracelet may be sent by maidens, it is only on occasions of urgent necessity and danger. The adopted brother may hazard his life in his adopted sister's cause, and yet never receive a mite in reward; for he cannot even see the fair object, who, as brother of her adoption, has constituted him her defender."[1]

"The . . . 'Bracelet-bound Brother' feels himself called upon to espouse the cause of the lady from

---

[1] Cited from "Tod's Travels, Journal Indian Archipelago, Vol. V., No. 12," in Balfour's *Cycl. of India*, s. v., "Brother."

whom he has received the gift, and to defend her
against all her enemies, whenever she shall demand
his assistance." Thus, the Great Mogul, Hoomâyoon,
father of the yet more celebrated Akbar, was in his
early life bound, and afterwards loyally recognized his
binding, as " the sworn knight of one of the princesses
of Rajasthan, who, according to the custom of her
country, secured the sword of the prince in her service
by the gift of a bracelet." When he had a throne of
his own to care for, this princess, Kurnivati, being be-
sieged at Cheetore, sent to Hoomâyoon, then prosecu-
ting a vigorous campaign in Bengal; and he, as in duty
bound, "instantly obeyed the summons"; and
although he was not in season to rescue her, he
" evinced his fidelity by avenging the fall of the city."[1]
It is noteworthy, just here, that the Oriental biogra-
pher of the Mogul Akbar calls attention to the fact,
that while the Persians describe close friendship as
chiefly subsisting between men, " in Hindostan it is
celebrated between man and woman ";[2] as, indeed, it
is among the Arab tribes east of the Jordan.[3]

In the Norseland, an oath of fidelity was taken on a
ring, or a bracelet, kept in the temple of the gods;
and the gift and acceptance of a bracelet, or a ring,

[1] See Elliott and Roberts's *Views in India*, II., 64.

[2] *Ayeen Akbery*, II., 453.

[3] See citation from Wetzstein, at page 9 f., *supra*.

was a common symbol of a covenant of fidelity. Thus, in "Hávamál," the high song of Odin, we find:

> "Odin, I believe,
> A ring-oath gave.
> Who in his faith will trust?"

And in "Viga Glum's Saga," it is related: "In the midst of a wedding party, Glum calls upon Thorarin, his accuser, to hear his oath, and taking in his hand a silver ring which had been dipped in sacrificial blood, he cites two witnesses to testify to his oath on the ring, and to his having appealed to the gods in his denial of the charge made against him." In the "Saga of Fridthjof the Bold," when Fridthjof is bidding farewell to his beloved Ingeborg, he covenants fidelity to her by the gift of

> "An *arm-ring*, all over famous;
> Forged by the halting Volund, 'twas,—the old North-story's Vulcan . . .
> Heaven was grav'd thereupon, with the twelve immortals' strong castles—
> Signs of the changing months, but the skald had Sun-houses named them."

As Fridthjof gave this pledge to Ingeborg, he said:

> "Forget me never; and,
> In sweet remembrance of our youthful love,
> This arm-ring take; a fair Volunder-work,
> With all heaven's wonders carved i' th' shining gold.
> Ah! the best wonder is a faithful heart . . .
> How prettily becomes it thy white arm—
> A glow-worm twining round a lily stem."

And the subsequent story of that covenanting arm-ring, fills thrilling pages in Norseland lore.[1]

Yet again, in the German cycle of the " Nibelungen Lied," Gotelind, the wife of Sir Rudeger, gives bracelets to the warrior-bard Folker, to bind him as her knightly champion in the court of King Etzel, to which he goes. Her jewel casket is brought to her.

" From this she took twelve bracelets, and drew them o'er his hand;
' These you must take, and with you bear hence to Etzel's land,
And for the sake of Gotelind the same at court must wear,
That I may learn, when hither again you all repair,
What service you have done me in yon assembly bright.'
The lady's wish thereafter full well perform'd the knight."

And when the fight waxed sore at the court of Etzel, the daring and dying Folker called on Sir Rudeger to bear witness to his bracelet-bound fidelity:

" For me, most noble margrave ! you must a message bear;
These bracelets red were given me late by your lady fair,
To wear at this high festal before the royal Hun.
View them thyself, and tell her that I've her bidding done."[2]

It would, indeed, seem, that from this root-idea of the binding force of an endless covenant, symbolized in the form, and in the primitive name, of the bracelet, the armlet, the ring,—there has come down to us the use of the wedding-ring, or the wedding-bracelet, and

[1] See Anderson's *Norse Mythol.*, p. 149; his *Viking Tales*, pp. 184, 237, 272 f.; Wood's *Wedding Day in all Ages and Countries*, p. 139.

[2] Lettsom's *Nibelungen Lied*, pp. 299, 388.

of the signet-ring as the seal of the most sacred covenants. The signet-ring appears in earliest history.
When Pharaoh would exalt Joseph over all the land
of Egypt, "Pharaoh took off his ring from his hand,
and put it upon Joseph's hand."[1] Similarly with
Ahasuerus and Haman: "The king took his ring from
his hand, and gave it unto Haman;" and the irrevocable decrees when written were "sealed with the king's
ring." When again Haman was deposed and Mordecai was exalted, "the king took off his ring, which he
had taken from Haman, and gave it unto Mordecai."[2]
The re-instatement of the prodigal son, in the parable,
was by putting "a ring on his hand."[3] And these
illustrations out of ancient Egypt, Persia, and Syria,
indicate a world-wide custom, so far. One's signet-
ring stood for his very self, and represented, thus, his
blood, as his life.

The use of rings, or bracelets, or armlets, in the
covenant of betrothal, or of marriage, is from of old,
and it is of wide-spread acceptance.[4] References to it
are cited from Pliny, Tertullian, Juvenal, Isidore; and
traces of it are found, earlier or later, among the peoples of Asia, Africa, Europe, and the Islands of the
Sea. In Iceland, the covenanting-ring was large
enough for the palm of the hand to be passed through;

[1] Gen. 41: 41, 42.   [2] Esther 3: 10–12; 8: 2.   [3] Luke 15: 22.
[4] See Wood's *Wedding Day;* also Jones's *Finger Ring Lore.*

so, in betrothal "the bridegroom passed four fingers
and his palm through one of these rings, and in this
manner he received the hand of the bride." In Ireland, long ago, "a usual gift from a woman to her be-
trothed husband was a pair of bracelets made of her
own hair"; as if a portion of her very self—as in the
case of one's blood—entered into the covenant rite.
Again in Ireland, as also among the old Romans, the
wedding-ring was in the form of two hands clasped
(called a "*fede*") in token of union and fidelity.

Sometimes, in England, the wedding-ring was worn
upon the thumb, as extant portraits illustrate ; and as
suggested in Butler's Hudibras :

> " Others were for abolishing
> That tool of matrimony, a ring,
> With which the unsanctify'd bridegroom
> Is marry'd only to a thumb."

In Southern's "Maid's Last Prayer," the heroine
says : "Marry him I must, and wear my wedding-ring
upon my thumb too, that I'm resolved." [1] These
thumb-weddings were said to be introduced from the
East [2]; and Chardin reports a form of marriage in
Ceylon, by the binding together of the thumbs of the
contracting parties; [3] as, according to the classics, the
thumbs were bound together in the rite of blood-covenanting. [4] Indeed, the selection of the ring-finger for

[1] Cited in Jones's *Finger Ring Lore*, p. 289.   [2] See *Ibid.*, pp. 87-90.
[3] *Persian- und Ost-Indische Reise*, II., 196.   [4] See pp. 59 f., 62, *supra*.

the wedding-covenant has commonly been attributed
to the relation of that finger to the heart as the blood-
centre, and as the seat of life. "Aulus Gellius tells us,
that Appianus asserts, in his Egyptian books, that a
very delicate nerve runs from the fourth finger of the
left hand to the heart, on which account this finger is
used for the marriage-ring." Macrobius says that in
Roman espousals the woman put the covenant ring "on
the third finger of her left hand [not counting the thumb],
because it was believed that a nerve ran from that finger
to the heart." And as to the significance of this point,
it has been said: "The *fact* [of the nerve connection with
the heart] has nothing to do with the question: that the
ancients *believed* it, is all we require to know."[1]

Among the Copts of Egypt, both the blood and the
ring have their part in the covenant of marriage.
Two rings are employed, one for the bride and one for
the bridegroom. At the door of the bridegroom's
house, as the bride approaches it, a lamb or a sheep
is slaughtered; and the bride must have a care to step
over the covenanting-blood as she enters the door,
to join the bridegroom. It is after this ceremony,
that the two contracting parties exchange the rings,
which are as the tokens of the covenant of blood.[2]

[1] See Godwyn's *Romanæ Historiæ*, p. 69; Brewer's *Dict. of Phrase and
Fable*, s. vv. "Ring," "Ring Finger"; Jones's *Finger Ring Lore*, p. 275.
See also Appendix, *infra*.   [2] Lane's *Mod. Egypt.*, II., 293.

In Borneo, among the Tring Dayaks, the marriage ceremony includes the smearing with a bloody sword, the
clasped hands of the bride and groom, in conjunction
with an invoking of the protecting spirits.[1]   In this case,
the wedding-ring would seem to be a bond of blood.

Again, in Little Russia, the bride gives to the bridegroom a covenanting draught in "a cup of wine, in
which a ring has been put ";[2] as if in that case the wine
and the blood-bond of the covenant were commingled
in a true *assiratum*.[3]   That this latter custom is an
ancient one, would seem to be indicated by the indirect
reference to it in Sir Walter Scott's ballad of "The
Noble Moringer," a mediæval lay—where the long
absent knight returns from the Holy Land just in
time to be at the wedding-feast of his enticed wife.
He appears unrecognized at the feast, as a poor
palmer.   A cup of wine is sent to him by the bride.

> " It was the noble Moringer that dropped amid the wine
>   A bridal ring of burning gold so costly and so fine :
>   Now listen, gentles, to my song, it tells you but the sooth,
>   'Twas with that very ring of gold he pledged his bridal truth."

Clearly this was not the ring he gave at his bridal,
but the one which he accepted, in the covenanting-cup,
from his bride.   The cup was carried back from the
palmer to the bride, for her drinking.

[1] See Bock's *Head Hunters of Borneo*, p. 221 f.
[2] *Finger Ring Lore*, p. 174.   [3] See page 63 f., *supra*.

"The ring hath caught the Lady's eye ; she views it close and near ;
Then might you hear her shriek aloud, 'The Moringer is here!'
Then might you see her start from seat, while tears in torrents fell ;
But whether 'twas from joy or woe, the ladies best can tell."

To the present day, an important ceremony at the coronation of a sovereign of Great Britain, is the investiture of the sovereign *per annulum*, or "by the ring." The ring is placed on the fourth finger of the sovereign's right hand, by the Archbishop of Canterbury; and it is called "The Wedding Ring of England," as it symbolizes the covenant union of the sovereign and his people. A similar practice prevails at the coronation of European sovereigns generally. It also runs back to the days of the early Roman emperors, and of Alexander the Great.[1]

That a ring, or a circlet, worn around a thumb, or a finger, or an arm, in token of an endless covenant between its giver and receiver, has been looked upon, in all ages, as the symbol of an inter-union of the lives thereby brought together, is unmistakable; whether the covenanting life-blood be drawn for such inter-commingling, directly from the member so encircled, or not. The very covenant itself, or its binding force, has been sometimes thought to depend on the circlet representing it; as if the life which was pledged passed into the token of its pledging. Thus Lord

[1] See *Finger Ring Lore,* pp. 177–197.

Bacon says: "It is supposed [to be] a help to the continuance of love, to wear a ring or bracelet of the person beloved;"[1] and he suggests that "a trial should be made by two persons, of the effect of compact and agreement; that a ring should be put on for each other's sake, to try whether, if one should break his promise the other would have any feeling of it in his absence." In other words, that the test should be made, to see whether the inter-union of lives symbolized by the covenant-token be a reality. On this idea it is, that many persons are unwilling to remove the wedding-ring from the finger, while the compact holds.[2]

It is not improbable, indeed, that the armlets, or bracelets, which were found on the arms of Oriental kings, and of Oriental divinities as well, were intended to indicate, or to symbolize, the personal inter-union claimed to exist between those kings and divinities. Thus an armlet worn by Thotmes III. is preserved in the museum at Leyden. It bears the cartouche of the King, having on it his sacred name, with its reference to his inter-union with his god. It was much the same in Nineveh.[3] Lane says, that upon the seal ring commonly worn by the modern Egyptian "is engraved the wearer's name," and that this name "is usually ac-

---

[1] Cited in Jones's *Credulities Past and Present*, p. 204 f. [2] See *Appendix*.

[3] See Wilkinson's *Anc. Egypt.*, II., 340–343; Layard's *Nineveh and its Remains*, II., 250, 358; also 2 Sam. 1 : 10.

companied by the words 'His servant' (signifying 'the
servant, or worshiper of God'), and often by other
words expressive of the person's trust in God."[1]

As the token of the blood-covenant is sometimes
fastened about the *arm*, and sometimes about the *neck*;
so the encircling necklace, as well as the encircling
armlet, is sometimes counted the symbol of a covenant
of very life. This is peculiarly the case in India;
where the bracelet-brotherhood has been shown to be
an apparent equivalent of the blood-brotherhood.
Among the folk-lore stories of India, it is a common
thing to hear of a necklace which holds the soul of the
wearer. That necklace removed, the wearer dies.
That necklace restored, the wearer lives again. "Sodewa Bai was born with a golden necklace about her
neck, concerning which also her parents consulted as-
trologers, who said, 'This is no common child; the
necklace of gold about her neck contains your daughter's soul; let it therefore be guarded with the utmost
care; for if it were taken off, and worn by another
person, she would die.'" On that necklace of life, the
story hangs. The necklace was stolen by a servant,
and Sodewa Bai died. Being placed in a canopied
tomb, she revived, night by night, when the servant
laid off the stolen necklace which contained the soul
of Sodewa Bai. The loss was at last discovered by

[1] *Modern Egyptians*, I., 39.

her husband; the necklace was restored to her, and she lived again.[1]   And this is but one story of many.

In the Brahman marriage ceremony the bridegroom receives his bride by binding a covenanting necklace about her neck. " A small ornament of gold, called *tahly*, which is the sign of their being actually in the state of marriage, . . . is fastened by a short string dyed yellow with *saffron*."[2]   And a Sanskrit word for " saffron " is also a word for " blood."[3]

The importance of this symbolism of the token of the blood-covenant, in its bearing on the root-idea of an inter-union of natures by an inter-commingling of blood, will be more clearly shown by and by.

8. THE RITE AND ITS TOKEN IN EGYPT.

Going back, now, to the world's most ancient records, in the monuments of Egypt, we find evidence of the existence of the covenant of blood in those early days. Even then it seems to have been a custom to covenant by tasting the blood from another's arm; and this inter-transference of blood was supposed to carry an inter-commingling, or an inter-merging, of natures. So far was this symbolic thought carried, that the ancient Egyptians spoke of the departed spirit as having entered into the nature, and, indeed,

---

[1] Frere's *Old Deccan Days*, pp. 225–245.
[2] Dubois' *Des. of Man. and Cust. of India*, Part II., chap. 7.
[3] See p. 194, *infra*.

7*

into the very being, of the gods, by the rite of tasting blood from the divine arm.

"The Book of the Dead," as it is commonly called, or "The Book of the Going Forth into Day,"—("The path of the just is as the shining light, that shineth more and more unto the perfect day,"[1])—is a group, or series, of ancient Egyptian writings, representing the state and the needs and the progress of the soul after death.[2]   A copy of this Funereal Ritual, as it is sometimes called, "more or less complete, according to the fortune of the deceased, was deposited in the case of every mummy."[3]   "As the Book of the Dead is the most ancient, so it is undoubtedly the most important, of the sacred books of the Egyptians;"[4] it is, in fact, "according to Egyptian notions, essentially an inspired work;"[5] hence its contents have an exceptional dogmatic value.   In this Book of the Dead, there are several obvious references to the rite of blood-covenanting.   Some of these are in a chapter of the Ritual which was found transcribed in a coffin of the

[1] Prov. 4: 18.

[2] See Lepsius's *Todtenbuch;* Bunsen's *Egypt's Place in Universal History*, V., 125–133; Renouf's *The Religion of Ancient Egypt*, pp. 179–208.

[3] See Lenormant and Chevallier's *Ancient History of the East*, I., 308.

[4] Renouf's *The Religion of Ancient Egypt*, p. 208.

[5] Bunsen's *Egypt's Place*, V., 133.

Eleventh Dynasty; thus carrying it back to a period prior to the days of Abraham.[1]

"Give me your arm; I am made as ye," says the departed soul, speaking to the gods.[2] Then, in explanation of this statement, the pre-historic gloss of the Ritual goes on to say: "The blood is that which proceeds from the member of the Sun, after he goes along cutting himself;"[3] the covenant blood which unites the soul and the god is drawn from the flesh of

---

[1] See *Egypt's Place*, V., 127.   [2] *Ibid.*, V., 174 f.

[3] This is the rendering of Birch. Ebers has looked for an explanation of this gloss in the rite of circumcision (*Ægypten u. d. Bücher Mose's*, p. 284 f.); but the primary reference to the "arm" of the god, and to the union secured through the interflowing blood, point to the blood-covenant as the employed figure of speech; although circumcision, as will be seen presently, was likewise a symbol of the blood-covenant —for one's self and for one's seed. Brugsch also sees a similar meaning to that suggested by Ebers in this reference to the blood. His rendering of the original text is: "Reach me your hands. I have become that which ye are" (*Religion u. Mythol. d. alt. Ægypt.*, I., 219). Le Page Renouf, looking for the symbolisms of *material* nature in all these statements, would find here "the crimson of a sunset" in the "blood which flows from the Sun-god Rā, as he hastens to his suicide" (*Trans. of Soc. of Bib. Arch.*, Vol. VIII., Part 2, p. 211). This, however, does not conflict with the *spiritual* symbolism of oneness of nature through oneness of blood. And no one of these last three suggested meanings accounts for the oneness with the gods through blood which the deceased claims, unless the symbolism of blood-covenanting be recognized in the terminology. That symbolism being recognized, the precise source of the flowing blood becomes a minor matter.

Rā, when he has cut himself in the rite of that covenant. By this covenant-cutting, the deceased becomes
one with the covenanting gods. Again, the departed
soul, speaking as Osiris,—or as the Osirian, which
every mummy represents,[1]—says: "I am the soul in
his two halves." Once more there follows the explanation: "The soul in his two halves is the soul of the
Sun [of Rā], and the soul of Osiris [of the deceased]."
Here is substantially the proverb of friendship cited
by Aristotle, "One soul in two bodies," at least two
thousand years before the days of the Greek philoso-
pher. How much earlier it was recognized, does not
yet appear.

Again, when the deceased comes to the gateway
of light, he speaks of himself as linked with the
great god Seb; as one "who loves his arm,"[2] and
who is, therefore, sure of admittance to him, within
the gates. By the covenant of the blood-giving arm,
"the Osiris opens the turning door; he has opened
the turning door." Through oneness of blood, he has
come into oneness of life with the gods; there is no
longer the barrier of a door between them. The
separating veil is rent.

An added indication that the covenant of blood-

---

[1] See Wilkinson's *Anc. Egypt.*, III., 473; Renouf's *Relig. of Anc.
Egypt*, pp. 191–193 ; Lenormant's *Chaldean Magic*, p. 88.

[2] See *Todtenbuch*, chap. LXVIII.; *Egypt's Place*, V., 211.

friendship furnished the ancient Egyptians with their
highest conception of a union with the divine nature
through an interflowing of the divine blood—as the
divine life—is found in the amulet of this covenant;
corresponding with the token of the covenant of blood-
friendship, which, as fastened to the arm, or about the
neck, is deemed so sacred and so precious in the
primitive East to-day. The hieroglyphic character
(⎓) which is translated "arm" is also translated
"bracelet," or "armlet," (⎓ ○)[1] as if in suggestion
of the truth, already referred to,[2] that the blood-fur-
nishing arm was represented by the token of the arm-
encircling, or of the neck-encircling, bond, in the
covenant of blood. Moreover, a "red talisman," or
red amulet, stained with "the blood of Isis," and
containing a record of the covenant, was placed at the
neck of the mummy as an assurance of safety to his
soul.[3] "When this book [this amulet-record] has

[1] See Pierret's *Vocabulaire Hiéroglyphique*, p. 721 f.; also, Birch's
"Dict. of Hierog." in *Egypt's Place*, V., 519.

[2] See page 65 f., *supra.*

[3] See *Todtenbuch*, chap. CLVI.; *Egypt's Place*, V., 315; *Trans. of
Soc. of Bib. Arch.*, VIII., 2, 211.

Another indication of the connection of these terms with this primitive rite, is in the fact that the hieroglyphic group which represents an
amulet (𐤟 𐤟 𐤟) seems to have the root-idea of "word;" as if it were
applied to the text of the blood-covenant.

The amulet as constructed for the mummy, was stained with the

been made," says the Ritual, " it causes Isis to protect
him [the Osirian], and Horus he rejoices to see him."
" If this book [this covenant-token] is known," says
Horus, " he [the deceased] is in the service of Osiris.
. . . His name is like that of the gods."

There are various other references to this rite, or
other indications of its existence, than those already
cited, in the Book of the Dead. " I have welcomed
Thoth (or the king) with blood; taking the gore from
the blessed of Seb,"[1] is one of these gleams. Again,

---

water or liquid of the tree called *ankh am* (⚲✝♆). The amulet itself,
according to Brugsch, was also called *ankh merer* (✝ ⚱). But
ankh (✝) means either to *live* (the ordinary meaning), or to *swear*,
to *make oath* (more rarely), and *merer* (⚱) is a reduplicated form
of *mer* (⚱) *to love, love, friendship.* The meaning of *ankh merer*
as applied to the blood-amulet may be oath, or covenant, or pledge
of love or friendship. The word *merer*, in the compound *ankh merer*,
is followed with the determinative of the flying scarabæus (🪲),
which was commonly placed (*Anc. Egypt.*, III., 346) upon the breast,
in lieu of the heart of the dead (*Ibid.*, III., 486). See page 100, *infra*.

And here the inquiry is suggested, Was the *ankh am* the same as the
modern *henneh ?* Note the connection of *henneh* with the marriage
festivities in the East to-day.

> " Paint one hand with henna, mother;
> Paint one hand and leave the other.
> Bracelets on the right with henna;
> On the left give drink to henna."

(Jessup's *Syrian Home Life*, p. 34.)

[1] See *Egypt's Place*, V., 232.

there are incidental mentions of the tasting of blood by gods and by men ;[1] and of the proffering, or the uplifting, of the blood-filled arm, in covenant with the gods.[2]

On a recently deciphered stéle of the days of Rameses IV., of the Twentieth Dynasty, about twelve centuries before Christ, there is an apparent reference to this blood-covenanting, and to its amulet record. The inscription is a specimen of a funereal ritual, not unlike some portions of the Book of the Dead. The deceased is represented as saying, according to the translation of Piehl[3]: "I am become familiar with Thoth, by his writings, on the day when he spat upon his arm." The Egyptian word, *khenmes,* here translated "familiar," means "united with," or "joined with." The word here rendered "writings," is *hetepoo;* which, in the singular, *hetep,* in the Book of Dead, stands for the record of the covenant on the blood-stained amulet.[4] The word *peqas* (🔲), rendered "spat," by Piehl, is an obscure term, variously rendered "moistened," "washed," "wiped," "healed."[5] It is clear therefore that this passage may fairly be read: "I am become united with Thoth, by the covenant-record, on the day when he moistened, or healed his arm "; and

---

[1] See *Egypt's Place,* V., 174, 254, 282.   [2] *Ibid.,* V., 323.

[3] See *Zeitschrift für Ægyptische Sprache,* erstes Heft, 1885, p. 16.

[4] See page 81 f., *supra.*   [5] See Pierret, Brugsch, Birch, *s. v.*

if the arm were healed, it had been cut, and so moistened. Indeed, it is quite probable that this word *peqas* has a root connection with *peq, peqa, peqau,* "a gap," "an opening," "to divide"; and even with *penqu,* ( ) "to bleed." Apparently, the unfamiliarity of Egyptologists with this rite of blood-covenanting by the cutting of the arm, has hindered the recognition of the full force of many of the terms involved.

Ebers, in his "Uarda," has incidentally given an illustration of the custom of blood-covenanting in ancient Egypt. It is when the surgeon Nebsecht has saved the life of Uarda, and her soldier-father, Kaschta, would show his gratitude, and would pledge his life-long fidelity in return.

"'If at any time thou dost want help, call me, and I will protect thee against twenty enemies. Thou hast saved my child—good! Life for life. I sign myself thy blood-ally—there!'

"With these words he drew his poniard out of his girdle. He scratched his arm, and let a few drops of his blood run down on a stone at the feet of Nebsecht.

"'Look!' he said. 'There is my blood! Kaschta has signed himself thine; and thou canst dispose of my life as of thine own. What I have said, I have said.'"[1]

[1] *Uarda*, I., 192.

9. OTHER GLEAMS OF THE RITE.

In this last cited illustration, from Uarda, there would, at first glance, seem to be the covenant proffered, rather than the covenant entered into; the covenant all on one side, instead of the mutual covenant. But this is, if it were possible, only a more unselfish and a more trustful mode than the other, of covenanting by blood; of pledging the life, by pledging the blood, to one who is already trusted absolutely. And this mode of proffering the covenant of blood, or of pledging one's self in devotedness by the giving of one's blood, is still a custom in the East; as it has been, in both the East and the West, from time immemorial.

For example, in a series of illustrations of Oriental manners, prepared under the direction of the French ambassador to Turkey, at the beginning of the eighteenth century, there appears a Turkish lover gashing his arm in the presence of his lady-love, as a proof of his loving attachment to her; and the accompanying statement is made, that the relative flow of blood thus devoted indicates the measure of affection—or of affectionate devotedness.[1]

A custom akin to this was found in Otaheite, when the South Sea Islands were first visited by English

[1] Ferriol's *Recueil de cent Estampes representant differentes Nations du Levant,* Carte 43, and Explication, p. 16.

missionaries.   The measure of love, in time of joy or
in time of grief, was indicated by the measure of blood
drawn from the person of the loving one.   Particularly
was this the case with the women; perhaps because
they, in Otaheite as elsewhere, are more loving in their
nature, and readier to give of their very life in love.

"When a woman takes a husband," says a historian
of the first missionary work in Otaheite, "she immediately provides herself with a shark's tooth, which is
fixed, with the bread-fruit gum, on an instrument that
leaves about a quarter of an inch of the tooth bare,
for the purpose of wounding the head, like a lancet.
Some of these have two or three teeth, and struck for-
cibly they bring blood in copious streams; *according*
to the love they bear the party, and the violence of their
grief, *the strokes are repeated on the head;* and this
has been known to bring on fever, and terminate in
madness.   If any accident happen to the husband, [to]
his relations, or friends, or their child, the shark's tooth
goes to work; and even if the child only fall down
and hurt itself, the blood and tears mingle together.
. . .   They have a very similar way of expressing
their joy as well as sorrow; for whether a relation dies,
or a dear friend returns from a journey, the shark's
tooth instrument . . . is again employed, and the
blood streams down. . . .   When a person of
eminence dies . . .   the relatives and friends . . .

repeat before it [the corpse] some of the tender
scenes which happened during their life time, and wiping the blood which the shark's teeth has drawn, de-
posit the cloth on the tupapow as the proof of their
affection." [1]

In illustration of this custom, the same writer says,
in the course of his narrative: "When we had got
within a short mile of the Isthmus, in passing a few
houses, an aged woman, mother to the young man who
carried my linen, met us, and to express her joy at
seeing her son, struck herself several times on the head
with a shark's tooth, till the blood flowed plentifully
down her breast and shoulders, whilst the son beheld
it with entire insensibility [he saw in it only the common proof of his mother's devoted love]. . . . The
son seeing that I was not pleased with what was done,
observed coolly, that it was the custom of Otaheite." [2]

This custom is again referred to by Mr. Ellis, as observed by him, in the Georgian and the Society Islands,
a generation later than the authority above cited. He
speaks of the shark's tooth blood-letter as employed
by men as well as by women; although more commonly by the latter. He adds another illustration of
the truth, that it is *the blood itself,* and not any suffering caused by its flowing, that is counted the proof of

[1] *First Miss. Voyage to the So. Sea Islands,* pp. 352–363.
[2] *Ibid.,* p. 196.

affection, by its representing the outpoured life, in pledge of covenant fidelity.

Describing the scenes of blood-giving grief over the dead bodies of the mourned loved ones, he says: "The females on these occasions sometimes put on a kind of short apron, of a particular sort of cloth; which they held up with one hand, while they cut themselves with the other. In this apron they caught the blood that flowed from these grief-inflicted wounds, until it [the apron] was almost saturated. It was then dried in the sun, and given to the nearest surviving relatives, as a proof of the affection of the donor, and was preserved by the bereaved family as a token of the estimation in which the departed had been held."[1] There is even more of vividness in this memorial than in that suggested by the Psalmist, when he says:

"Put thou my tears into thy bottle."[2]

There would seem to be a suggestion of this same idea in one of Grimm's folk-lore fairy tales of the North. A queen's daughter is going away from her home, attended by a single servant. Her loving mother would fain watch and guard her in her absence. Accordingly, "as soon as the hour of departure had arrived, the mother took her daughter into a chamber, and there, with a knife, she cut her [own] finger with

[1] Ellis's *Polynesian Researches*, I., 529.   [2] Psa. 56: 8.

it, so that it bled. Then she held her napkin beneath,
and let three drops of blood fall into it; which she
gave to her daughter, saying : ' Dear child, preserve
this well, and it will help you out of trouble.' " [1]   That
blood represented the mother's very life.   It was accustomed to speak out in words of counsel and warning to the daughter.   But by and by the napkin which
held it was lost, and then the power of the young
princess over her mother's servant was gone, and the
poor princess was alone in the wide world, at the mercy
of strangers.

Acting on the symbolism of this covenanting with
another by the loving proffer of one's blood, men have
reached out toward God, or toward the gods, in
desire for a covenant of union, and in expression of
fidelity of devotedness, by the giving of their blood
God-ward.   This, also, has been in the East and in
the West, in ancient days and until to-day.

There was a gleam of this in the Canaanitish
worship of Baal, in the contest between his priests and
the prophet Elijah, before King Ahab, at Mount Car-
mel.   First, those priests shed the blood of the substitute bullock, at the altar of their god, and " called on
the name of Baal from morning even until noon,
saying, O Baal, hear us !   But there was no voice,
nor any that answered."   Then they grew more earnest

---

[1] " The Goose Girl," in Grimm's *Household Tales.*

in their supplications, and more demonstrative in their proofs of devotedness. "They leaped [or, limped] about the altar which was made. . . . And they cried aloud, and cut themselves after their manner with knives and lances, till the blood gushed out upon them."[1] Similar methods of showing love for God are in vogue among the natives of Armenia to-day. Describing a scene of worship by religious devotees in that region, Dr. Van Lennep says: "One of them cuts his forehead with a sword, so that 'the blood gushes out.' He wears a sheet in front, to protect his clothes, and his face is covered with clots of blood."[2] Clearly, in this case, as in many others elsewhere, it is not as a means of self-torture, but as a proof of self-devotedness, that the blood is poured out—the life is proffered —by the devotee, toward God.

Among the primitive peoples of North and of South America, it was the custom of priests and people to draw blood from their own bodies, from their tongues, their ears, their noses, their limbs and members, when they went into their temples to worship, and to anoint with that blood the images of their gods.[3] The thorns

---

[1] 1 Kings 18: 26–28.   [2] Van Lennep's *Bible Lands*, pp. 767–769.

[3] See Herrera's *Gen. Hist. of Cont. and Isl. of America*, III., 209, 211, 216, 300 f.; Clavigero's *Hist. of Mex.*, Bk. VI., chaps. 22, 38; Montolinia's *Hist. Ind. de Nueva España*, p. 22; Landa's *Relat. Yucatan*, XXXV.; Ximenez's *Hist. Ind. Gautem.*, pp. 171–181; Palacio's *San*

of the maguey—a species of aloe—were, in many regions, kept ready at places of sacrifice, for convenient
use in this covenant blood-letting.[1] A careful student
of these early American customs has said of the obvious purpose of this yielding of one's blood in worship,
that it "might be regarded as an act of individual
devotion, a gift made to the gods by the worshiper
himself, out of his own very substance [of his very
life, as in the blood-covenant]. . . . The priests in
particular owed it to their special character [in their
covenant relation to the divinities], to draw their blood
for the benefit of the gods [in renewed pledge to the
gods]; and nothing could be stranger than the refined
methods they adopted to accomplish this end. For
instance, they would pass strings or splinters through
their lips or ears, and so draw a little blood. But then
a fresh string, or a fresh splinter, must be added every
day, and so it might go on indefinitely; for the more
there were, the more meritorious was the act;"[2] pre-

Salv. and Hond. (in Squier's *Coll.*, I.) 65 ff., 106, 116; Simon's *Ter.
Not. Conq. Tier. Firm. en Nue Gran.* (in Kingsborough's *Antiq. of
Mex.*, VIII.) 208, 248; all cited in Spencer's *Des. Soc.* II., 20–26, 28, 33.
See, also, Bancroft's *Native Races of Pacif Coast*, I., 665, 723; II.,
259, 306, 708, 710.

[1] Serving the purpose of the Otaheitan shark's teeth. See page 86 f.,
supra.

[2] Réville's *Native Religions of Mexico and Peru*, p. 84 f.

ciscly as is the standard of love-showing by blood-letting among Turkish lovers and Otaheitan wives and
mothers, in modern times.

A similar giving of blood, in proof of devotedness,
and in outreaching for inter-communion with the gods
through blood, is reported in India, in recent times.
Bishop Caldwell, of Madras, referred to it, a generation ago, in his description of the "Devil Dance"
among the Tinnevelly Shawars.[1] The devotee, in this
dance, "cuts and lacerates himself till the blood flows,
lashes himself with a huge whip, presses a burning
torch to his breast, drinks the blood which flows from
his own wounds, or drains the blood of the sacrifice;
putting the throat of a decapitated goat to his mouth."
Hereby he has given of his own blood to the gods, or
to the devils, and has drunk of the substitute blood
of the divinities—in the consecrated sacrifice; as if in
consummation of the blood-covenant with the supernal
powers. "Then as if he had acquired new life [through
inter-union with the object of his worship], he begins
to brandish his staff of bells, and to dance with a
quick but wild unsteady step. Suddenly the afflatus
descends; there is no mistaking that glare or those
frantic leaps. He snorts, he swears, he gyrates.
The demon has now taken bodily possession of him.
[The twain are one. The two natures are inter-

[1] Cited in Adam's *Curiosities of Superstition.*

mingled]. . . . The devil-dancer is now worshiped as a present deity, and every bystander consults him respecting his diseases, his wants, the welfare of his absent relations, the offerings to be made for the accomplishment of his wishes, and in short everything for which superhuman knowledge is supposed to be available." In this instance, the *mutual* covenant is represented; the devotee both giving and receiving blood, as a means of union.

On this idea of giving one's self to another, by giving of one's blood, it is that the popular tradition was based, that witches and sorcerers covenanted with Satan by signing a compact in their own blood. And again it was in recognition of the idea that two natures were inter-united in such a covenant, that the compact was sometimes said to be signed in Satan's blood.

Among the many women charged with witchcraft in England by the famous Matthew Hopkins, the " witch- finder " in the middle of the seventeenth century, was one, at Yarmouth, of whom it is reported, that her first temptation came to her when she went home from her place of employment discouraged and exasperated by her trials. "That night when she was in bed, she heard a knock at the door, and going to her window, she saw (it being moonlight) a tall black man there: and asked what he would have? He told her that she was discontented, because she could not get work; and that he would put her into a way that she should never want anything. On this she let him in, and asked him what he had to say to her. He told her he must first see her hand; and taking out something like a penknife, he gave it a little scratch, so that a little blood followed; a scar being still visible when she told the story. Then he took some of the blood in a pen, and pulling a book out of his pocket, bid her write her name; and when she said she could not, he said he would guide her hand. When this was done, he bid her now ask what she would have."[1] In signing with her own blood, she had pledged her very life to the "tall black man."

Cotton Mather, in his "Wonders of the Invisible World," cites a Swedish trial for witchcraft, where the possessed children, who were witnesses, said that the witches, at the trysting-place where they were observed, were compelled "to give themselves unto the devil, and vow that they would serve him. Hereupon they cut their fingers, and with blood writ their names in his book." In some cases "the mark of the cut finger was [still] to be found." Moreover, the devil gave meat and drink both to the witches and to the children they brought with them. Again, Mather cites the testimony of a witness who had been invited to covenant with the Devil, by signing the Devil's book.

[1] Cited in Benson's *Remarkable Trials and Notorious Characters*, p. 11.

"Once, with the book, there was a pen offered him, and an inkhorn with liquor in it that looked like blood."[1] Another New England writer on witchcraft says that "the witch as a slave binds herself by vow, to believe in the Devil, and to give him either body or soul, or both, under his handwriting, or some part of *his* blood."[2]

It is, evidently, on this popular tradition, that Goethe's Faust covenants in blood with Mephistopheles.

MEPHISTOPHELES.

"But one thing!—accidents may happen; hence
A line or two in writing grant, I pray."

FAUST.

. . . .

"Spirit of evil! what dost thou require?
Brass, marble, parchment, paper, dost desire?
Shall I with chisel, pen, or graver, write?
Thy choice is free; to me 'tis all the same."

MEPHISTOPHELES.

. . . .

"A scrap is for our compact good.
Thou under-signest merely with a drop of blood."

. . . .

"Blood is a juice of very special kind."[3]

Even "within modern memory in Europe," there have been traces of the primitive rite of covenanting

---

[1] Cited in Drake's *The Witchcraft Delusion in New England*, I., 187; II., 214. [2] *Ibid.*, I., xviii. See, also Appendix, *infra*.

[3] *Faust*, Swanwick's translation, Part I., lines 1360–1386.

with God by the proffer of one's blood. In the Russian province of Esthonia, he who would observe this rite, " had to draw drops of blood from his fore finger," and at the same time to pledge himself in solemn covenant with God. " I name thee [I invoke thee] with my blood, and [I] betroth thee [I entrust myself to thee] with my blood,"—was the form of his covenanting. Then he who had given of his blood in self-surrendering devotedness, made his confident supplications to God with whom he had thus covenanted; and his prayer in behalf of all his possessions was: " Let them be blessed through my blood and thy might." [1]

Thus, in ancient Egypt, in ancient Canaan, in ancient Mexico, in modern Turkey, in modern Russia, in modern India, and in modern Otaheite; in Africa, in Asia, in America, in Europe, and in Oceanica: Blood-giving was life-giving. Life-giving was love-showing. Love-showing was a heart-yearning after union in love and in life and in blood and in very being. That was the primitive thought in the primitive religions of all the world.

[1] See Tylor's *Primitive Culture*, II., 402; citing Boecler's *Ehsten Abergläubische Gebräuche*, 4.

LECTURE II.

SUGGESTIONS AND PERVERSIONS OF THE RITE.

II.

SUGGESTIONS AND PERVERSIONS OF THE RITE.

APART from, and yet linked with, the explicit proofs of the rite of blood-covenanting throughout the primitive world, there are many indications of the root-idea of this form of covenanting; in the popular estimate of blood, and of all the marvelous possibilities through blood-transference. These indications, also, are of old, and from everywhere.

To go back again to the earlier written history of the world; it is evident that the ancient Egyptians recognized blood as in a peculiar sense life itself; and that they counted the heart,—as the blood-source and the blood-centre,—the symbol and the substance of life. In the Book of the Dead, the deceased speaks of his heart—or his blood-fountain—as his life; and as giving him the right to appear in the presence of the gods: " My heart was my mother; my heart was my mother; my heart was my being on earth; placed

within me; returned to me by the chief gods, placing
me before the gods "[1] [in the presence of the gods].
In the process of embalming, the heart was always
preserved with jealous care;[2] and sometimes it was
embalmed by itself in a sepulchral vase.[3] It was the
heart—as the life, which is the blood—that seems to
have been put into the scales of the divine Judge for
the settling of the soul's destiny;[4] according to all the
Egyptian pictures of the judgment. Throughout the
Book of the Dead, and in all the sacred teachings and
practices of the ancient Egyptians, with reference to
human life and human destiny, the heart is obviously
recognized as the analogon of blood, and blood as the
analogon of life. Moreover, the life, which is represented by the blood and by the heart, appears to be
counted peculiarly the gift and the guarded treasure
of Deity, and as being in itself a resemblance to, if
not actually a part of, the divine nature.[5]

[1] *Egypt's Place*, V. 188.

[2] This is illustrated by Ebers, in his romance of "Uarda;" where
the surgeon, Nebsecht, finds such difficulty in obtaining a human heart,
in order to its anatomical study. See, also, Birch's statement, in *Egypt's
Place*, V., 135, and Pierret's *Dict. d'Arch. Égypt.*, s.v. "Cœur."

[3] *Anc. Egypt.*, III., 472, note 6.   [4] *Ibid.*, III., 466, note 3.

[5] In the Book of the Dead, Chapter xxxvi. tells "How a Person has
his Heart made (or given) to him in the Hades." And in preparing
the mummy, a scarabaeus,—a symbol of the creative or life-giving god
—was put in the place of the heart. (See Rubric, chapter xxx., Book of
the Dead; *Anc. Egypt.*, III., 346, 486; also, note in *Uarda*, I., 305 f.).

Even of the lower animals, the heart and the heart's blood were counted sacred to the gods, and were not to be eaten by the Egyptians; as if life belonged only to the Giver of life, and, when passing out from a lower organism, must return, or be returned, only to its original Source.

When the soul stands before the forty-two judges, in the Hall of the Two Truths, to give answer concerning its sins, one of its protesting avowals, as recorded in the Book of the Dead, is : " Oh Glowing Feet, coming out of the darkness! I have not eaten the heart ; "[1] In my earthly life-course, I have not committed the sacrilege of heart-eating. Yet, of the sacrificial offering of " a red cow," as prescribed in the Book of the Dead, " of the blood squeezed from the heart, one hundred drops,"[2] make a portion for the gods. In one of the tombs of Memphis, there is represented a scene of slaughtering animals. As the heart of an animal is taken out, the butcher who holds it says,—as shown by the accompanying hieroglyphics, —" Take care of this heart ; "[3] as if that were a portion to be guarded sacredly. " Keep thy heart with all diligence [or, as the margin has it, " above all thou guardest "]; for out of it are the issues of life."[4] It may, indeed, have been from the lore of Egypt that

[1] *Egypt's Place*, V., 14.
[2] *Ibid.*, V., 283.
[3] *Anc. Egypt.*, II., 27, note.
[4] Prov. 4: 23.

Solomon obtained this proverb of the ages, to pass it onward to posterity with his stamp of inspiration.

It would even seem that the blood of animals was not allowed to be eaten by the Egyptians; although there has been a question at that point, among Egyptologists. Wilkinson thinks that they *did* employ it in cooking;[1] but this is only his inference from a pictured representation of the blood being caught in a vessel, when an animal is slaughtered for the table. On the other hand, that same picture shows the vessel of blood being borne away, afterwards, on uplifted hands;[2] as it would have been if it were designed for a sacred libation. Again, the other picture, reported by Birch as showing the butcher's care of the heart, represents the blood as "collected in a jar with a long spout"; such as was used for sacred libations.[3] It is evident that blood *was* offered to the gods of Egypt in libation, as was also wine.[4] Indeed, the common Egyptian word for blood ($\overline{}$, *senf*) is regularly followed by the determinative of outpouring ( ). The word *tesher,* " red," is sometimes used as a synonym for *senf;* in this case (and in this only) the determinative of outpouring is added to

---

[1] *Anc. Egypt.*, II., 27, 31 ; III., 409.

[2] *Ibid.*, II., 32, Plate No. 300.   [3] *Ibid.*, II., 27 note **I.**

[4] Comp. *Ibid.*, III., 409, 416 f.

the hieroglyphics for *tesher*. Moreover, among the forty-two judges, before whom the dead appears, he who is " Eater of Blood " comes next in order before the " Eater of Hearts ";[1] as if blood-eating, like heart-eating, were a prerogative of the gods.

If proof were still wanting that, in ancient Egypt, it was the *heart* which was deemed the epitome of life, and that the heart had this pre-eminence because of its being the fountain of *blood*—which is life—that proof would be found in " The Tale of the Two Brothers "; a story that was prepared in its present form by a tutor of the Pharaoh of the exodus, while the latter was yet heir presumptive to the throne. This story has been the subject of special study by De Rougé, Chabas, Maspero, Brugsch, Birch, Goodwin, and Le Page Renouf. It is from the latter's translation that I draw my facts for this reference.[2]

Anpu and Bata were brothers. Bata's experience with the wife of Anpu was like that of Joseph in the house of Potiphar. He was true, like Joseph. Like Joseph, he was falsely accused, his life was sought, and his innocence was vindicated. Then, for his better protection, Bata took his *heart* out from his body, and put that in a safe place, while he made his home near it. To his brother he had said :

" I shall take my heart, and place it in the top of

[1] See *Egypt's Place*, V., 254.   [2] *Rec. of Past*, II., 137–152.

the flower of the cedar, and when the cedar is cut down it will fall to the ground. Thou shalt come to seek it. If thou art seven years in search of it, let not thy heart be depressed, and when thou hast found it thou shalt place it in a cup of cold water. Oh, then I shall live (once more)."

After a time the cedar, through the treachery of Bata's false wife, was cut down. As it fell, with the heart of Bata, the latter dropped dead. For more than three years Anpu sought his brother's heart; then he found it. "He brought a vessel of cold water, dropped the heart into it, and sat down according to his daily wont. But when the night was come, the heart absorbed the water. Bata [whose body seems to have been preserved—like a mummy—all this time] trembled in all his limbs, and continued looking at his elder brother, but his heart was faint. Then Anpu took the vessel of cold water which his brother's heart was in. And when the latter [Bata] had drunk it up, his heart rose in its place; and he became as he had been before. Each embraced the other, and each one of them held conversation with his companion."

The revivified Bata was transformed into a sacred bull, an Apis. That bull, by the treachery, again, of Bata's wife, was killed. "And as they were killing him, and he was in the hands of his attendants, he shook his neck, and two drops of blood fell upon the two door-posts of His Majesty [in whose keeping was the sacred bull]; one was on the one side of the great staircase of His Majesty, the other upon the other side; and they grew up into two mighty persea trees, each of which stood alone." Thus the blood was both life and life-giving, and the heart was as the very soul of its possessor, in the estimation of the ancient Egyptians.

In primitive America also, as in ancient Egypt, the blood and the heart were held pre-eminently sacred. Among the Dakotas, in North America, the heart of the deer, and of other animals killed in hunting, was offered to the spirits.[1] In Central America and in South America, it was the blood and the heart of the human victims offered in sacrifice which were counted the peculiar portion of the gods.[2] In description of a human sacrifice among the Nahuas of Central America,[3] a Mexican historian says: " The high priest then approached, and with a heavy knife of obsidian cut open the miserable man's breast. Then, with a dexterity acquired by long practice, the sacrificer tore forth the yet palpitating heart, which he first offered

---

[1] See Lynd's *Hist. of Dakotas*, p. 73.

[2] See citations from various original sources, in Bancroft's *Native Races of Pacific Coast*, II., 306–310, 707–709.

[3] The Nahuas were "skilled ones," or "experts," who had emigrated Northward from the Maya land (Réville's *Native Religions*, p. 20).

to the sun, and then threw at the feet of the idol. Taking it up, he again offered it to the god, and afterwards burned it; preserving the ashes with great care and veneration. Sometimes the heart was placed in the mouth [of the idol] with a golden spoon. It was customary also to anoint the lips of the image and the cornices of the door with the victim's blood." [1]

Of the method among the Maya nations,[2] south of the Gulf of Mexico, a Spanish historian [3] says: " The bleeding and quivering heart was held up to the sun, and then thrown into a bowl prepared for its reception. An assistant priest sucked the blood from the gash in the chest, through a hollow cane; the end of which he elevated towards the sun, and then discharged its contents into a plume-bordered cup held by the captor of the prisoner just slain. This cup was carried around to all the idols in the temples and chapels, before whom another blood-filled tube was held up, as if to give them a taste of the contents. This ceremony performed, the cup was left at the palace."

Yet another record stands: " The guardian of the temple . . . opened the left breast of the victim,

---

[1] Clavigero's *Anc. Hist. of Mex.*, II., 45–49, cited in Bancroft's *Native Races*, II., 307.

[2] The proper centre of the Maya nations lay in Yucatan (Réville's *Native Religions of Mexico and Peru*, p. 18).

[3] Gomara, cited in Bancroft's *Native Races*, II., 310 f.

tore out the heart, and handed it to the high priest,
who placed it in a small embroidered purse which he
carried. The four [assisting] priests received the blood
of the victim in four jicaras or bowls, made from the
shell of a certain fruit; and descending, one after the
other, to the court yard, [they] sprinkled the blood
with their right hand in the direction of the cardinal
points [of the compass]. If any blood remained over,
they returned it to the high priest, who placed it, with
the purse containing the heart, in the body of the victim, through the wound that had been made; and the
body was interred in the temple."[1]

Commenting on these customs in Central America,
Réville—the representative comparative-religionist of
France—says: " Here you will recognize that idea, so
widely spread in the two Americas, and indeed almost
everywhere amongst uncivilized peoples [nor is it
limited to the uncivilized], that the heart is the epitome, so to speak, of the individual—his soul in some
sense—so that to appropriate his heart is to appropriate his whole being."[2] What else than this gave rise
to the thought of preserving the *heart* of a hero, or
of a loved one, as a symbol of the living presence of
the dead? It was by his heart, that King Robert

[1] Herrera, cited in Bancroft's *Native Races*, II., 706 f.

[2] *Native Religions of Mexico and Peru* (Hibbert Lectures, 1884),
p. 43 f. See, also, pp. 45, 46, 82, 99.

Bruce was to lead his army to the Holy Land; and how many times, in history, have men bequeathed their hearts to those dear to them, as the poet Shelley's heart was preserved by his friends, and by them given to Mrs. Shelley.

In the Greek and Roman sacrifices, it was the blood of the victim, which, as the life of the victim, was poured out unto the gods, as unto the Author of life.[1] Moreover, there is reason for supposing that the *heart* was always given the chief place, as representing the very life itself, in the examination and in the *tasting* of the "entrails" ($\sigma\pi\lambda\acute{a}\gamma\chi\nu a$, *splangchna*) in connection with the sacrifices of those classic peoples.[2] An indication of this truth is found in a statement by Cicero, concerning the sacrifices at the time of the inauguration of Cæsar: "When he [Cæsar] was sacrificing on that day in which he first sat in the golden chair, and made procession in the purple garment, there was no *heart* among the entrails of the sacrificial ox. (Do you think, therefore, that any animal which has blood can exist without a heart?) Yet he [Cæsar] was not terrified by the phenomenal nature of the event, although Spurinna declared, that

[1] See Pindar's *Olympian Odes*, Ode 1, line 146; Sophocles's *Trachiniæ*, line 766; Virgil's *Æneid*, Bk. XI., line 81 f.

[2] Homer's *Odyssey*, Bk. III., lines 11, 12, 461–463; *Iliad*, Bk. II., lines 427, 428.

it was to be feared that both mind [literally ' counsel '] and life were about to fail him [Cæsar]; for both of these [mind and life] do issue from the heart." [1]

Similarly it has been, and to the present day it is, with primitive peoples everywhere. Blood libations were made a prominent feature in the offerings in ancient Phoenicia,[2] as in Egypt. In India, the Brahmans have a saying, in illustration of the claim that Vishnu and Siva are of one and the same nature: " The heart of Vishnu is Sivâ, and the heart of Sivâ is Vishnu; and those who think they differ, err." [3] The Hindoo legends represent the victim's heart as being torn out and given to the one whom in life he has wronged.[4] In China, at the great Temple of Heaven, in Peking, where the emperors of China are supposed to have conducted worship without material change in its main features for now nearly three thousand years,[5] the blood of the animal sacrifice is buried in the earth [6] while the body of the sacrificial victim is offered as a whole burnt offering.[7]

---

[1] Cicero's *De Divinatione*, Bk. I., chap. 52, § 119.

[2] See Sanchoniathon's references to blood libations, in Cory's *Ancient Fragments*, pp. 7, 11, 16.

[3] See " The Hindu Pantheon," in Birdwood's *Indian Arts*, p. 96.

[4] Frere's *Old Deccan Days*, p. 266.

[5] Williams's *Middle Kingdom*, I., 194.

[6] Edkins's *Religion in China*, p. 22.

[7] Williams's *Mid. King.*, I., 76–78.

The blood is the life; the heart as the fountain of blood is the fountain of life; both blood and heart are sacred to the Author of life. The possession, or the gift, of the heart or of the blood, is the possession, or the gift, of the very nature of its primal owner. That has been the world's thought in all the ages.

2. VIVIFYING POWER OF BLOOD.

The belief seems to have been universal, not only that the blood is the life of the organism in which it originally flows, but that in its transfer from one organism to another the blood retains its life, and so carries with it a vivifying power. There are traces of this belief in the earliest legends of the Old World, and of the New; in classic story; and in medical practices as well, all the world over, from time immemorial until the present day.

For example, in an inscription from the Egyptian monuments, the original of which dates back to the early days of Moses, there is a reference to a then ancient legend of the rebellion of mankind against the gods; of an edict of destruction against the human race; and of a divine interposition for the rescue of the doomed peoples.[1] In that legend, a prominent

---

[1] The inscription was first found, in 1875, in the tomb of Setee I., the father of Rameses II., the Pharaoh of the oppression. A translation of it appeared in the *Transactions of the Society of Biblical Arch-*

part is given to human blood, mingled with the juice of mandrakes[1]—instead of wine—prepared as a drink of the gods, and afterwards poured out again to overflow and to revivify all the earth. And the ancient text which records this legend, affirms that it was in conjunction with these events that there was the beginning of sacrifices in the world.

An early American legend has points of remarkable correspondence with this one from ancient Egypt. It relates, as does that, to a pre-historic destruction of the race, and to its re-creation, or its re-vivifying, by means of transferred blood. Every Mexican province

æology, Vol. 4, Part I. Again it has been found in the tomb of Rameses III. Its earliest and its latest translations were made by M. Edouard Naville, the eminent Swiss Egyptologist. Meantime, Brugsch, De Bergmann, Lauth, Lefébure, and others, have aided in its elucidation (See *Proceed. of Soc. of Bib. Arch.*, for March 3, 1885).

Is there not a reference to this legend in the Book of the Dead, chapter xviii., sixth section?

[1] Mandrakes, or "love-apples," among the ancient Egyptians, as also among the Orientals generally, from the days of Jacob (Gen. 30: 14–17) until to-day, carried the idea of promoting a loving union; and the Egyptian name for mandrakes—*tetmut*—combined the root-word *tet* already referred to as meaning "arm," or "bracelet," and *mut*—with the signification of "attesting," or "confirming." Thus the blood and the mandrake juice would be a true *assiratum*. (See Pierret's *Vocabulaire Hiéroglyphique*, p. 723.) "Belief in this plant [the mandrake] is as old as history." (Napier's *Folk-Lore*, p. 90.) See, also, Lang's *Custom and Myth*, pp. 143–155.

told this story in its own way, says a historian; but
the main features of it are alike in all its versions.

When there were no more men remaining on the
earth, some of the gods desired the re-creation of mankind; and they asked help from the supreme deities
accordingly. They were then told, that if they were
to obtain the bones or the ashes of the former race,
they could revivify those remains by their own blood.
Thereupon Xolotl, one of the gods, descended to the
place of the dead, and obtained a bone (whether a *rib*,
or not, does not appear). Upon that vestige of humanity the gods dropped blood drawn from their own
bodies; and the result was a new vivifying of mankind.[1]

An ancient Chaldean legend, as recorded by Berosus,
ascribes a new creation of mankind to the mixture, by
the gods, of the dust of the earth with the blood that
flowed from the severed head of the god Belus. "On
this account it is that men are rational, and partake of
divine knowledge," says Berosus.[2] The blood of the
god gives them the life and the nature of a god. Yet,
again, the early Phœnician, and the early Greek, the-
ogonies, as recorded by Sanchoniathon[3] and by Hes-
iod,[4] ascribe the vivifying of mankind to the outpoured

[1] Mendieta's *Hist. Eccl. Ind.*, 77 ff.; cited in Spencer's *Des. Soc.*, II.,
38; also Brinton's *Myths of the New World*, p. 258.
[2] See Cory's *Anc. Frag.*, p. 59 f.   [3] *Ibid.*, p. 15.
[4] Comp. Fabri's *Evagatorium*, III., 218.

blood of the gods. It was from the blood of Ouranos, or of Saturn, dripping into the sea and mingling with its foam, that Venus was formed, to become the mother of her heroic posterity. "The Orphics, which have borrowed so largely from the East," says Lenormant,[1] "said that the immaterial part of man, his soul [his life], sprang from the blood of Dionysus Zagreus, whom . . . Titans had torn to pieces, partly devouring his members."

Homer explicitly recognizes this universal belief in the power of blood to convey life, and to be a means of revivifying the dead. When Circé sent Odysseus

> " To consult
> The Theban seer, Tiresias, in the abode
> Of Pluto and the dreaded Proserpine,"

she directed him, in preparation, to

> "Pour to all the dead
> Libations,—milk and honey first, and next
> Rich wine, and lastly water ; "

and after that to slay the sacrificial sheep. But Circé's caution was :

> " Draw then the sword upon thy thigh, and sit,
> And suffer none of all those airy forms
> To touch the blood, until thou first bespeak
> Tiresias. He will come, and speedily,—
> The leader of the people,—and will tell
> What voyage thou must make."

---

[1] *Beginnings of History*, p. 52, note.
10*

Odysseus did as he was directed. The bloodless shades flocked about him, as he sat there guarding the life-renewing blood; but even those dearest to him he forbade to touch that consecrated draught.

> "And then the soul of Anticleia came,—
> My own dead mother, daughter of the king
> Autolycus, large minded.   Her I left
> Alive, what time I sailed for Troy, and now
> I wept to see her there, and pitied her,
> And yet forbade her, though with grief, to come
> Near to the blood till I should first accost
> Tiresias.   He too came, the Theban seer,
> Tiresias, bearing in his hand a wand
> Of gold; he knew me and bespake me thus :—
> ' Why, O unhappy mortal, hast thou left
> The light of day to come among the dead,
> And to this joyless land?   Go from the trench
> And turn thy sword away, that I may drink
> The blood, and speak the word of prophecy.'
> He spake; withdrawing from the trench, I thrust
> Into its sheath my silver-studded sword,
> And, after drinking of the dark red blood,
> The blameless prophet turned to me and said—" [1]

Then came the prophecy from the blood-revivified seer.

The wide-spread popular superstition of the vampire and of the ghoul seems to be an outgrowth of this universal belief that transfused blood is re-vivification. The bloodless shades, leaving their graves at night, seek renewed life by drawing out the blood of

---

[1] Bryant's *Odyssey*, Bks. x. and xi.

those who sleep ; taking of the life of the living, to
supply temporary life to the dead. This idea was
prevalent in ancient Babylon and Assyria.[1] It has
shown itself in the Old World and in the New,[2] in all
the ages ; and even within a little more than a century,
it has caused an epidemic of fear in Hungary, "resulting in a general disinterment, and the burning or stak-
ing of the suspected bodies."[3]

An added force is given to all these illustrations of
the universal belief that transferred blood has a vivifying power, by the conclusions of modern medical
science concerning the possible benefits of blood-
transfusion.[4] On this point, one of the foremost living
authorities in this department of practice, Dr. Roussel,
of Geneva, says : "The great vitality of the blood of
a vigorous and healthy man has the power of improving the quality of the patient's blood, and can restore
activity to the centres of nervous force, and the organs
of digestion. *It would seem that health itself can be*

---

[1] See Sayce's *Anc. Emp. of East*, p. 146.

[2] Among the ancient Peruvians, there was said to be a class of devil-
worshipers, known as *canchus*, or *rumapmicuc*, the members of which
sucked the blood from sleeping youth, to their own nourishing and to
the speedy dying away of the persons thus depleted. (See Arriaga's
Extirpacion de la Idolatria del Piru, p. 21 f. ; cited in Spencer's *Des.
Soc.*, II., 48.). See, also, Ralston's *Russian Folk Tales*, pp. 311–328.

[3] Farrer's *Primitive Manners and Customs*, p. 23 f.

[4] The primitive belief seems to have had a sound basis in scientific fact.

transfused with the blood of a healthy man";[1] death itself being purged out of the veins by inflowing life. And in view of the possibilities of new life to a dying one, through new blood from one full of life, this writer insists that "every adult and healthy man and woman should be ready to offer an *arm*, as the natural and mysteriously inexhaustible source of the wonder-working elixir."[2]   Blood-giving can be life-giving. The measure of one's love may, indeed, in *such* a case, be tested by the measure of his yielded blood.[3]

Roussel says that blood transfusion was practised by the Egyptians, the Hebrews, and the Syrians, in ancient times;[4] and he cites the legend that, before Naaman came to Elisha to be healed of his leprosy,[5] his physicians, in their effort at his cure, took the blood from his veins, and replaced it with other blood. Whatever basis of truth there may be in this legend, it clearly gained its currency through the prevailing conviction that new blood is new life.   There certainly is ample evidence that baths of human blood were anciently prescribed as a cure for the death-representing leprosy; as if in recognition of this root idea of the re-vivifying power of transferred blood.

Pliny, writing eighteen centuries ago concerning

---

[1] *Transfusion of Human Blood*, pp. 2–4.   [2] *Ibid.*, p. 5.
[3] See pages 85–88, *supra*.   [4] *Transf. of Blood*, p. 5.
[5] 2 Kings 5: 1–14.

leprosy, or elephantiasis, says[1] : " This was the peculiar disease of Egypt; and when it fell upon princes, woè to the people; for, in the bathing chambers, tubs were prepared, with human blood, for the cure of it." Nor was this mode of life-seeking confined to the Egyptians. It is said that the Emperor Constantine was restrained from it only in consequence of a vision from heaven.[2]

In the early English romance of Amys and Amylion, one of these knightly brothers-in-arms consents, with his wife's full approbation, to yield the lives of his two infant children, in order to supply their blood for a bath, for the curing of his brother friend's leprosy.[3] In this instance, the leprosy is cured, and the children's lives are miraculously restored to them; as if in proof of the divine approbation of the loving sacrifice.

It is shown, indeed, that this belief in the life-bringing power of baths of blood to the death-smitten lepers, was continued into the Middle Ages; and that it finally "received a check from an opinion gradually gaining ground, that only the blood of those would be efficacious, who offered themselves freely and voluntarily for a beloved sufferer."[4] There is something

---

[1] *Hist. Nat.* xxvi., 5.

[2] See *Notes and Queries*, for Feb. 28, 1857 ; with citation from Soane's *New Curiosities of Literature*, I., 72.

[3] *Ibid.;* also Mills's *History of Chivalry*, chap. IV., note.

[4] See citation from Soane, in *Notes and Queries*, supra.

very suggestive in this thought of the truest potency
of transferred life through transferred blood! It is this
thought which finds expression and illustration in
Longfellow's Golden Legend.   In the castle of Vauts-
berg on the Rhine, Prince Henry is sick with a strange
and hopeless malady.   Lucifer appears to him in the
garb of a traveling physician, and tells him of the only
possible cure for his disease, as prescribed in a venerable tome:

> " 'The only remedy that remains
>   Is the blood that flows from a maiden's veins,
>   Who of her own free will shall die,
>   And give her life as the price of yours!'
>   That is the strangest of all cures,
>   And one, I think, you will never try;
>   The prescription you may well put by,
>   As something impossible to find
>   Before the world itself shall end!"

Elsie, the lovely daughter of a peasant in the Oden-
wald, learns of the Prince's need, and declares she will
give her blood for his cure.   In her chamber by night,
her self-surrendering prayer goes up:

> " 'If my feeble prayer can reach thee,
>   O my Saviour, I beseech thee,
>   Even as thou hast died for me,
>   More sincerely
>   Let me follow where thou leadest,
>   Let me, bleeding as thou bleedest,

Die, if dying I may give
Life to one who asks to live,
And more nearly,
Dying thus, resemble thee!' "

Her father, Gottlieb, consents to her life-surrender,
saying to the Prince :

" 'As Abraham offered, long ago,
His son unto the Lord, and even
The Everlasting Father in heaven
Gave his, as a lamb unto the slaughter,
So do I offer up my daughter.' "

And Elsie adds :

" ' My life is little,
Only a cup of water,
But pure and limpid.
Take it, O Prince !
Let it refresh you,
Let it restore you.
It is given willingly
It is given freely ;
May God bless the gift !' "

The proffered sacrifice is interfered with before its consummation ; but its purposed method shows the estimate which was put, from of old, on voluntarily yielded
life for life.

There is said to be an Eastern legend somewhat
like the story of Amys and Amylion ; with a touch
of the ancient Egyptian and Mexican legends already
cited. "The Arabian chronicler speaks of a king,

who, having lost a faithful servant by his transformation into stone, is told that he can call his friend back to life, if he is willing to behead his two children, and to sprinkle the ossified figure with their blood. He makes up his mind to the sacrifice; but as he approaches the children with his drawn sword, the will is accepted by heaven for the deed, and he suddenly sees the stone restored to animation." [1] This story, in substance, (only with the slaying and the resuscitating of the children, as in the English romance,) appears in Grimm's folk-lore tales, under the title of "Faithful John";[2] but whether its origin was in the East or in the North, or in both quarters, is not apparent. Its reappearance East, North, and West, is all the more noteworthy.

In the romances of King Arthur and his knights, there is a story of a maiden daughter of King Pellinore, a sister of Sir Percivale, who befriends the noble Sir Galahad, and then accompanies him and his companions on their way to the castle of Carteloise, and beyond, in their search for the Holy Grail.

"And again they went on to another castle, from which came a band of knights, who told them of the custom of the place, that every maiden who passed by

---

[1] Citation from "Saturday Review," for Feb. 14, 1857, in *Notes and Queries*, supra.

[2] See Grimm's *Household Tales*, I., 23–30.

must yield a dish full of her blood. ' That shall she not do,' said Galahad, ' while I live ' ; and fierce was the struggle that followed ; and the sword of Galahad, which was the sword of King David, smote them down on every side, until those who remained alive craved peace, and bade Galahad and his fellows come into the castle for the night ; 'and on the morn,' they said, 'we dare say ye will be of one accord with us, when ye know the reason for our custom.' So awhile they rested, and the knights told them that in the castle there lay a lady sick to death, who might never gain back her life, until she should be anointed with the blood of a pure maiden who was a king's daughter. Then said Percivale's sister, ' I will yield it, and so shall I get health to my soul, and there shall be no battle on the morn.' And even so was it done ; but the blood which she gave was so much that she might not live ; and as her strength passed away, she said to Percivale, ' I die, brother, for the healing of this lady.' . . . Thus was the lady of the castle healed ; and the gentle maiden, [Percivale's sister,] . . . died." [1]

In the old Scandinavian legends, there are indications of the traditional belief in the power of transferred life through a bath of blood. Siegfried, or Sigurd, a descendant of Odin, slew Fafner, a dragon-shaped guardian of ill-gotten treasure. In the hot blood of

[1] Cox and Jones's *Popular Romances of the Middle Ages*, pp. 85–87.

that dragon he bathed himself, and so took on, as it were, an outer covering of new life, rendering himself sword-proof, save at a single point where a leaf of the linden-tree fell between his shoulders, and shielded the flesh from the life-imparting blood.[1]   On this incident it is, that the main tragedy in the Nibelungen Lied pivots; where Siegfried's wife, Kriemhild, tells the treacherous Hagan of her husband's one vulnerable point:

> " Said she, My husband 's daring, and thereto stout of limb ;
> Of old, when on the mountain he slew the dragon grim,
> In its blood he bathed him, and thence no more can feel,
> In his charmed person, the deadly dint of steel.
>
> .   .   .   .
>
> " As from the dragon's death-wounds gushed out the crimson gore,
> With the smoking torrent, the warrior washed him o'er.
> A leaf then 'twixt his shoulders fell from the linden bough ;
> There, only, steel can harm him ; for that I tremble now." [2]

Even among the blood-reverencing Brahmans of India there are traces of this idea, that life is to be guarded by the outpoured blood of others.   In the famous old work, " Kalila wa-Dimna," there is the story of a king, named Beladh, who had a vision in the night, which so troubled him that he sought coun- sel of the Brahmans.   Their advice was, that he should sacrifice his favorite wife, his best loved son,

[1] Cox and Jones's *Romances of the Middle Ages*, p. 292.

[2] Lettsom's *Nibel. Lied*, p. 158.

his nephew, and his dearest friend, in conjunction with other valued offerings to the gods. " It will be necessary for you, O King," they said, " when you have put to death the persons we have named to you, to fill a cauldron with their blood, and sit upon it; and when you get up from the cauldron, we, the Brahmans, assembled from the four quarters of the kingdom, will walk around you, and pronounce our incantations over you, and we will spit upon you, and wipe off from you the blood, and will wash you in water and sweet-oil, and then you may return to the palace, trusting in the protection of heaven against the danger which threatens you." [1]

Here the king's offering to the gods was to be of that which was dearest to him; and the bath of blood was to prove to him a cover of life. King Beladh wisely said that, if that were the price of his safety, he was ready to die. He would not prolong his life at such a cost. But the story shows the primitive estimate of the life-giving power of blood among the Hindoos.

In China, also, blood has its place as a life-giving agency. A Chinese woman, on the Kit-ie River, tells a missionary of her occasional seasons of frenzy, under the control of spirits, and of her ministry of blood, at such seasons, for the cure of disease. " Every

---

[1] *Kalila wa-Dimna*, p. 315–319.

year when there is to be a pestilence, or when cholera is to prevail, she goes into this frenzy, and cuts her tongue with a knife, letting some drops of her blood fall into a hogshead of water. This [homœopathically-treated] water the people drink as a specific against contagion." Its sacred blood is counted a shield of life. "With the rest of the blood, she writes charms, which the people paste [as words of life] upon their door-posts, or wear upon their persons, as preventives of evil."[1]

Receiving new blood as a means of receiving new life, seems to have been sought interchangeably, in olden time, in various diseases, by blood lavations, by blood drinking, and by blood transfusion. It is recorded that, in 1483, King Louis XI., of France, struggled for life by drinking the blood of young children, as a means of his revivifying. "Every day he grew worse," it is said; "and the medicines profited him nothing, though of a strange character; for he vehemently hoped to recover by the human blood which he took and swallowed from certain children."[2] Again there is a disputed claim, that, in 1492, a Jewish physician endeavored to save the life of Pope Innocent VIII. by giving him in transfusion the blood of three

[1] Fielde's *Pagoda Shadows*, p. 88.

[2] *Croniques de France*, 1516, feuillet c c i j, cited from Soane, in *Notes and Queries*, supra.

young men successively. The Pope was not recovered, but the three young men lost their lives in the experiment.[1] Yet blood transfusion as a means of new life to the dying was not always a failure, even in former centuries; for the record stands, that "at Frankfort, on the Oder, the surgeons Balthazar, Kaufman, and Purmann, healed a leper, in 1683, by passing the blood of a lamb into his veins."[2]

Even to-day, in South Africa, "when the Zulu king is sick, his immediate personal attendants, or *valets*, are obliged to allow themselves to be wounded; that a portion of their blood may be introduced into the king's circulation, and a portion of his into theirs."[3] In this plan, the idea seems to be, that health may have power over disease, and that death may be swallowed up in life, by equalizing the blood of the one who is in danger, and of the many who are in strength and safety. Moreover, among the Kafirs those who are still in health are sometimes "washed in blood to protect them against wounds";[4] as if an outer covering of life could be put on, for the protec-

---

[1] Roussel's *Trans. of Blood*, p. 6. A different version of this story is given in Bruy's *Histoire des Papes*, IV., 278; but the other version is supported by two independent sources, in *Infessuræ Diarium*, and *Burchardi Diarium*. See *Notes and Queries*, 5th Series, III., 496, and IV., 38; also Hare's *Walks in Rome*, p. 590.

[2] *Dict. Méd. et Chirurg. Prat.*, Art. "Transfusion."

[3] Shooter's *Kafirs of Natal*, p. 117.   [4] *Ibid.*, p. 216.

11*

tion of their life within. Transfused human blood is also said to be a common prescription of the medicine-men of Tasmania, for the cure of disease.[1]

And so it would appear, that, whatever may be its basis in physiological science, the opinion has prevailed, widely and always, that there is a vivifying power in transferred blood; and that blood not only represents but carries life.

3. A NEW NATURE THROUGH NEW BLOOD.

It was a primeval idea, of universal sway, that the taking in of another's blood was the acquiring of another's life, with all that was best in that other's nature. It was not merely that the taking away of blood was the taking away of life; but that the taking in of blood was the taking in of life, and of all that that life represented. Here, again, the heart, as the fountain of blood, and so as the centre and source of life, was pre-eminently the agency of transfer in the acquiring of a new nature.

Herodotus tells us of this idea in the far East, twenty-four centuries ago. When a Scythian, he said, killed his first man in open warfare, he drank in his blood as a means of absorbing his fairly acquired life; and the heads of as many as he slew, the Scythian carried

[1] Bonwick's *Daily Life and Origin of Tasmanians*, p. 89; cited in Spencer's *Des. Soc.*, III., 43.

in triumph to the king;[1] as the American Indian bears away the scalps of his slain, to-day. Modern historians, indeed, show us other resemblances than this between the aboriginal American and the ancient Scythian.

The Jesuit founder of the Huron Mission to the American Indians, "its truest hero, and its greatest martyr," was Jean de Brébeuf. After a heroic life among a savage people, he was subjected to frightful torture, and to the cruelest death. His character had won the admiration of those who felt that duty to their gods demanded his martyrdom; and his bearing under torture exalted him in their esteem, as heroic beyond compare. "He came of a noble race," says Parkman,[2]—"the same [race], it is said, from which sprang the English Earls of Arundel; but never had the mailed barons of his line confronted a fate so appalling, with so prodigious a constancy. To the last he refused to flinch, and ' his death was an astonishment to his murderers.'" "We saw no part of his body," wrote an eye-witness,[3] "from head to foot, which was not burned [while he was yet living], even to his eyes, in the sockets of which these wretches had placed live coals." Such manhood as he displayed under these tortures, the Indians could appre-

[1] *Hist.*, IV., 64.   [2] *Jesuits in No. Am. in 17th Cent.*,p. 389 f.
[3] Ragueneau; cited by Parkman.

ciate. Such courage and constancy as his, they longed
to possess for themselves.   When, therefore, they perceived that the brave and faithful man of God was
finally sinking into death, they sprang toward him,
scalped him, "laid open his breast, and came in a
crowd to drink the blood of so valiant an enemy;
thinking to imbibe with it some portion of his courage.   A chief then tore out his heart, and devoured it."

Not unlike this has been a common practice among
the American Indians, in the treatment of prisoners of
war.   "If the victim had shown courage," again says
Parkman, concerning the Hurons, "the heart was first
roasted, cut into small pieces, and given to the young
men and boys, who devoured it, to increase their own
courage."[1]   So, similarly, with the Iroquois.[2]   And
Burton says of the Dakotas:[3] "They are not cannibals, except when a warrior, after slaying a foe, eats,
porcupine-like, the heart or liver, with the idea of in-
creasing his own courage."   Schomburgk, writing
concerning the natives of British Guiana, says: "In
order to increase their courage, and [so their] con-
tempt of death, the Caribs were wont to cut out the
heart of a slain enemy, dry it on the fire, powder it,
and mix the powder in their drink."[4]

---

[1] *Jesuits in No. Am.*, Introduction, p. xxxix.   [2] *Ibid.*, p. 250.
[3] *City of the Saints*, p. 117.   See also Appendix.
[4] *Reisen in Brit. Guian.*, II., 430; cited in Spencer's *Des. Soc.*, VI., 36.

The native Australians find, it is said, an inducement to bloodshed, in their belief—like that of the ancient Scythians—that the life, or the spirit, of the first man whom one slays, enters into the life of the slayer, and remains as his helpful possession thereafter.[1] The Ashantee fetishmen, of West Africa, apparently acting on a kindred thought, make a mixture of the hearts of enemies, mingled with blood and consecrated herbs, for the vivifying of the conquerors. "All who have never before killed an enemy eat of the preparation; it being believed that if they did not, their energy would be secretly wasted by the haunting spirits of their deceased foes."[2] The underlying motive of the bloody "head-hunting" in Borneo, is the Dayak belief, that the spirits of those whose heads are taken are to be subject to him who does the decapitating. The heads are primarily simply the proof—like the Indian's scalps—that their owner has so many lives absorbed in his own.[3]

A keen observer of Fellâheen life in Palestine has reported:[4] "There is an ugly expression used among

[1] *Trans. of Ethn. Soc.* new series, III., 240, cited in Spencer's *Des. Soc.*, III., 36.

[2] Beecham's *Ashantee and the Gold Coast*, p. 211; cited in Spencer's *Des Soc.*, IV., 33.

[3] See Tylor's *Primitive Culture*, I., 459; also Bock's *Head Hunters of Borneo*, passim.

[4] Mrs. Finn's "Fellaheen of Palestine" in *Surv. of West. Pal.* "Special Papers," p. 360.

the fellâheen of South Palestine, in speaking of an enemy slain in war—'*Dhabbahhtho bisnâny*' ('I slew him with my teeth')[1]; and it is said that there have been instances of killing in battle in this fashion by biting at the throat. In the Nablous district (Samaria), where the people are much more ferocious, the expression is, 'I have drunk his blood'; but that is understood figuratively."

An ancient Greek version of the story of Jason, telling of that hero's treatment of the body of Apsyrtos—whom he had slain—says: " Thrice he tasted the blood, thrice [he] spat it out between his teeth ; " and a modern collator informs us that the scholiast here finds "the description of an archaic custom, popular among murderers."[2] This certainly corresponds with the Semitic phrases lingering among the Fellâheen of Palestine.

In the old German epic, the Nibelungen Lied, it is told of the brave Burgundians, when they were fighting desperately in the burning hall of the Huns, that they were given new courage for the hopeless conflict by drinking the blood of their fallen comrades; which " quenched their thirst, and made them fierce."[3] With

---

[1] This is Mrs. Finn's rendering of it; but it should be " I *sacrificed* him with my teeth." The Arabic word is obviously *dhabaha* (ذبح), identical with the Hebrew *zabhakh* (זָבַח) " to sacrifice."

[2] Lang's *Custom and Myth*, p. 95 f.; also Grimm's *Household Tales*, p. lxviii.

[3] Cox and Jones's *Pop. Rom. of Mid. Ages*, p. 310.

their added life, from the added blood of heroes, they
battled as never before.

> "It strung again their sinews, and failing strength renewed.
> This, in her lover's person, many a fair lady rued." [2]

Is there not, indeed, a trace of the primitive custom
—thus recognized in all quarters of the globe—of
absorbing the life of a slain one by drinking in his
blood, in our common phrase, "blood-thirstiness,"
as descriptive of a life-seeker? That phrase certainly
gains added force and appropriateness in the light of
this universal idea.

It is evident that the wide-spread popular belief in
nature-absorption through blood-appropriation, has
included the idea of a *tribal* absorption of new life in
vicarious blood. Alcedo, a Spanish-American writer,
has illustrated this in his description of the native
Araucanians of South America. When they have
triumphed in war, they select a representative prisoner
for official and vicarious execution. After due preparation, they "give him a handful of small sticks and a
sharp stake, with which they oblige him to dig a hole
in the ground; and in this they order him to cast the
sticks one by one, repeating the names of the principal
warriors of his country, while at the same time the
surrounding soldiers load these abhorred names with
the bitterest execrations. He is then ordered to cover

[2] Lettsom's *Nibel. Lied*, p. 373.

the hole, as if to bury therein the reputation and valor of their enemies, whom he has named. After this ceremony, the toqui, or one of his bravest companions to whom he relinquishes the honor of the execution, dashes out the brains of the prisoner with a club. The *heart* is immediately taken out, and presented palpitating to the general, who sucks a little of the *blood*, and passes it to his officers, who repeat in succession the same ceremony."[1] And in this way the life of the conquered tribe passes, symbolically, into the tribal life of the conquerors.

Burckhardt was so surprised at a trace of this idea in Nubia, that he could hardly credit the information concerning it; "although several persons asserted it to be a fact," he says; and he "heard no one contradict it."[2] As he learned it: "Among the Hallenga, who draw their origin from Abyssinia, a horrible custom is said to attend the revenge of blood. When the slayer has been seized by the relatives of the deceased, a family feast is proclaimed, at which the murderer is brought into the midst of them, bound upon an angareyg; and while his throat is slowly cut with a razor, the blood is caught in a bowl, and handed round amongst the guests; every one of whom is

[1] Thompson's *Alcedo's Geog. and Hist. Dict. of America*, I., 408; cited in Spencer's *Des. Soc.*, VI., 19.

[2] *Travels in Nubia*, p. 356.

bound to drink of it, at the moment the victim breathes his last." The forfeited life of the murderer here seems to be surrendered to, and formally appropriated by, the family, or clan, which he had, to the same extent, depleted of character and life.

A practice not unlike this is reported of the Australians, in their avenging the blood of a murdered person. They devour their victims; who are selected from the tribe of the murderer, although they may be personally innocent of the murder. The tribe depleted by the murder replaces its loss by blood—which is life—from the tribe of the murderer. Indeed, "when any one of a tribe [in New South Wales] dies a natural death, it is usual to avenge [or to cancel] the loss of the deceased by taking blood from one or other of his friends."[1] In this way, the very life and being of those whose blood is taken, go to restore to the bereaved ones the loss that death has brought to them.

Strange as this idea may seem to us, its root-thought, as a fact, is still an open question in the realm of physiological science. The claim is positive, in medical works, that insanity has been cured by the transfusion of a sane man's blood;[2] that a normal mind has been

[1] *Trans. of Ethn. Soc.,*II., 246, and Angas's *Austr. and New Zeal.,*I., 73, 227, 462, cited in Spencer's *Des. Soc.* III., 26.

[2] See *Dict. Méd. et Chir. Prat.*, Art. "Transfusion"; also Roussel's *Transf. of Blood*, pp. 78–88.

restored, through a normal life gained in new blood. Moreover, the question, how far the nature, or the characteristics, of an organism, are affected, in blood transfusion, by the nature, or the characteristics, of the donor of the transfused blood, is by no means a settled one among scientists. Referring to a series of questions in this line, propounded by Robert Boyle, more than two centuries ago, Roussel has said, within the past decade: "No one has been able to give any positive answers to them, based upon well-conducted operations"; and, "they still await solution in 1877, as in 1667."[1]

4. LIFE FROM ANY BLOOD, AND BY A TOUCH.

Because blood is life, all blood, and any blood, has been looked upon as a vehicle of transferred life. And because blood is life, and the heart is a fountain of blood, and so is a fountain of life,—a touch of blood, or, again, the minutest portion of a vital and vivifying heart, has been counted capable of transferring life, with all that life includes and carries; just as the merest cutting of a vine, or the tiniest seed of the mightiest tree, will suffice as the germ of that vine or that tree, in a new planting. The blood, or the heart, of the lower animals, has been deemed the vehicle of life and strength, in its transference; and a touch from

[1] *Transf. of Blood*, p. 19.

either has been counted potent in re-vivifying and in improving the receiving organism.

Thus, for example, Stanley, in the interior of Africa, having received "a fine, fat ox as a peace-offering," from "the great magic doctor of Vinyata," when making a covenant of blood with him,[1] was requested to return the heart of the ox to the donor; and he acceded to this request. After this, Stanley's party was several times assailed by the Wanyaturu, from the neighborhood of Vinyata. Thereupon his ally Mgongo Tembo explained, says Stanley, "that we ough⁺ not to have bestowed the *heart* of the presented ox upon the magic doctor of Vinyata; as by the loss of that diffuser of blood, the Wanyaturu believed we had left our own bodies weakened, and would be an easy prey to them."[2]

Another modern traveler in Equatorial Africa finds fresh bullock's blood counted a means of manhood. While the young Masâi man is passing his novitiate into warrior life, he seeks new strength by taking in new blood. Having employed medical means to rid his system of the remains of all other diet, says Thompson, the novice went to a lonely place with a single attendant; they taking with them a living bullock. There "they killed the bullock, either with a blow from a rungu, or by stabbing it in the back of

---

[1] See page 20, *supra*.   [2] *Thro. Dark Cont.*, I., 123–131.

the neck.   They then opened a vein and drank the
blood fresh from the animal."   After this, the young
man gorged himself with the bullock's flesh.[1]   And
whenever the Masâi warriors "go off on war-raids they
also contrive to eat a bullock [after this fashion], by
way of getting up their courage."[2]

Again, it is said that Arab women in North Africa
give their male children a piece of the lion's heart to
eat, to make them courageous.[3]   And an English
traveler in South Africa[4] describing the death of a lion
shot by his party, says: "Scarcely was the breath out
of his body than the Caffres rushed up, and each took
a mouthful of the blood that was trickling from the
numerous wounds; as they believe that it is a specific
which imparts strength and courage to those who partake of it."

That the transference of life, with all that life carries, can be made by the simplest blood-anointing, as
surely as by blood absorption, is strikingly illustrated
by a custom still observed among the Hill Tribes of
India.   The Bheels are a brave and warlike race of
mountaineers of Hindostan. They claim to have been,
formerly, the rulers of all their region; but, whether
by defeat in war, or by voluntary concession, to have

[1] Thompson's *Thro. Masâi Land*, p. 430.   [2] *Ibid.*, p. 452.

[3] Shooter's *Kafirs of Natal*, notes, p. 399.

[4] H. A. L., in *Sport in Many Lands*.

yielded their power to other peoples—whom they now
authorize to rule in their old domain. "The extraor-
dinary custom, common to almost all the countries [of
India] that have been mentioned," says Sir J. Malcolm,[1]
"of the *tika,* or mark that is put upon the forehead of
the Rajput prince, or chief, when he succeeds to
power, being moistened with blood taken from the toe
or thumb of a Bhill, may be received as one among
many proofs of their having been formerly in possession of the principalities, where this usage prevails.
    . . . The right of giving the blood for this cere-
mony, is claimed by particular families ; and the belief, that the individual, from whose veins it is supplied,
never lives beyond a twelvemonth, in no degree oper-
ates to repress the zeal of the Bhills to perpetuate an
usage, which the Rajput princes are, without exception, desirous should cease." The Bheels claim that
the right to rule is vested in their race ; but they transfer that right to the Rajpoot by a transfer of blood—
which is a transfer of life and of nature. Thus the
Bheels continue to rule—in the person of those who
have been vivified by their blood.

So, again, among the ancient Caribs, of South
America, "' as soon as a male child was brought into
the world, he was sprinkled with some drops of his

[1] See *Trans. Royal Asiat. Soc.*, I., 69; cited in Spencer's *Des. Soc.*,
V., 26 f.

father's blood'; the father 'fondly believing, that the same degree of courage which he had himself displayed, was by these means transmitted to his son.'"[1] Here it is evident that the voluntary transfusion of blood is deemed more potent to the strengthening of personal character, than is the transmission of blood by natural descent.

In South Africa, among the Amampondo, one of the Kaffir tribes, it is customary for the chief, on his accession to authority, " to be washed in the blood of a near relative, generally a brother, who is put to death on the occasion, and his skull used as a receptacle for his blood."[2]   In order to give more life and more character than the ordinary possession to the newly elevated chieftain, the family blood is withdrawn from the veins of one having less need of it, that it may be absorbed by him who can use it more imposingly.

In the Yoruba country, in Central Africa, "when a beast is sacrificed for a sick man, the blood is sprinkled on the wall, and smeared on the patient's forehead, with the idea, it is said, of thus transferring to him the [divinely] accepted victim's life." Life is life, and whether that life be in the blood of one organism or

[1] Edwards's *Hist. of Brit. West Ind.*, I., 47 ; cited in Spencer's *Des. Soc.*, VI., 36.
[2] Shooter's *Kafirs of Natal*, p. 216.

of another, of man or of an inferior animal, its transference carries with it all that life includes. That
seems to be the thought in Yoruba ; and, as all life is
of supernatural origin and preservation, its transference
can be by a touch as easily as by any other method.[1]

5. INSPIRATION THROUGH BLOOD.

Because blood, as life, belongs to, and, in a peculiar
sense, represents, the Author of life, blood has been
counted a means of inspiration. The blood of the
gods, in myth and legend, and again the blood of
divinely accepted sacrifices, human and animal, in
ancient and modern religious rituals, has been relied
on as the agency whereby the Author of life speaks
in and through the possessor of that blood.

The inspiring power of blood is a thought that runs
all through the early Norseland legends. Thus, Kvaser,
according to the Scandinavian mythology, was a being
created by the gods with preternatural intelligence.
Kvaser traversed the world, teaching men wisdom ;
but he was treacherously murdered by the dwarfs
Fjalar and Gala. The dwarfs let Kvaser's blood run
into two cups and a kettle. " The name of the kettle
is Odrœrer, and the names of the cups are Son and
Bodn. By mixing up his blood with honey, they

---

[1] See Tylor's *Prim. Cult.*, II., 382, referring to Bastian's *Psychologie.*

composed a drink of such surpassing excellence, that whoever partakes of it acquires the gift of song."[1] And that was the origin of poetry in the world; although there have been a good many imitations of the real article since that day.

So, again, in the Elder Edda, the hero Sigurd killed Fafner, at the instigation of Fafner's brother Regin. Regin cut out the heart of his brother, and gave it to Sigurd to roast, while he drank the blood of the murdered one. Touching the bleeding heart with his fingers, and then putting his fingers into his mouth, Sigurd found that he was now able to understand the voice of birds; and thenceforward he was a hero inspired.[2] Afterwards he gave his bride, Gudrun, "to eat of the remnant of Fafnir's heart; so *she* grew wise and great-hearted."[3]

Down to the present time, there are those in the far East, and in the far West, who seek inspiration by blood-drinking. All along the North Pacific coast, the shamanism of the native tribes shows itself in a craving for blood as a means and as an accompaniment of preternatural frenzy. The chief sorcerer, or medicine-man, has his seasons of demoniacal posses-

---

[1] See Anderson's *Norse Mythol.*, p. 247.

[2] *Ibid.*, p. 380; Lettsom's *Nibel. Lied*, Preface, p. ix.; Cox and Jones's *Pop. Rom. of Mid. Ages*, p. 254 f.

[3] *Pop. Rom. of Mid. Ages*, p. 260; also *Nib. Lied*, p. x.

sion, when he can communicate with the powers of
the air. At such times he is accustomed to spring
upon the members of his tribe, and bite out from their
necks or bodies the bleeding flesh, as a help to inspiration and debauch. None would venture to resist
these blood-thirsty assaults; but the scars which result
are always borne with pride.[1]

Another phase of this universal idea is reported by
a recent traveler in the Himalayan districts of India;
where, as he thinks, the forms of religion ante-date in
their origin those of Hindooism, or of Brahmanism,
and "have descended from very early ages." When
a favor is sought from a local divinity, "it is the *chela*
[or primitive seer] who gasps out the commands of
the *deoty* [the 'deity'], as he [the chela] shivers under
the divine afflatus, and [under] the vigorous application of the *soongul*, or iron scourge." But before the
chela can have "the divine afflatus" he must drink of
living blood. Thus, this traveler witnessed an appeal
to the snake-god, Kailung Nag, for fine weather for
the sowing of the crops. The sacrificial sheep was
procured by the people; the ceremonies of wild worship, including music, dancing, incense-burning, and
bodily flagellations, proceeded. "At length, all being
ready, the head of the victim was struck off with an

[1] See Bancroft's *Native Races*, III., 150; Brinton's *Myths of New
World*, p. 274 f.; Jackson's *Alaska*, p. 103 f.

axe. The body was then lifted up by several men, and the chela, seizing upon it like a tiger, drank the blood as it spurted from the neck. When all the blood had been sucked from the carcass, it was thrown down upon the ground, amid yells and shouts of '*Kail-ung Maharaj ki jai!*' ['Victory to the great king Kailung']. The dancing was then renewed, and became more violent, until, after many contortions, the chela [now blood-filled] gasped out that the deota accepted the sacrifice, and that the season would be favorable. This was received with renewed shouts, and the chela sank down upon the ground in a state of exhaustion."[1]

In the folk-lore of Scotland, as representing the primitive traditions of Western Europe, there are illustrations of the idea that the blood of the gods was communicated to earthly organisms. Thus, a scientific antiquarian of Scotland records in this line : " There was a popular saying that the robin "—the robin redbreast—" had a drop of God's blood in its veins, and that therefore to kill or hurt it was a sin, and that some evil would befall any one who did so ; and, conversely, any kindness done to poor robin would be repaid in some fashion. Boys did not dare to harry a robin's nest." On the other hand, the yellow-hammer

[1] Charles F. Oldham's " Native Faiths in the Himalayah," in *The Contemporary Review* for April, 1885.

and the swallow were said, each "to have a drop of
the Devil's blood in its veins"; so the one of these
birds—the yellow-hammer—was "remorselessly har-
ried"; and the other—the swallow—"was feared, and
therefore let alone."[1]   A similar legendary fear of the
swallow, and the guarding of his nest accordingly,
exists in Germany and in China.[2]

Another indication of the belief that human blood
has a vital connection with its divine source, and is
under the peculiar oversight of its divine Author, is
found in the wide-spread opinion that the blood of a
murdered man will bear witness against the murderer,
by flowing afresh at his touch; the living blood crying out from the dead body, by divine consent, in testimony of crime against the Author of life.   Ancient
European literature teems with incidents in the line of
this "ordeal of touch."

Thus it was, according to the Nibelungen Lied, that
Kriemhild fastened upon Hagan the guilt of murder-
ing her husband Siegfried; when Hagan and his asso-
ciates were gathered for the burial of the hero.

"Firmly they made denial; Kriemhild at once replied,
'Whoe'er in this is guiltless, let him this proof abide.
In sight of all the people let him approach the bier,
And so to each beholder shall the plain truth appear.'

[1] Napier's *Folk-Lore of the West of Scotland*, p. 111 f.

[2] Farrer's *Prim. Man. and Cust.*, p. 276 f.

"It is a mighty marvel, which oft e'en now we spy,
  That, when the blood-stain'd murderer comes to the murder'd nigh,
  The wounds break out a-bleeding; then too the same befell,
  And thus could each beholder the guilt of Hagan tell.
  The wounds at once burst streaming, fast as they did before;
  Those who then sorrowed deeply, now yet lamented more." [1]

Under Christian II., of Denmark, the " Nero of the North," early in the sixteenth century, there was a notable illustration of this confidence in the power of blood to speak for itself. A number of gentlemen being together in a tavern, one evening, they fell to quarreling, and " one of them was stabbed with a poniard. Now the murderer was unknown, by reason of the number [present]; although the person stabbed accused a pursuivant of the king's who was one of the company. The king, to find out the homicide, caused them all to come together in the stove [the tavern], and, standing round the corpse, he commanded that they should, one after another, lay their right hand on the slain gentleman's naked breast, swearing that they had not killed him. The gentlemen did so, and no sign appeared against them. The pursuivant only remained, who, condemned before in his own conscience, went first of all and kissed the dead man's feet. But, as soon as he had laid his hand upon his breast, the blood gushed forth in abundance, both out

[1] Lettsom's *Nibel. Lied*, p. 183; also Cox and Jones's *Pop. Rom. of Mid. Ages*, p. 47 f.

of his wound and his nostrils; so that, urged by this evident accusation, he confessed the murder, and was, by the king's own sentence, immediately beheaded."[1]

A striking example of the high repute in which this ordeal of touch was formerly held, and of the underlying idea on which its estimate was based, is reported from the State Trials of Scotland. It was during the trial of Philip Standsfield, in 1688, for the murder of his father, Sir James. The testimony was explicit, that when this son touched the body, the blood flowed afresh, and the son started back in terror, crying out, "Lord, have mercy upon me!" wiping off the blood, from his hand, on his clothes. Sir George M'Kenzie, acting for the State, at the inquest, said concerning this testimony and its teachings: "But they, fully persuaded that Sir James was murdered by his own son, sent out [with him] some surgeons and friends, who having raised the body, did see it bleed miraculously upon his touching it. In which, God Almighty himself was pleased to bear a share in the testimonies which we produce: that Divine Power which makes the blood circulate during life, has oft times, in all nations, opened a passage to it after death upon such occasions, but most in this case."[2]

[1] Benson's *Remarkable Trials*, p. 94, note.

[2] Cobbett's *State Trials*, XI., 1371; cited in *Anecdotes of Omens and Superstitions*, p. 47 f.

Mr. Henry C. Lea, in his erudite work on Superstition and Force, has multiplied illustrations of the ordeal of touch, or of "bier-right," all along the later centuries.[1] He recalls that "Shakspeare introduces it, in King Richard III., where Gloster interrupts the funeral of Henry VI., and Lady Anne exclaims:

> 'O gentlemen, see, see! dead Henry's wounds
> Open their congealed mouths, and bleed afresh.'"

He refers to the fact that it was an old-time Jewish custom to ask pardon of a corpse for any offenses committed against the living man, laying hold of the great toe of the corpse while thus asking; and if the asker had really inflicted any grievous injury on the deceased, the body was supposed to signify that fact by a copious hemorrhage from the nose.[2] "This, it will be observed," he adds, "is almost identical with the well-known story which relates that, when Richard Cœur-de-Lion hastened to the funeral of his father, Henry II., and met the procession at Fontevraud, the blood poured from the nostrils of the dead king, whose end he had hastened by his disobedience and rebellion." Mr. Lea shows that in some instances the bones of a murdered man are said to have given out

---

[1] *Superstition and Force*, pp. 315–323.

[2] Cited from Gamal. ben Pedahzur's *Book of Jewish Ceremonies*, p. 11.

fresh blood when handled by a murderer as long as twenty years, or even fifty, after the murder; and he gives ample evidence that a belief in this power of blood to speak for itself against the violator of God's law, still exists among the English-speaking people, and that it has manifested itself as a means of justice-seeking, in the United States, within a few years past.

6. INTER-COMMUNION THROUGH BLOOD.

Beyond the idea of inspiration through an interflow of God-representing blood, there has been in primitive man's mind (however it came there) the thought of a possible inter-communion with God through an inter-union with God by blood. God is life. All life is from God, and belongs to God. Blood is life. Blood, therefore, as life, may be a means of man's inter-union with God. As the closest and most sacred of covenants between man and man; as, indeed, an absolute merging of two human natures into one,—is a possibility through an inter-flowing of a common blood; so the closest and most sacred of covenants between man and God; so the inter-union of the human nature with the divine,—has been looked upon as a possibility, through the proffer and acceptance of a common life in a common blood-flow.

Whatever has been man's view of sin and its punishment, and of his separation from God because of unforgiven sin (I speak now of man as he is found, without the specific teachings of the Bible on this subject), he has counted blood—his own blood, in actuality or by substitute—a means of inter-union with God, or with the gods. Blood is not death, but life. The shedding of blood, Godward, is not the taking of life, but the giving of life. The outflowing of blood toward God is an act of gratitude or of affection, a proof of loving confidence, a means of inter-union. This seems to have been the universal primitive conception of the race. And an evidence of man's trust in the accomplished fact of his inter-union with God, or with the gods, by blood, has been the also universal practice of man's inter-communion with God, or with the gods, by his sharing, in food-partaking, of the body of the sacrificial offering, whose blood is the means of the divine-human inter-union.

Perhaps the most ancient existing form of religious worship, as also the simplest and most primitive form, is to be found in China, in the state religion, represented by the Emperor's worship at the Temple of Heaven, in Peking. And in that worship, the idea of the worshiper's inter-communion with God, through the body and blood of the sacrificial offering, is disclosed, even if not always recognized, by all the representative Western authorities on the religions of China.

"The Chinese idea of a sacrifice to the supreme

spirit of Heaven and of Earth is that of a banquet.
There is no trace of any other idea," says Dr. Edkins.[1]
Dr. Legge,[2] citing this statement, expands its significance by saying: "The notion of the whole service
[at the Temple of Heaven] might be that of a banquet; but a sacrifice and a banquet are incompatible
ideas."[3] He then shows that the Chinese character
tsî, signifying "sacrifice," "covers a much wider space
of meaning than our term sacrifice [as he seems to
view our use of that term]." Morrison gives as one
of the meanings of *tsî,* "That which is the medium
between, or brings together, men and gods"; and
Hsü Shan "says, that *tsî* is made up of two ideo-
grams;—one the primitive for spiritual beings, and the
other representing a right hand and a piece of flesh."
Legge adds: "The most general idea symbolized by
it is—an offering whereby communication and communion with spiritual beings [God, or the gods] is
effected."[4]

Dr. S. Wells Williams says that "no religious system has been found among the Chinese which taught

[1] *Religion in China,* pp. 23, 32.   [2] *The Religions of China,* p. 55.

[3] Dr. Legge here seems to use the word "sacrifice" in the light of a
single meaning which attaches to it. There is surely no incompatibil-
ity in the terms "banquet" and "sacrifice," as we find their two-fold
idea in the banquet-sacrifice of the Mosaic peace-offering (see Lev.
7: 11–15).

[4] *The Relig. of China,* Notes to Lect. I., p. 66.

13*

the doctrine of the atonement by the shedding of blood"; and this he counts "an argument in favor of their [the Chinese] antiquity"; adding that "the state religion . . . has maintained its main features during the past three thousand years."[1] Williams here, evidently, refers to an expiatory atonement for sin; and Legge has a similar view of the facts.[2] The idea of an approach to God through blood—blood as a means of favor, even if not blood as a canceling of guilt—is obvious in the outpouring of blood by the Emperor when he approaches God for his worship in the Temple of Heaven. The symbolic sacrifice in that worship, which precedes the communion, is of a whole "burnt offering, of a bullock, entire and without blemish";[3] and the blood of that offering is reverently poured out into the earth,[4] to be buried there, according to the thought of man and the teachings of God in all the ages. It is even claimed that as early as 2697 B. C., it was the blood of the first-born which must be poured out toward God—as a means of favor —in the Emperor's approach for communion with

[1] *The Mid. King.*, II., 194. See also Martin's *The Chinese*, p. 258.

[2] *The Relig. of China*, p. 53 f. Gray thinks differently (*China*, I., 87.)

[3] *The Mid. King.*, I., 76–78; *The Chinese*, p. 99; *Relig. in China*, p. 21; *The Relig. of China*, p. 25; *Confucianism and Taouism*, p. 87.

[4] *Relig. in China*, p. 22. The same is true in sacrifices to Confucius (Gray's *China*, I., 87).

God; "a first-born male" being offered up "as a whole burnt sacrifice," in this worship.[1] Surely, in this surrender of the first-born, there must have been some idea of an affectionate offering, in the gift of that which was dearest, even if there was no idea of substitution by way of expiation; something in addition to the simple idea of "a banquet"; something which was an essential preliminary to the banquet.

Access to God being attained by the Emperor, the Emperor enjoys communion with God in the Temple of Heaven. It is after the outpouring of blood, and the offering of the holocaust, that—in a lull of the orchestral music, in the great annual sacrifice—"a single voice is heard, on the upper terrace of the altar, chanting the words, 'Give the cup of blessing, and the meat of blessing.' In response, the officer in charge of the cushion advances and kneels, spreading the cushion. Other officers present the cup of blessing and the meat of blessing [which have already been presented Godward] to the Emperor, who partakes of the wine and returns them. The Emperor then again prostrates himself, and knocks his forehead three times against the ground, and then nine times more, to represent his thankful reception of the wine and meat [in communion]."[2]

[1] *Chow le*, cited by Douglas in *Confuc. and Taou.*, p. 82 f.
[2] Edkins's *Relig. in China*, p. 27.

The evidence is abundant, that the main idea of this primitive and supreme service in the religions of China is the inter-communion of the Emperor with God. And there is no lack of proof that in China, as elsewhere all the world over, blood—as life—is the means of covenanting in an indissoluble inter-union; of which inter-union, inter-communion is a result and a proof.

In China, as also in India,[1] when the sacrifice of human beings was abolished, it was followed by the sacrifice of the horse.   And the horse-sacrifice is still practised in some parts of the Chinese Empire, on important occasions.   A white horse is brought to the brink of a stream, or a lake, and there sacrificed, by decapitating it, "burying its head below low-water mark, but *reserving its carcase for food.*"[2]   In a description of this sacrifice, in honor of a certain goddess, as witnessed by Archdeacon Gray,[3] it is said: "Its *blood* was received in a large earthenware jar, and a portion carried to the temple of the aforesaid goddess; when all the villagers rushed tumultuously to secure a sprinkling of blood on the charms which they had

[1] See page 156 f., *infra.*

[2] " The flesh of the horse is eaten both by the Chinese and the Mongolians."   (Gray's *China*, II., 174.)

[3] See C. F. Gordon Cumming's article "A Visit to the Temple of Heaven at Peking," in *Lond. Quart. Rev.*, for July, 1885.

already purchased. The rest of the blood was mingled with sand," and taken, with various accessories, in a boat. "This boat headed a long procession of richly carved and gilded boats, in which were priests, both Buddhist and Taouists, and village warriors discharging matchlocks to terrify the water-devils; while the men in the first boat sprinkle the waters, as they advance, with blood-stained sand."

So, again, it is the blood of a cock,—not the body but the blood,—which is made the propitiatory offering to the goddess known as " Loong-moo, or the Dragon's Mother," on the river junks of China. The blood is sprinkled on the deck, near a temporary altar, where libations of wine have already been poured out by the master of this junk, who is the sacrificer. Afterwards, bits of silver paper are " sprinkled with the blood, and then fastened to the door-posts and lintels of the cabin ";[1] as if in token of the blood-covenant between those who are within those doors and the goddess whose substitute blood is there affixed. And this precedes the feast of inter-communion.[2]

Nor are indications wanting, that the idea of inter-union with the gods by blood was originally linked with, if it were not primarily based upon, the rite of blood-covenanting between two human friends. Thus, Archdeacon Gray unconsciously discloses traces of

[1] See Exod. 12: 7–10.   [2] Gray's *China*, II., 271 f.

this rite, in his description of the exorcising of demons from the body of a child, by a Taouist priest, in Canton.[1]   Certain preliminary ceremonies were concluded, which were supposed to drive out the demons. "The priest then proceeded to uncover his [own] arm, and made an incision with a lancet in the fleshy part. The blood which flowed from the wound, was allowed to mingle with a small quantity of water in a cup. The seal of the temple, the impression of which was the name of the idol, was then dipped into the blood, and stamped upon the wrists, neck, back and forehead[2] of the poor heathen child." By this means, that child was symbolically sealed in covenant relations with the god of that temple, by the substitute blood of that god's representative priest.

Thus, also, Dr. Legge, referring to old-time covenantings in China, says :[3] "Many covenants were made among the feudal princes,—made over the blood of a victim, with which each covenanting party smeared the corners of his mouth [which is one form of tasting];[4] while an appeal was addressed to the invisible powers to inflict vengeance on all who should violate the conditions agreed upon [the ordinary imprecatory prayers in the rite of blood-covenanting]." A symbolic inter-

---

[1] Gray's *China*, I., 102.

[2] See Rev. 7 : 3; 9 : 4; 13 : 16; 14 : 1; 20 : 4; 22 : 4.

[3] *The Relig. of China*, p. 289.   [4] See The Rite in Burmah, in Appendix.

union of blood is a basis of inter-communion between two human beings, as also between the human and the divine beings even in China—where, perhaps, that idea would be least likely to be looked for.

It is a common opinion, that in no part of the world is there a more general prejudice against blood-shedding, or the taking of animal life, than in India. And it certainly is a fact, that the great religious systems, of Brahmanism and of Booddhism, which have controlled the moral sense of the peoples of India for a score or two of centuries, have exerted themselves, in the main, to the inculcation of these views as to the sacredness of blood and of life—or of blood which is life. Hence, we would naturally look, in India, only for traces, or vestiges, of the primitive, world-wide idea of inter-communion with God, or with the gods, through a divine-human inter-union by blood. Nor are such traces and vestiges lacking in the religious customs of India.

In India, as in China, human sacrifices, especially the sacrifice of the first-born son, were formerly made freely, as a means of bringing the offerer into closer relations with the gods, through the outpoured blood.[1] It was the blood, as the life, which was believed to be the common possession of gods, men, and beasts;

---

[1] See Dubois's *Des. Man. and Cust. of People of India*, Part III., chap. 7; also Monier Williams's *Hinduism*, p. 36 f.

hence the final substitution, in India, of beasts for men, in the blood-covenanting with the gods. On this point, the evidence seems clear.

The Vedas, or sacred books of the Brahmans, teach, indeed, that the gods themselves were mere mortals, until by repeated offerings of blood in sacrifice, to the Supreme Being, they won immortality from him; which is only another way of making the claim, put forward by the immortalized-mortal, in the Book of the Dead, of ancient Egypt, that the mortal became one with the gods through an interflow of a common life in the common blood of the two. Mortals gave the blood of their first-born sons in sacrifice to the Supreme Being. Then the Supreme Being gave the blood of his first-born male in sacrifice. Thus, the nature of the favored mortals and the nature of the Supreme Being became one and the same. Dr. Monier Williams cites freely from the Vedas in the direction of this great truth; although he does not note its bearing on the blood-covenant rite. Thus, in "the following free translation of a passage of the Satapatha-brāhmana:

> 'The gods lived constantly in dread of Death—
> The mighty Ender—so, with toilsome rites
> They worshiped, and repeated sacrifices,
> Till they became immortal.'"

"And again in the Taittirīya-brahmana: 'By means of

the sacrifice the gods obtained heaven.'" In the Tān-
dya-brāhmanas : "The lord of creatures offered himself a sacrifice for the gods." "And again, in the
Satapatha-brāhmana : 'He who, knowing this, sacrifices with the *Purusha-medha,* or sacrifice of the primeval male, becomes everything.'"[1]

That it was the *blood,* which was the chief element
in the covenanting-sacrifice, is evident from all the
facts in the case. Thus, in the Aitareya-brāhmana, it
is said : "The gods killed a man for their victim [of
sacrifice]. But from him thus killed, the part which
was fit for a sacrifice went out and entered a horse.
Thence, the horse became an animal fit for being sacrificed. The gods then killed the horse, but the part
of it fit for being sacrificed went out of it and entered an
ox. The gods then killed the ox, but the part of it fit
for being sacrificed went out of it and entered a
sheep. Thence it entered a goat. The sacrificial part
remained for the longest time in the goat ; thence it
[the goat] became pre-eminently fit for being sacrificed!" Indian history shows that this has been the progress of reform, from the days of human sacrifice down-
ward. "It is remarkable that in Vedic times, even a cow
. . . was sometimes killed ; and goats, as is well
known, are still sacrificed to the goddess Kālī."[2] Kālī,
also called Doorgā, is the blood-craving goddess. The

[1] Monier Williams's *Hinduism,* p. 35 f.   [2] *Ibid.,* p. 37 f.

14

blood of one human victim, it is said, "gives her a gleam of pleasure that endures a thousand years; and the sacrifice of three men together, would prolong her ecstasy for a thousand centuries."[1]

Bishop Heber indicates the "sacrificial part" of the goat as he saw it offered at a temple of Kālī in Umeer. He was being shown by his guide through that city, on his first visit there, and the guide proposed a look at the temple. "He turned short, and led us some little distance up the citadel, then through a dark, low arch into a small court, where, to my surprise, the first object which met my eyes was a pool of blood on the pavement, by which a naked man stood with a bloody sword in his hand. . . . The guide . . . cautioned me against treading in the blood, and told me that a goat was sacrificed here every morning. In fact a second glance showed me the headless body of the poor animal lying before the steps of a small shrine, apparently of Kali. The Brahman was officiating and tinkling his bell. . . . The guide told us, on our way back, that the tradition was, that, in ancient times, a man was sacrificed here every day; that the custom had been laid aside till Jye Singh [the builder of Umeer] had a frightful dream, in which the destroying power appeared to him, and asked why her image was suffered to be dry [It is *blood*, not *flesh*,

[1] Dubois's *Des. of Man. and Cust. in India*, Part III., chap. vii.

that moistens]. The Rajah, afraid to disobey, and re-
luctant to fulfil the requisition to its ancient extent of
horror, took counsel and substituted a goat [in which
as well as in man there is blood—which is life—which
is the chief thing in a sacrifice Godward] for the
human victim; with which the

> 'Dark goddess of the azure flood,
>> Whose robes are wet with infant tears,
>> Skull-chaplet wearer, whom the blood
>> Of man delights three thousand years,'

was graciously pleased to be contented." [1]

" I had always heard, and fully believed till I came
to India," says Bishop Heber, " that it was a grievous
crime, in the opinion of the Brahmans, to eat the flesh
or shed the blood of any living creature whatever. I
have now myself seen Brahmans of the highest caste
cut off the heads of goats, as a sacrifice to Doorga;
and I know from the testimony of Brahmans, as well
as from other sources, that not only hecatombs of
animals are often offered in this manner, as a most
meritorious act (a Rajah, about twenty-five years back
[say about A. D. 1800], offered sixty thousand in one
fortnight); but that any persons, Brahmans not excepted, eat readily [in inter-communion] of the flesh
which has been offered up to one of their divinities." [2]

Clearly, the idea of inter-communion with the gods,

---

[1] Heber's *Travels in India*, II., 13 f.   [2] *Ibid.*, II., 285.

on the basis of the inter-flow of blood, exists in many Brahmanic practices of to-day. It still finds its expression in the occasional "Sacrifice of the Yajna, at which a ram is immolated." It is claimed by the Brahmans that "this sacrifice is the most exalted and the most meritorious of all that human beings can devise. It is the most grateful to the gods. It calls down all sorts of temporal blessings, and blots out all the sins that can have been accumulated for four generations." The ram chosen for this sacrifice must be "entirely white, and without blemish: of about three years old." Only Brahmans who are free from physical infirmities and from ceremonial defects can have a part in its offering, "at which no man of any other caste can be present." Because of the Brahmanic horror of the shedding of blood, the victim is smothered, or "strangled"; after which it is cut in pieces, and burned as an oblation. "A part, however, is preserved for him who presides at the sacrifice, and part for him who is at the expense of it. These share their portions with the Brahmans who are present; amongst whom a scuffle ensues, each striving for a small bit of the flesh. Such morsels as they can catch they tear with their hands, and devour as a sacred viand [the meat of inter-communion with the gods]. This practice is the more remarkable, as being the only occasion in their [the Brahmans'] lives when they can venture to touch animal food." "This most renowned sacrifice . . . is one of the six privileges of the Brahmans"; and it would seem that its offering may now be directed to any one of the divinities, at the preference of the offerer. Formerly there was also the "*Great* Sacrifice of the Yajna," which is no longer in use. "At this sacrifice," in its day, "every species of victim was immolated; and it is beyond doubt that human beings even were offered up; but the horse and the elephant were the most common."[1] So, there has never been an entire absence from the Brahmanic practices of an inter-communion with the gods through an inter-union by blood.

Even more remarkable than this canonical sacrifice of the Yajna, with its accompanying inter-communion, are some of the occult sacrifices to the gods of the Hindoo Pantheon, in which all the ordinary barriers of caste are disregarded, in the un-canonical but greatly prized services of inter-communion with the gods on the basis of an inter-flow of blood. The offerings of blood-flowing sacrifices, including even the cow, are made before the image of Vishnoo; or, more probably, of Krishna as one of the forms of Vishnoo. The spirituous liquors of the country are also presented as drink-offerings. Then follows the inter-communion. "He who administers [at the offering to the god] tastes

[1] Dubois's *Des. of Man. and Cust. of India*, Part II., chap. xxxi.

14*

each species of meat and of liquor; after which he gives permission to the worshipers to consume the rest. Then may be seen men and women rushing forward, tearing and devouring. One seizes a morsel, and while he gnaws it, another snatches it out of his hands, and thus it passes on from mouth to mouth till it disappears, while fresh morsels, in succession, are making the same disgusting round. The meat being greedily eaten up, the strong liquors and the opium [which have all been offered to the gods] are sent round. All drink out of the same cup, one draining what another leaves, in spite of their natural abhorrence of such a practice. . . . All castes are confounded, and the Brahman is not above the Pariah. . . . Brahmans, Sudras, Pariahs, men and women, swill the arrack which was the offering to the Saktis, regardless of the same glass being used by them all, which in ordinary cases would excite abhorrence. Here it is a virtuous act to participate in the same morsel, and to receive from each other's mouths the half-gnawn flesh." [1]

The fact that this service is of so disgusting a character, does not lessen its importance as an illustration of a primitive custom degraded by successive generations of defiling influences. It still stands as one of the proofs of the universal custom of an

[1] Dubois's *Des. of Man. and Cust. of India,* Part II., chap. xi.

attempted inter-communion with the gods through
an inter-union by blood. Indeed, there are many
traces, in India, of the survival of this primitive idea.
Referring to the worship of Krishna, under the form
of Jagan-natha (or Juggernaut, as the name is popu-
larly rendered) a recent writer on India says: " Before this monstrous shrine, all distinctions of caste
are forgotten, and even a Christian may sit down and
eat with a Brahman. In his work on Orissa, Dr. W.
W. Hunter says that at the 'Sacrament of the Holy
Food' he has seen a Puri priest receive his food from a
Christian's hand. . . . This rite is evidently also a
survival of Buddhism [It goes a long way back of
that]. It is remarkable that at the shrine of Vyan-
koba, an obscure form of Siva, at Pandharpur, in the
Southern Maratha country, caste is also in abeyance,
all men being deemed equal in its presence. Food is
daily sent as a gift from the god to persons in all parts
of the surrounding country, and the proudest Brahman gladly will accept and partake of it from the
hands of the Sudra, or Mahar, who is usually its
bearer. There are two great annual festivals in
honor of Jagan-natha. . . . They are held everywhere; but at Puri they are attended by pilgrims from
every part of India, as many as 200,000 often being
present. All the ground is holy within twenty miles
of the pagoda, and the establishment of priests

amounts to 3000. The 'Sacrament of the Holy Food' is celebrated three times a day."[1]

Thus it is evident that the idea of inter-communion with the gods has not been lost sight of in India, even through the influence of Brahmanism and Booddhism against the idea of divine-human inter-union by blood—which is life. Indeed, this idea so pervades the religious thought of the Hindoos, that the commands are specific in their sacred books, that a portion of all food must be offered to the spirits, before any of it is partaken of by the eater. "It is emphatically declared that he who partakes of food before it has been offered in sacrifice as above described, eats but to his own damnation;"[2] unless he discerns there the principle of divine-human inter-communion, he eats to his own spiritual destruction.[3]

And just here it is well to notice an incidental item of evidence that in India, as in the other lands of the East, the sacrifices to the gods were in some way linked with the primitive rite of human covenanting by blood. An Oriental scholar has called attention to the origin of the nose-ring, so commonly worn in India, as described in the Hindoo Pāga-Vatham.[4] The story runs, that at the incarnation of Vishnoo as

---

[1] "The Hindu Pantheon," in Birdwood's *Indian Arts*, p. 76 f.

[2] *Ibid.*, p. 42. [3] 1 Cor. 11 : 29.

[4] See Roberts's *Oriental Illus. of Scriptures*, pp. 484–489.

Krishna, the holy child's life was sought, and his mother exchanged her infant for the child of another woman, in order to his protection. In doing so, she "bored a hole in the nose of her infant, and put a ring into it as an impediment and a sign. The blood which came from the wound was as a sacrifice to prevent him from falling into the hand of his enemies." And, to this day, the nose-ring has two names, indicative of its two-fold purpose. "The first [name] is *nate-kaddan*, which signifies 'the obligation or debt a person is under by a vow'; the second [name] is *mooka-taddi*, literally 'nose-impediment or hindrance,' that is, to sickness or death." The child's blood is given in covenant obligation to the gods, and the nose-ring is the token of the covenant-obligation, and a pledge of protected life. When a Hindoo youth who has worn a nose-ring would remove it, on the occasion of his marriage, he must do so with formal ceremonies at the temple, and by the use of a liquid "which represents blood," composed of saffron,[1] of lime, and of water. A young tree must also be planted in connection with this ceremony, as in the ceremony of blood-covenanting in some portions of the East.[2] These symbolisms can hardly fail to be recognized as based on the universal primitive rite of blood-covenanting.[3]

The very earliest records of Babylon and Assyria,

[1] See page 77, *supra*. [2] See page 53, *supra*. [3] See also page 194 ff., *infra*.

indicate the outreaching of man for an inter-union with God, or with the gods, by substitute blood, and the confident inter-communion of man with God, or with the gods, on the strength of this inter-union by blood. There is an Akkadian poem which clearly "goes back to pre-Semitic times," with its later Assyrian translation, concerning the sacrifice, to the gods, of a first-born son.[1] It says distinctly: "His offspring for his life he gave." Here is obviously the idea of vicarious substitution, of life for life, of the blood of the son for the blood of the father, but this substitution does not necessarily involve the idea of an *expiatory* offering for sin; even though it does include the idea of *propitiation.* Abraham's surrender of his first-born son to God was in proof of his loving trust, not of his sense of a penalty due for sin. Jephthah's surrender of his daughter was on a vow of devotedness, not as an exhibit of remorse, or of penitence, for unexpiated guilt. In each instance, the outpouring of substitute blood was in evidence of a desire to be in new covenant oneness with God. Thus Queen Manenko and Dr. Livingstone made a covenant of blood vicariously, by the substitution of her husband on the one part, and of an attendant of Livingstone, on the other part.[2] So also the Akkadian king may have sought

---

[1] See Sayce's paper, in *Trans. Soc. Bib. Arch.*, Vol. I., Part 1, pp. 25-31.

[2] See page 13 f., *supra.*

a covenant union with his god—from whom sin had separated him—by the substitute blood of his first-born and best loved son.

Certain it is, that the early kings of Babylon and Assyria were accustomed to make their grateful offerings to the gods, and to share those offerings with the gods, by way of inter-communion with the gods, apart from any sense of sin and of its merited punishment which they may have felt.[1]   Indeed, it is claimed, with a show of reason, that the very word (*surqinu*) which was used for "altar" in the Assyrian, was primarily the word for "table"; that, in fact, what was later known as the "altar" to the gods, was originally the table of communion between the gods and their worshipers.[2]   There seems to be a reference to this idea in the interchanged use of the words "altar" and "table" by the Prophet Malachi: "And ye say, Wherein have we despised thy name? Ye offer polluted bread upon mine *altar*.   And ye say, Wherein have we polluted thee? In that ye say, The *table* of the Lord is contemptible."[3]   So again, in Isaiah

---

[1] "Whether he has overcome his enemies or the wild beasts, he pours out a libation from the sacred cup," says Layard (*Nineveh and its Remains*, Vol. II., chap. 7) concerning the old-time King of Nineveh.

[2] See H. Fox Talbot's paper, in *Trans. Soc. Bib. Arch.*, Vol. IV, Part I, p. 58 f.

[3] Mal. I : 6, 7. See also Isa. 65 : II.

65 : 11 : "But ye that forsake the Lord, that forget
my holy mountain, that prepare a *table* for Fortune,
and that fill up mingled wine unto Destiny; I will
destine you to the sword, and ye shall all bow down
to the slaughter."

See, in this connection, the Assyrian inscription of
Esarhaddon, the son of Sennacherib,[1] in description of
his great palace at Nineveh: "I filled with beauties the
great palace of my empire, and I called it 'The Palace
which Rivals the World.' Ashur, Ishtar of Nineveh,
and the gods of Assyria, all of them, I feasted within
it. Victims precious and beautiful I sacrificed before
them, and I caused them to receive my gifts. I did
for those gods whatever they wished."[2]   It is even
claimed by Assyrian scholars, that in this inter-communion with the gods, worshipers might partake of
the flesh of animals which was forbidden to them at
all other times[3]—as among the Brahmans of India
to-day.

In farther illustration of the truth that inter-communion with the gods was shown in partaking of
sacred food with the gods, H. Fox Talbot, the Assyriologist, says of the ancient Assyrian inscription:

[1] 2 Kings 19: 37; Ezra 4: 2; Isa. 37: 38. See also 1 Cor. 10: 21.

[2] *Rec. of Past.* III., 122 f.

[3] Sayce's *Anc. Emp. of East*, p. 201; also, W. Robertson Smith's *Old
Test. in Jew. Ch.*, notes on Lect. xii.

"There is a fine inscription, not yet fully translated, describing the soul in heaven, clothed in a white radiant garment, seated in the company of the blessed, and fed by the gods themselves with celestial food."[1]

Among the Parsees, or the Zoroastrians, who intervene, as it were, between the primitive peoples of Assyria and India, and the later inhabitants of the Persian empire, there prevailed the same idea of divine-human inter-union through blood, and of divine-human inter-communion through sharing the flesh of the proffered and accepted sacrifice, at the altar, or at the table, of the gods, Ormuzd and Ahriman. The horse was a favorite substitute victim of sacrifice, among the Parsees; as also among the Hindoos and the Chinese. Its blood was the means of divine-human inter-union. "The flesh of the victim was eaten by the priest and the worshipers; the 'soul' [the life, the blood] of it only was enjoyed by Ormazd."[2] The communion-drink, in the Parsee sacrament, as still observed, is the juice of the *haoma*, or *hom.* "Small bread [or wafers] called Darun, of the size of a dollar, and covered with a piece of meat, incense, and Haoma, or Hom," the juice of the plant known in India as Soma, are used in this sacrament. "The Darun and the Hom [having been presented to the gods] are afterwards eaten by

[1] *Rec. of Past*, III., 135. [2] Sayce's *Anc. Emp. of East*, p. 266.

15

the priests," as in communion.[1]   This is sometimes
called the " Sacrament of the Haoma."[2]

In ancient Egypt, it seems to have been much as in
China, and India, and Assyria.   Substitute blood was a
basis of inter-union between man and the gods; and a
divine-human inter-communion was secured as a proof
and as a result of that inter-union.   That it was human
blood which was, of old, in Egypt, poured out as a
means of this inter-union (in some cases at least) seems
clear.   It is declared by Manetho, and Diodorus, and
Athenæus, and Plutarch, and Porphyry.[3]   It is recognized as proven, by Kenrick[4] and Ebers[5] and other
Egyptian scholars.   Wilkinson, it is true, was unwilling to accept its reality, because, in his opinion, " it is
quite incompatible with the character of a nation
whose artists thought acts of clemency towards a foe
worthy of record, and whose laws were distinguished
by that humanity which punished with death the murder even of a slave ";[6] and he prefers to rest on " the
improbability of such a custom among a civilized people."   Yet, a single item of proof from the monuments

---

[1] Schaff-Herzog's *Encyc. of Relig. Knowl.*, art. " Parseeism."

[2] *Anc. Emp. of East,* p. 266.

[3] See Wilkinson's *Anc. Egypt.*, III., 30, 400.

[4] Kenrick's *Anc. Egypt,* I., 369 ff.

[5] Ebers's *Ægypt. u. d. Büch. Mose's,* p. 245 f.

[6] Wilkinson's *Anc. Egypt.*, III., 402.

would seem sufficient to settle this question, if it were still deemed a question. The ideogram which was employed on the seal of the priests, authorizing the slaying of an animal in sacrifice, " bore the figure of a man on his knees, with his hands tied behind him, and a sword pointed at his throat." [1]

Herodotus,[2] describing the magnificent festival of Isis, at Busiris, says that a bull was sacrificed on that occasion ; and we know that in every such sacrifice the blood of the victim was poured out as an oblation, at the altar.[3] When the duly prepared offering was consumed upon the altar, those portions of the victim which had been reserved were eaten by the priest and others.[4] Herodotus says, moreover, that some of the Greeks who were present at this festival were in the habit of causing their own blood to flow during the consuming of the sacrifice, as if in proof of their desire for inter-union with the goddess, as precedent to their inter-communion with her. He says: " But as many of the Karians as are dwelling in Egypt, do yet more than these [native Egyptians], inasmuch as

[1] Cited from Castor, in Plutarch, in Wilkinson's *Anc. Egypt.*, III., 407. See also Ebers's *Ægypt. u. d. Büch. Mose's*, p. 246.

[2] *Hist.*, II., 59.

[3] Wilkinson's *Anc. Egypt.*, III., 409. See also page 102, *supra*.

[4] Wilkinson's *Anc. Egypt.*, III., 109; 410; Kenrick's *Anc. Egypt.*, I., 373. See Herodotus, *Hist.*, II., 47.

they cut their foreheads with swords;[1] and so they are shown to be foreigners and not Egyptians."[2]

It would even seem that in Egypt, as in other parts of the primitive world, the prohibition of the eating of many sacred animals applied to the eating of them when not offered in sacrifice. Because those animals became, as it were, on the altar, or on the table, of the gods, a portion of the gods themselves, they must not be eaten except by those who discerned in them the body of the gods, and who were entitled to share them in inter-communion with the gods.[3]

The monumental representations of the other world show the gods sharing food and drink with the souls of the deceased.[4] And the idea of a divine-human inter-communion through the partaking by gods and men of the food provided for, or accepted by, the former, runs all through the Egyptian record. A remarkable illustration of this idea is found in an extended inscription from the tomb of Setee I., whose daughter is supposed to have been the finder of the infant Moses. In this inscription, which is sometimes called the Book of Hades, or more properly the Book of Amenti, the Sun-god Rā is represented as passing through Amenti—or the under world—on his noctur-

---

[1] *Hist.*, II., 61.   [2] See references to this custom at page 85 ff., *supra.*

[3] See Wilkinson's *Anc. Egypt.*, III., 404–406.

[4] Renouf's *The Relig. of Anc. Egypt*, pp. 138–147.

nal circuit, and speaking words of approval to his disembodied worshipers there.[1] "These are they who worshiped Rā on the earth, . . . who offered their oblations. . . . They are [now] masters of their refreshments; they take their meat; they seize their offerings in the porch of him, whose being is mysterious. . . . Rā says to them, Your offerings are yours; take your refreshment." Again and again the declaration is made of "the elect," of those who are greeted by Rā in Amenti: "Their food is (composed) of Rā's bread; their drink [is] of his liquor *tesher* [a common word for " red," often standing for " blood " [2]]. And yet again: "Their food is to hear the word of this god."[3] " Their food is that of the veridical [the truth-speaking] ones. Offerings are [now] made to them on earth; because the true word is in them."[4]

Thus there was inter-communion between man and the gods in ancient Egypt, on the basis of a blood-made inter-union between man and the gods; as there was also in primitive Assyria and Babylon, in primitive India, and in primitive China.

Turning now from the far East to the far West, we

[1] See *Rec. of Past*, X., 79–134.   [2] See page 102 f., *supra*.

[3] " Man doth not live by bread only, but by every word that proceedeth out of the mouth of the Lord doth man live." (Deut. 8: 3. See, also, Matt. 4: 4; Job 23: 12; John 4: 34.)

[4] See John 8: 31, 32; 16: 13; 17: 19.

find that Central American and South American history and legends tend to illustrate the same primitive belief, that inter-communion with the gods was to be secured by the hearty surrender of self—as evidenced by the tender of personal, or of substitute *blood*. A Guatemalan legend has its suggestion of that out-reaching of man for fire from heaven which is illustrated in the primitive and the classic myths of the ages.[1]   The men of Guatemala were without the heaven-born fire, and they turned, in their longing, to the Quiché god, Tohil, seeking it from him, on such terms as he might prescribe.   "The condition finally named by the god was, that they consent to ' unite themselves to me, under their armpit, and under their girdle, and that they embrace me, Tohil '; a condition not very clearly expressed [says a historian], but which, as is shown by what follows, was an agreement to worship the Quiché god, and sacrifice to him their *blood*, and, if required, their *children*.   They accepted the condition, and received the fire."[2]

In the light of the prevailing customs of the world, concerning this rite of blood-covenanting, the require-

[1] See Réville's *Native Relig. of Mex. and Peru*, pp. 63, 163 ; Cory's *Anc. Frag.*, p. 5 ; Dubois's *Des. Man. and Cust. of India*, Part II., chap. 31 ; Tylor's *Prim. Cult.*, II., 278 ff. ; Dorman's *Orig. of Prim. Supers.*, p. 150; Anderson's *Lake Ngami*, p. 220.

[2] Bancroft's *Native Races*, V., 547 f.

ments of the Quiché god were clearly based on the symbolism of that rite; as the historian did not perceive, from his unfamiliarity with the rite. If men would be in favor with that god, and would receive his choicest gifts, they must unite themselves to him; must enter into oneness of nature with him, by giving of their blood, from "under their armpit, and under their girdle"; from the source of life, and at the issue of life; for themselves and for their seed; and they must lovingly embrace their covenant-god, accordingly. And in the counsel given to those new worshipers, it was said: "Make first your thanksgiving; prepare the holes in your ears; [blood was drawn from the ears, as well as from other parts of the body, in Central American worship; indeed one of their festivals was 'the feast of piercing the ears,' suggesting a similar religious custom in India;[1]] pierce your elbows; and offer sacrifice. This will be your act of gratitude before God."[2]

Among all these aboriginal races of Central America, not only was the flesh of the sacrificial offerings eaten as in communion with the gods; but the blood of the offerings, and also the blood of the offerers themselves, was sometimes sprinkled upon, or commingled with, those articles of food, which were made

---

[1] Monier Williams's *Hinduism*, p. 60.

[2] Bancroft's *Native Races*, V., 548.

a means of spiritual inter-communion with their deities. Cakes of maize sprinkled with their own blood, drawn from "under the girdle," during their religious worship, were "distributed and eaten as blessed bread."[1] Moreover, an image of their god, made with certain seeds from the first fruits of their temple gardens, with a certain gum, and with the blood of human sacrifices, was partaken of by them reverently, under the name, "Food of our soul."[2]   At the conclusion of one of the great feasts of the year at Cuzco, in Peru, the worshipers "received the loaves of maize and the sacrificial blood, which they ate as a symbol of brotherhood with the Ynca"[3]—who claimed to be of divine blood and of divine power.

Herrera describes one of these ceremonies of inter-communion with the gods, by means of a blood-moistened representation of a god.   "An idol made of all the varieties of the seeds and grain of the country, was made, and moistened with the blood of children and virgins.   This idol was broken into small bits, and given by way of communion to men and women to eat; who, to prepare for that festival, bathed, and

---

[1] Bancroft's *Native Races*, II., 710.

[2] Mendieta's *Hist. Eccles. Ind.*, p. 108 f.; cited in Spencer's *Des. Soc.*, II., 20.

[3] Acosta's *Hist. Nat. Mor. Ind.*, Bk. V., chap. 27, cited in Spencer's *Des. Soc.*, II., 26.

dressed their heads, and scarce slept all the night. They prayed, and as soon as it was day [they] were all in the temple to receive that communion, with such singular silence and devotion, that though there was an infinite multitude, there seemed to be nobody. If any of the idol was left, the priests ate it." [1]

So marked, indeed, was the sacramental character of these Peruvian communion feasts, that a Spanish Jesuit missionary to that country, three centuries ago, was disposed to see in them an invention of Satan, rather than a survival of a world-wide primitive custom. He said: "That which is most admirable in the hatred and presumption of Sathan is, that he not only counterfeited in idolatry and sacrifices, but also in certain ceremonies, our sacraments, which Jesus Christ our Lord instituted, and the Holy Church uses; having, especially, pretended to imitate, in some sort, the sacrament of the communion, which is the most high and divine of all others." [2]

Yet again, a prisoner of war would be selected to represent one of the gods, and so to be partaken of, in inter-communion through his blood. He would receive the name of the god; and for a longer or a

[1] Herrera's *Gen. Hist. of America*, II., 379; cited in Dorman's *Orig. of Prim. Supers.*, p. 152 f.

[2] Acosta's *Hist. Nat. Mor. Ind.*, Bk. V., chap. 23; cited in Prescott's *Conquest of Peru*, I., 108, note.

shorter time,—"sometimes a year, sometimes six
months, and sometimes less,"—he would be min-
istered to, and would receive honors and reverence as
a god. Then he would be offered in sacrifice. His
heart would be presented to the god. His blood
would be employed reverently—as was the case with
all sacrifices—in token of covenanting. His flesh
would be eaten by the worshipers of the god whom
he represented.[1] This "rite of dressing and worshiping the sacrifices like the deities themselves, is related
as being performed at the festivals of many gods and
goddesses."[2]

A remarkable illustration of the unity of the race,
and of the universal sweep of these customs in conjunction with the symbolism of the blood-covenant,
is found in the similarity of this last named Central
American practice, with a practice charged upon the
Jews by Apion, as replied to by Josephus. The charge
is, that "Antiochus found, upon entering the temple
[at Jerusalem], a man lying upon a bed, with a table
before him, set out with all the delicacies that either
sea or land could afford." This captive's story was:
"I am a Greek, and wandering up and down in quest

[1] Herrera's *Gen. Hist.*, III., 207 f.; cited in Spencer's *Des. Soc.*
II., 20.

[2] Spencer's *Des. Soc.*, II., 20. See also Southey's *Hist. of Brazil*, II., 370.

of the means of subsistence, was taken up by some
foreigners, brought to this place, and shut up. . . .
They gave me to understand, that the Jews had a custom among them, once a year, upon a certain day pre-
fixed, to seize upon a Grecian stranger, and when they
had kept him fattening one whole year, to take him
into a wood, and offer him up for a sacrifice according
to their own form, *taking a taste of his blood*, with a
horrid oath to live and die sworn enemies to the
Greeks."[1] Baseless as was this charge against the
Jews, its very framing indicates the existence in the
East,—possibly among the Phœnicians,—in days prior
to the Christian era, as well as in pre-historic times in
the West, of the custom of seeking inter-communion
with God, or with the gods, by the tasting of the blood
of a substitute human victim, offered in sacrifice to
God, or to the gods.

At the two extremes of the world, to-day, among
the primitive Bed'ween of the Desert of Arabia, and
among the primitive Indians of the prairies of North
America, there lingers a trace of this world-wide idea,
that the body of an offering covenanted to God by its
blood, can be a means of inter-communion with God
in its eating. Both the Bed'ween and the Indians connect in their minds the fact of sacrificing and of feasting; and they speak of the two things interchangeably.

[1] *Contra Apionem*, II., 7.

An Arab, when he makes a feast, speaks of sacrificing the animal which is the main feature of that feast. I saw an Arab wedding at Castle Nakhl, on the Arabian Desert. The bridegroom sacrificed a young dromedary in honor of the occasion, and to furnish, as it were, the sacramental feast. The blood of the victim was poured out unto the Lord, by being buried in the earth—as the Chinese bury the blood of their sacrifices in the Temple of Heaven. Portions of the dromedary were eaten by all the guests, and a portion was sent to the stranger encamping near them. And that is the common method of Arab sacrificing and feasting.

There is much of similarity in the ways of the Arabs and of the Indians. The Indian feasts are largely feasts of inter-communion with the gods. Whether it were the human victim, of former times, whose blood was drunk and whose heart was eaten, as preliminary to the feasting on his entire remains;[1] or, whether it be the preserved hearts and tongues of the buffaloes, which now form the basis of some of the sacred feasts of the Indians;[2]—the idea of divine-human inter-communion was and is inseparable from the idea of the feast. The first portion of the feast is always proffered to the spirits, in order to make it, in a pecu-

[1] See pages 105 f., 132, *supra.*
[2] See Clark's *Indian Sign Language,* s. v., "Feast."

liar sense, a sacred feast. Then, each person having
a part in the feast is expected to eat the full share
assigned to him;[1] unless indeed he be permitted to
carry a remainder of it away " as sacred food " for the
benefit of the others.[2]

And so the common root-idea shows itself, in lesser
or in larger degree, all the world over, and in all the
ages. It is practically universal.

One of the many proofs that the idea of a blood-
covenanting sacrifice is that of a loving inter-communion between man and God, or the gods, is the fact
that the animals offered in sacrifice are always those
animals which are suitable for eating, whether their
eating is allowed at other times than when sacrificed,
or not. "Animals offered in sacrifice [at the Temple
of Heaven, in China]," says Dr. Edkins, "must be
those in use for human food. There is no trace in
China of any distinction between clean and unclean
animals, as furnishing a principle in selecting them for

[1] " Should he fail [to eat his portion], the host would be outraged,
the community shocked, and the spirits roused to vengeance. Disaster
would befall the nation—death, perhaps, the individual." "A feaster
unable to do his full part, might, if he could, hire another to aid him ;
otherwise he must remain in his place till the work was done." (Parkman's *Jesuits in No. Am.*, p. xxxviii.)

[2] "At some feasts guests are permitted to take home some small portions for their children as sacred food, especially good for them because it
came from a feast." (Clark's *Ind. Sign Lang.*, p. 168.)

sacrifice. That which is good for food is good for
sacrifice, is the principle guiding in their selection." [1]
The same *principle* has been already noted as prevailing in the sacrifices of India, Assyria, and Egypt;
although in these last named countries many animals
which are " good for food " are not " in use for human
food " except as they are served up at the table of the
gods.[2]   In the primitive New World it was the same as
in the primitive Old World.   Referring to the sacrifices
in ancient Peru, Réville says, " It should be noted that
they only sacrificed edible animals, which [as he would
understand it] is a clear proof that the intention was
to feed the gods ";[3] and it certainly seems a clear
proof that the intention was to feed the worshipers
who shared the sacred food.

That this sharing of the proffered and accepted sacrifice, in divine-human inter-communion, was counted
a sharing of the divine nature, by the communicant,
seems evident, as widely as the world-wide custom
extended.   The inter-union was wrought by intermingled blood; the inter-communion gave a common
progress to the common nature.   The blood gave common life; the flesh gave common nourishment.   " Almost everywhere," says Réville,[4] "but especially

[1] Edkins's *Relig. in China*, p. 22, note.
[2] See pages 159, 168, 172, *supra.*
[3] Réville's *Native Relig. of Mex. and Peru*, p. 183.   [4] *Ibid.*, p. 76.

among the Aztecs, we find the notion, that the victim devoted to a deity, and therefore destined to pass into his substance, and to become by assimilation an integral part of him, is already co-substantial with him, has already become part of him; so that the worshiper in his turn, by himself assimilating a part of the victim's flesh, unites himself in substance with the divine being. And now observe [continues this student in the science of comparative religion] that in all religions the longing, whether grossly or spiritually apprehended, to enter into the closest possible union with the adored being, is fundamental. This longing is inseparable from the religious sentiment itself, and becomes imperious wherever that sentiment is warm; and this consideration is enough to convince us that it is in harmony with the most exalted tendencies of our nature, but may likewise, in times of ignorance, give rise to the most deplorable aberrations." This observation is the more noteworthy, in that it is made by so pronounced a rationalist as Réville.

It would even seem to be indicated, by all the trend of historic facts, that cannibalism—gross, repulsive, inhuman cannibalism—had its basis in man's perversion of this outreaching of his nature (whether that outreaching were first directed by revelation, or by divinely given innate promptings) after inter-union and inter-communion with God; after life in God's life, and after growth through the partaking of God's food, or of that food which represents God. The studies of many observers in widely different fields have led both the rationalistic and the faith-filled student to conclude, that in *their* sphere of observation it was a religious sentiment, and not a mere animal craving,—either through a scarcity of food, or from a spirit of malignity,—that was at the bottom of cannibalistic practices there; even if that field were an exception to the world's fields generally. And now we have a glimpse of the nature and workings of that religious sentiment which prompted cannibalism wherever it has been practised.

Man longed for oneness of life with God. Oneness of life could come only through oneness of blood. To secure such oneness of life, man would give of his own blood, or of that substitute blood which could best represent himself. Counting himself in oneness of life with God, through the covenant of blood, man has sought for nourishment and growth through partaking of that food which in a sense was life, and which in a larger sense gave life, because it was the food of God, and because it was the food which stood for God. In misdirected pursuance of this thought, men have given the blood of a consecrated human victim to bring themselves into union with God; and then they

have eaten of the flesh of that victim which had supplied the blood which made them one with God. This
seems to be the basis of *fact* in the premises; whatever may be the understood *philosophy* of the facts.
Why men reasoned thus, may indeed be in question.
That they reasoned thus, seems evident.

Certain it is, that, where cannibalism has been studied in modern times, it has commonly been found to
have had originally, a religious basis; and the inference is a fair one, that it must have been the same
wherever cannibalism existed in earlier times. Even
in some regions where cannibalism has long since
been prohibited, there are traditions and traces of its
former existence as a purely religious rite. Thus, in
India, little images of flour paste or clay are now
made for decapitation, or other mutilation, in the temples,[1] in avowed imitation of human beings, who were
once offered and eaten there. Referring to the fre-
quency of human sacrifices in India, in earlier and in
later times, and to these emblematic substitutes for
them, now employed, the Abbe Dubois says:[2] "In
the kingdom of Tanjore there is a village called
Tirushankatam Kudi, where a solemn festival is celebrated every year, at which great multitudes of people
assemble, each votary bringing with him one of those

---

[1] See page 176 f., *supra*.

[2] *Des. of Man. and Cust. of India*, Part III., chap. 7.

16*

little images of dough into the temple dedicated to Vishnu, and there cutting off the head in honor of that god. This ceremony, which is annually performed with great solemnity, was instituted in commemoration of a famous event which happened in that village.

"Two virtuous persons lived there, Sirutenden and his wife Vanagata-ananga, whose faith and piety Vishnu was desirous to prove. He appeared to them, and demanded no other service of them but that of sacrificing, with their own hands, their only and much beloved son Siralen, and *serving up his flesh for a repast.* The parents with heroic courage, surmounting the sentiments and chidings of nature, obeyed without hesitation, and submitted to the pleasure of the god. So illustrious an act of devotion is held worthy of this annual commemoration, at which the sacrifice is emblematically renewed. The same barbarous custom is preserved in many parts of India; and the ardor with which the people engage in it leaves room to suspect that they still regret the times when they would have been at liberty to offer up to their sanguinary gods the reality, instead of the symbol."

Such a legend as this, taken in conjunction with the custom which perpetuates it, and with all the known history of human sacrifices, in India and elsewhere, furnishes evidence that cannibalism as a religious rite was known to the ancestors of the present dwellers in India. And as it is in the far East, so it is in the far West; and so, also, in mid-ocean.

Thus, for example, in the latter field, among the degraded Feejee Islanders, where one would be least likely to look for the sway of a religious sentiment in the more barbarous customs of that barbarous people, this truth has been recognized by Christian missionaries, who would view the relics of heathenism with no undue favor. The Rev. Messrs. Williams and Calvert—the one after thirteen years, and the other after seventeen years of missionary service there—said on this subject: "Cannibalism is a part of the Fijian religion, and the gods are described as delighting in human flesh." And again: " Human flesh is still the most valued offering [to the gods], and their ' drink offerings of blood' are still the most acceptable [offerings to the gods] in some parts of Fiji." [1]

It was the same among the several tribes of the North American Indians, according to the most trustworthy testimony. A Dutch clergyman, Dominie Megapolensis, writing two centuries ago from near the present site of Albany, "bears the strongest testimony to the ferocity with which his friends the Mohawks treated their prisoners, . . . and is very explicit as to

[1] See Williams and Calvert's *Fiji and the Fijians*, pp. 35 f., 161–166, 181 f.

cannibalism.   'The common people,' he says 'eat the arms, buttocks, and trunk ; but the chiefs eat the head and the heart.'   This feast was of a religious character." [1]   Parkman says, of the " hideous scene of feasting [which] followed the torture of a prisoner," " it was, among the Hurons, partly an act of vengeance, and partly a religious rite." [2]   He cites evidence, also, that there was cannibalism among the Miamis, where " the act had somewhat of a religious character [and], was attended with ceremonial observances." [3]

Of the religious basis of cannibalism among the primitive peoples of Central and South America, students seem agreed.   Dorman who has carefully collated important facts on this subject from varied sources, and has considered them in their scientific bearings, is explicit in his conclusions at this point.   Reviewing all the American field, he says : " I have dwelt longer upon the painful subject of cannibalism than might seem desirable, in order to show its religious character and prevalence everywhere.   Instead of being confined to savage peoples, as is generally supposed, it prevailed to a greater extent and with more horrible rites among the most civilized.   Its religious inception was the cause of this." [4]   Again, he says, of the peoples of

[1] Cited in Parkman's *Jesuits in No. Am.*, p. 228, note.

[2] *Ibid.*, p. xxxix.   [3] *Ibid.*, p. xl., note.

[4] *Origin of Prim. Supers.*, p. 151 f.

Mexico and of the countries south of it: "All the Nahua nations practised this religious cannibalism. That cannibalism as a source of food, unconnected with religious rites, was ever practised, there is little evidence. Sahagun and Las Casas regard the cannibalism of the Nahuas as an abhorrent feature of their religion, and not as an unnatural appetite."[1]

Réville, treating of the native religions of Mexico and Peru, comes to a similar conclusion with Dorman; and he argues that the state of things which was there was the same the world over, so far as it related to cannibalism. "Cannibalism," he says,[2] "which is now restricted to a few of the savage tribes who have remained closest to the animal life, was once universal to our race. For no one would ever have conceived the idea of offering to the gods a kind of food which excited nothing but disgust and horror." In this suggestion, Réville indicates his conviction that the primal idea of an altar was a table of blood-bought communion. "Human sacrifices" however, he goes on to say, "prevailed in many places when cannibalism had completely disappeared from the habits and tastes of the population. Thus the Semites of Western Asia, and the Çivaïte Hindus, the Celts, and some of the populations

[1] *Origin of Prim. Supers.*, p. 150.
[2] *Native Relig. in Mex. and Peru*, p. 75 f.

of Greece and Italy, long after they had renounced cannibalism, still continued to sacrifice human beings to their deities." And he might have added, that some savage peoples continued cannibalism when the religious idea of its beginning had been almost swept away entirely by the brutalism of its inhuman nature and tendencies. Referring to the date of the conquest of Mexico, he says: "Cannibalism, in ordinary life, was no longer practised. The city of Mexico underwent all the horrors of famine during the siege conducted by Fernando Cortes. When the Spaniards finally entered the city, they found the streets strewn with corpses, which is a sufficient proof that human flesh was not eaten even in dire extremities. And, nevertheless, the Aztecs not only pushed human sacrifices to a frantic extreme, but they were *ritual cannibals*, that is to say, there were certain occasions on which they ate the flesh of the human victims they had immolated." [1]

And as it was in India and in America and in the Islands of the Sea, so it seems to have been wherever the primitive idea of cannibalism as a prevalent custom has been intelligently sought out.[2]

---

[1] *Native Relig. of Mex. and Peru,* p. 76.

[2] See references to cannibalism as a religious rite among the Khonds of Orissa, the people of Sumatra, etc., in Adams's *Curiosities of Superstition.*

7. SYMBOLIC SUBSTITUTES FOR BLOOD.

As the primitive and more natural method of commingling bloods, in the blood-covenant, by sucking
each other's veins, or by an inter-transference of
blood from the mutually opened veins, was in many
regions superseded by the symbolic laving, or sprinkling, or anointing, with blood; and as the blood of the
lower animals was often substituted, vicariously, for
human blood;—so the blood and wine which were
commingled for mutual drinking in the covenant-rite,
or which were together poured out in libation, when
the covenant was between man and the Deity, came, it
would appear, to be represented, in many cases, by
the wine alone. First, we find men pledging each
other in a sacred covenant, in ·the inter-drinking of
each other's blood mingled with wine. They called
their covenant-draught, " assiratum," or " vinum assiratum "; " wine, covenant-filled." By and by, apparently, they came to count simple wine—" the blood of
grapes " [1]—as the representative of blood and wine, in
many forms of covenanting.

This mutual drinking, as a covenant-pledge, has been
continued as an element in the marriage ceremony, the
world over, down to the present time. It would even

[1] Gen. 49: 11; Deut. 32: 14; Ecclesiasticus 39: 26; 50: 15;
1 Macc. 6: 34.

seem that the gradual changes in the methods of this symbolic rite could be tracked, through its various forms in this ceremony, in different portions of the world. Among the wide-spreading 'Anazeh Bed'ween, the pouring out of a blood libation is still the mode of completing the marriage-covenant. "When the marriage day is fixed," says Burckhardt,[1] "the bridegroom comes with a lamb in his arms to the tent of the father of his bride, and then, before witnesses, he cuts its throat. As soon as the blood falls upon the earth, the marriage ceremony is regarded as complete." Among the Bed'ween of Sinai, as Palmer tells us,[2] the bride is sprinkled with the blood of the lamb, before she is surrendered to the bridegroom. Lane's mention of the prominence of outpoured blood at the weddings of the Copts in Cairo, has already been cited.[3] Among the Arabs, since the days of Muhammad, wine has been generally abjured, and coffee now commonly takes its place as a drink, in all ordinary conferences for covenanting.

In Borneo, among the Dayaks, the bride and the bridegroom sit side by side, facing the rising sun. Their parents then besprinkle them with the blood of some animal, and also with water. "Each being next presented with a cup of arrack, they mutually pour half into each

---

[1] In *Beduinen und Wahaby*, p. 86 f.

[2] *Desert of the Exodus*, I., 90.   [3] See page 72, *supra*.

other's cup, take a draught, and exchange vessels."[1]
In Burmah, among the Karens, water is poured upon
the bride as she enters the bridegroom's house. When
she is received by the bridegroom, "each one then
gives the other to drink, and each says to the other,
'Be faithful to thy covenant.' This is the proper marriage ceremony, and the parties are now married."[2]

The blood of an ox, or a cow, is caused to flow at
the door of the bride's house, as a part of the marriage
ceremony, in Namaqua Land.[3] A similar custom
prevails among the Kafirs of Natal; and an observer
has said of this blood-flowing, in the covenanting
rite: "This appears to be the fixing point of the
ceremony"; this is "the real matrimonial tie."[4]

Again it is the sharing from the same dish in drinking, as well as in eating, that the bride and the bridegroom covenant in marriage, in the Feejee Islands.[5]
The liquor that is made the common draught, as a
substitute for the primitive blood-potion, is commonly
the spirituous drink of the region; whether that drink
be wine, or arrack, or whiskey, or beer. The symbolism is the same in every case.

[1] Wood's *Wedding Day*, p. 144.

[2] Mason, in *Journ. of Asiat. Soc. of Bengal*, Vol. XXXV., Part II.,
p. 17; cited in Spencer's *Des. Soc.*, V., 9.

[3] Andersson's *Lake Ngami*, p. 220 f.

[4] Shooter's *Kafirs of Natal*, p. 77.

[5] Williams and Calvert's *Fiji and the Fijians*, p. 134.

In the Sanskrit, the word *asrij* signifies both "blood," and "saffron."[1] In the Hindoo wedding ceremony, in Malabar, "a dish of a liquid like blood, made of saffron and lime," is held over the heads of the bride and groom. When the ceremony is concluded, the newly married couple sprinkle the spectators with this blood-like mixture;[2] which seems, indeed, not only here but in many other cases, in India, to have become a substitute for the covenanting blood. Reference has already been made to its use in connection with the covenant of the nose-ring; and the saffron colored cord of the wedding necklace, among the Brahmans, has also been mentioned.[3]

A still more remarkable illustration of this saffron mixture in lieu of blood, in formal covenanting, in India, is found in its use in the rite of "adoption." In India, as elsewhere throughout the East, the desire of every parent to have a son is very strong. A son is longed for, to inherit the parental name and possessions, to perform the funeral rites and the annual ceremonies in honor of his parents; and, indeed, "it is said in the Dattaka-Mimansa, 'Heaven awaits not one who is destitute of a son.'" When, therefore, parents have not a son of their own, they often formally adopt one; and, in this ceremony, saffron-water seems to

[1] See Monier Williams's *Sanskrit Dictionary*, s. v.

[2] See Pike's *Sub-Tropical Rambles*, p. 198.   [3] See pages 77, 165, *supra*.

take the place of blood, in the sacred and indissoluble covenant of transfer.[1] So prominent indeed is this element of the saffron-water drinking—as the substitute for blood-drinking—in the covenant of adoption, that the adopted children of parents are commonly spoken of as their " water-of-saffron children." " Is it good to adopt the child, and give it saffron-water ? " is a question that " occurs eight times in the book of fate called Sagā-thevan-sāsteram." Formal sacrifices precede the ceremony of adoption, and mutual feasting follows it. The natural mother of the child, in his transfer to his new parents by adoption, hands with him a dish of consecrated saffron-water ; and both the child and the blood-symbol are received by the adopting father, with his declaration that the son is now to enter into all that belongs to that father. " Then he and his wife, pouring a little saffron water into the hollow of their hands, and dropping a little into that of the adoptive child, pronounce aloud before the assembly : ' We have acquired this child to our stem, and we incorporate him into it.' Upon which they drink the saffron-water, and rising up, make a profound obeisance to the assembly ; to which the officiating Brahmans reply by the word, ' Asirva-

[1] This Oriental custom gives an added meaning to the suggestion, that Christ was sent to bring us to his Father, " that we might receive th adoption of sons " (Gal. 4: 5).

dam.' " [1]   It seems to me in every way probable, that
in primitive times the blood of the child adopted, and
of the parents adopting him, was partaken of by the
three parties (as now throughout the East, in the case
of the blood-covenanting of friends), in order that the
child and his new parents might be literally of one
blood.   But, with the prejudice which grew up against
blood-drinking in India, the saffron-water came to be
used as a substitute for blood; even as the blood of
the grape came to be used instead of human blood in
many other portions of the world.

In China, an important rite in the marriage ceremony is the drinking of " the wedding wine," from
" two singularly shaped goblets, sometimes connected
together by a red silk, or red cotton, cord, several
feet long." After their worship of their ancestral
tablets, the bride and the bridegroom stand face to
face. " One of the female assistants takes the two
goblets . . . from the table, and having partially
filled them with a mixture of wine and honey, she
pours some of their contents from one [goblet] into
the other, back and forth several times. She then
holds one to the mouth of the groom, and the other to

---

[1] The citations above made are from Roberts's *Oriental Illustrations
of the Scriptures*, p. 574, and from Dubois's *Des. of Man. and Cust.
of India*, Part II., chap. 22; the latter being from the Directory or
Ritual of the Purohitas.

the mouth of the bride; who continue to face each other, and who then sip a little of the wine. She then changes the goblets, and the bride sips out of the one just used by the groom, and the groom sips out of the one just used by the bride, the goblets oftentimes remaining tied together [by the red cord]. Sometimes she uses one goblet [interchanging its use between the two parties] in giving the wine."[1] The Rev. Chester Holcombe, who has been a missionary in China for a dozen years or more, writes me explicitly: " I have been told that in ancient times blood was actually used instead of the wine now used as a substitute," in this wedding-cup of covenanting.

Again, Professor Douglas says[2] that, for a thousand years or so, it has been claimed that, at the birth of each two persons who are to be married, the red cord invisibly binds their feet together; which is only another way of saying that their lives are divinely inter-linked, as by the covenant of blood.

In Central America, among the Chibchas, it was a primitive custom for the bridegroom to present himself by night, after preliminary bargainings, at the door of his intended father-in-law's home, and there let his presence be known. Then the bride would come out to him, bringing a large gourd of *chica*, a fermented drink made from the juice of Indian corn;

[1] Doolittle's *Social Life of the Chinese*, I., 85–87.   [2] *China*, p. 72 f.

"and coming close to him, she first tasted it herself, and then gave it to him. He drank as much as he could; and thus the marriage was concluded."[1] Among the Bheels of India, the drinking of the covenant is between the representatives of the bridegroom and the parents of the bride, at the time of the betrothal; but this is quite consistent with the fact that the bride herself is not supposed to have a primary part in the covenant.[2] It is much the same also among the Laplanders.[3]

Among the Georgians and Circassians,[4] and also among the Russians,[5] the officiating priest, at a marriage ceremony, drinks from a glass of wine, and then the bride and the groom drink three times, each, from the same glass. The Galatians wedded, with a *poculum conjugii,* "a wedding cup."[6] In Greece, the marriage ceremony concludes by the bride and the groom "drinking wine out of one cup."[7] In Switzerland, formerly, the clergymen "took two glasses of wine, mixed their contents, and gave one glass to the bride,

---

[1] Piedrahita's *Hist. New Granada,* Bk. I., chap. 6; cited in Spencer's *Des. Soc.,* II., 34.

[2] Malcolm, in *Trans. Royal Asiat. Soc.,* I., 83; cited in Spencer's *Des. Soc.,* V., 8.

[3] Wood's *Wedding Day,* p. 142.   [4] *Ibid.,* p. 66 f.

[5] *Ibid.,* p. 124 f.   [6] Rous and Bogan's *Archæologiæ Atticæ,* p. 167.

[7] Wood's *Wedding Day,* pp. 36, 39.

and the other to the bridegroom."[1] Among European
Jews in olden time, the officiating rabbi, having blessed
a glass of wine, tasted it himself, and then gave it first
to the one and then to the other of the parties covenanting in marriage.[2]

This custom of covenanting in the wine-cup, at a
wedding, is said to have come into England from the
ancient Goths.[3] Its symbolical significance and its
exceptional importance seem to have been generally
recognized. Ben Jonson calls the wedding-wine a
" knitting cup "[4]—an inter-binding cup. And a later
poet asks, forcefully :

> " What priest can join two lovers' hands,
> But wine must seal the marriage bands ? "[5]

In Ireland, as in Lapland and in India, it was at the
betrothal, instead of at the wedding, that the covenanting-cup—or the " agreement bottle " as it was called—
was shared ; and not unnaturally strong *usquebaugh*,
or " water of life," was there substituted for wine—as
the representative of life-blood.[6]

In Scotland, as in Arabia and in Borneo, the use of
blood in conjunction with the use of a wedding-cup
has continued down to recent times. The " agreement bottle," or " the bottling," as it was sometimes
called, preceded the wedding ceremony proper. At

---

[1] Wood's *Wedding Day*, p. 151.   [2] *Ibid.*, pp. 22, 23.

[3] *Ibid.*, p. 247.   [4] *Ibid.*, p. 247.   [5] *Ibid.*, p. 248.   [6] *Ibid.*, p. 173.

the wedding, the blood of a cock was shed at the
covenanting feast. A reference to this is found in
" The Wowing [the Wooing or the Vowing ?] of Jok
and Jynny," among the most ancient remains of Scottish minstrelsy :

> " Jok tuk Jynny be the hand,
>> And cryd ane feist, and slew ane cok,
>> And maid a brydell up alland ;
>> Now haif I gottin your Jynny, quoth Jok." [1]

Among the ancient Romans, as also among the
Greeks, the outpouring of sacrificial blood, and the
mutual drinking of wine, were closely linked, in the
marriage ceremony.   When the substitute victim was
ready for slaying, " the soothsayer drank wine out of
an earthen, or wooden, chalice, called in Latin, *simpu-
lum*, or *simpuvium*.   It was in fashion much like our
ewers, when we pour water into the basin.   This chalice was afterward carried about to all the people, that
they also might *libare*, that is, lightly taste thereof;
which rite hath been called *libation*."   The remainder
of the wine from the chalice was poured on to the
victim, which was then slain ; its blood being carefully
preserved.   And these ceremonies preceded the marriage feast.[2] The wedding wine-drinking is now, however, all that remains of them.

[1] Ross's *The Book of Scottish Poems*, I., 218.
[2] Godwyn's *Rom. Historiae*, p. 66 f.

Indeed, it would seem that the common custom of " drinking healths," or of persons " pledging " each other in a glass of wine, is but a degenerate modification, or a latest vestige, of the primitive rite of covenanting in a sacred friendship, by means of commingled bloods shared in a wine-cup. Certainly this custom prevailed among the old Norsemen, and among the ancient Romans and Greeks. That it originally included an idea of a possible covenant with Deity, and of a spiritual fellowship, is indicated in the fact that " the old Northmen drank the ' minni' [the loving friendship] of Thor, Odin, and Freya; and of kings, likewise, at their funerals." So again there were " such formulas as ' God's minnie!' [and] ' A bowl to God in heaven!'"[1]

The earlier method of this ceremony of pledging each other in wine, was by all the participants drinking, in turn, out of a common bowl; as Catiline and his fellow-conspirators drank their blood and wine in mutual covenant; and as the Romans drank at a wedding service. In the Norseland, to-day, this custom is continued by the use of a drinking-bowl, marked by pegs for the individual potation; each man as he receives it, on its round, being expected to " drink his peg." And even among the English and the Americans, as well as among the Germans, the touching of

[1] Tylor's *Prim. Cult.*, I., 85–97.

two glasses together, in this health-pledging, is a common custom; as if in symbolism of a community in the contents of the two cups. As often, then, as we drink each other's healths, or as we respond to any call for a common toast-drinking, we do show a vestige of the primeval and the ever sacred mutual covenanting in blood.

8. BLOOD-COVENANT INVOLVINGS.

And now that we have before us this extended array of related facts concerning the sacred uses and the popular estimates of blood in all the ages, it will be well for us to consider what we have learned, in the line of blood-rites and of blood-customs, and in the direction of their religious involvings. Especially is it important for us to see where and how all this bears on the primitive and the still extant ceremony of covenanting by blood, with which we started in this investigation.

From the beginning, and everywhere, blood seems to have been looked upon as pre-eminently the representative of life; as, indeed, in a peculiar sense, life itself. The transference of blood from one organism to another has been counted the transference of life, with all that life includes. The inter-commingling of blood by its inter-transference has been understood as equivalent to an inter-commingling of natures. Two natures thus inter-commingled, by the inter-commingling of blood, have been considered as forming, thenceforward, one blood, one life, one nature, one soul—in two organisms. The inter-commingling of natures by the inter-commingling of blood has been deemed possible between man and a lower organism; and between man and a higher organism,—even between man and Deity, actually or by symbol;—as well as between man and his immediate fellow.

The mode of inter-transference of blood, with all that this carries, has been deemed practicable, alike by way of the lips and by way of the opened and inter-flowing veins. It has been also represented by blood-bathing, by blood-anointing, and by blood-sprinkling; or, again, by the inter-drinking of wine—which was formerly commingled with blood itself in the drinking. And the yielding of one's life by the yielding of one's blood has often been represented by the yielding of the blood of a chosen and a suitable substitute. Similarly the blood, or the nature, of divinities, has been represented, vicariously, in divine covenanting, by the blood of a devoted and an accepted substitute. Inter-communion between the parties in a blood-covenant, has been a recognized privilege, in conjunction with any and every observance of the rite of blood-covenanting. And the body of the divinely accepted offering, the blood of which is a means of divine-human inter-union, has been counted a very part of the divinity; and to partake of that body as food has been deemed equivalent to being nourished by the very divinity himself.

Blood, as life, has been looked upon as belonging, in the highest sense, to the Author of all life. The taking of life has been seen to be the prerogative of its Author; and only he who is duly empowered, for a season and for a reason, by that Author, for blood-taking in any case, has been supposed to have the right to the temporary exercise of that prerogative. Even then, the blood, as the life, must be employed under the immediate direction and oversight of its Author. The heart of any living organism, as the blood-source and the blood-fountain, has been recognized as the representative of its owner's highest personality, and as the diffuser of the issues of his life and nature.

A covenant of blood, a covenant made by the inter-commingling of blood, has been recognized as the closest, the holiest, and the most indissoluble, compact conceivable. Such a covenant clearly involves an absolute surrender of one's separate self, and an irrevocable merging of one's individual nature into the dual, or the multiplied, personality included in the compact. Man's highest and noblest outreachings of soul have, therefore, been for such a union with the divine nature as is typified in this human covenant of blood.

How it came to pass that men everywhere were so generally agreed on the main symbols of their religious yearnings and their religious hopes, in this realm of their aspirations, is a question which obviously admits of two possible answers. A common revelation from God may have been given to primitive man; and all these varying yet related indications of religious strivings and aim may be but the perverted remains of the lessons of that misused, or slighted, revelation. On the other hand, God may originally have implanted the germs of a common religious thought in the mind of man, and then have adapted his successive revelations to the outworking of those germs. Whichever view of the probable origin of these common symbolisms, all the world over, be adopted by any Christian student, the importance of the symbolisms themselves, in their relation to the truths of revelation, is manifestly the same.

On this point, Kurtz has said, forcefully: "A comparison of the religious symbols of the Old Testament with those of ancient heathendom shows that the ground and the starting point of those forms of religion which found their appropriate expressions in symbols, was the same in all cases; while the history of civilization proves that, on this point, priority cannot be claimed by the Israelites. But when instituting such an inquiry, we shall also find that the symbols

18

which were transferred from the religions of nature to that of the spirit, first passed through the fire of divine purification, from which they issued as the distinctive theology of the Jews; the dross of a pantheistic deification of nature having been consumed."[1] And as to even the grosser errors, and the more pitiable perversions of the right, in the use of these world-wide religious symbolisms, Kurtz says, again: "Every error, however dangerous, is based on some truth misunderstood, and . . . every aberration, however grievous, has started from a desire after real good, which had not attained its goal, because the latter was sought neither in the right way, nor by right means."[2] To recognize these truths concerning the outside religions of the world gives us an added fitness for the comparison of the symbolisms we have just been considering with the teachings of the sacred pages of revelation on the specific truths involved.

Proofs of the existence of this rite of blood-covenanting have been found among primitive peoples of all quarters of the globe; and its antiquity is carried back to a date long prior to the days of Abraham. All this outside of any indications of the rite in the text of the Bible itself. Are we not, then, in a position to turn intelligently to that text for fuller light on the subject?

[1] Kurtz's *History of the Old Covenant*, I., 235.   [2] *Ibid.*, I., 268.

LECTURE III.

INDICATIONS OF THE RITE IN THE BIBLE.

III.

INDICATIONS OF THE RITE IN THE BIBLE.

I. LIMITATIONS OF INQUIRY.

AND now, before entering upon an examination of
the Bible text in the light of these disclosures of
primitive and universal customs, it may be well for me
to say that I purpose no attempt to include or to explain all the philosophy of sacrifice, and of the involved
atonement. All my thought is, to ascertain what new
meaning, if any, is found in the Bible teachings concerning the uses and the symbolism of blood, through
our better understanding of the prevailing idea, among
the peoples of the ancient world, that blood represents
life; that the giving of blood represents the giving of
life; that the receiving of blood represents the receiving of life; that the inter-commingling of blood represents the inter-commingling of natures; and that
a divine-human inter-union through blood is the basis
of a divine-human inter-communion in the sharing
of the flesh of the sacrificial offering as sacred food.

Whatever other Bible teachings there are, beyond these, as to the meanings of sacrifice, or as to the nature of the atonement, it is not my purpose, in this investigation, to consider.

In the days of Moses, when the Pentateuch is supposed to have been prepared, there were—as we have already found—certain well-defined views, the world over, concerning the sacredness of blood, and concerning the methods, the involvings, and the symbolisms, of the covenant of blood. This being so, we are not to look to the Bible record, as it stands, for the original institution of every rite and ceremony connected with blood-shedding, blood-guarding, and blood-using; but we may fairly look at every Bible reference to blood in the light of the primitive customs known to have prevailed in the days of the Bible writing.

2. PRIMITIVE TEACHINGS OF BLOOD.

The earliest implied reference to blood in the Bible text is the record of Abel's sacrifice. "And Abel was a keeper of sheep, but Cain was a tiller of the ground. And in process of time it came to pass that Cain brought of the fruit of the ground an offering unto the Lord. And Abel, he also brought of the firstlings of his flock and of the fat thereof. And the Lord had respect unto Abel and to his offering: but unto Cain and to his offering he had not respect." [1]   An inspired comment on this incident is: " By faith Abel offered unto God a more excellent sacrifice than Cain, through which he had witness borne to him that he was right-eous, God bearing witness in respect of [or, over] his gifts: and through it he [Abel] being dead yet speak-eth." [2]

Now, on the face of it, in the light of all that we know of primitive customs in this matter of the blood-covenant, and apart from any added teachings in the Bible concerning the nature and meanings of different sacrifices, this narrative shows Abel lovingly and trustfully reaching out toward God with substitute blood, in order to be in covenant oneness with God ; while Cain merely proffers a gift from his earthly pos-sessions.   Abel so trusts God that he gives *himself* to him.   Cain defers to God sufficiently to make a *present* to him.   The one shows unbounded faith ; the other shows a measure of affectionate reverence.   It is the same practical difference as that which distinguished Ruth from Orpah when the testing time of their love for their mother-in-law, Naomi, had come to them alike.   "And Orpah kissed her mother-in-law ; but Ruth clave unto her." [3]   No wonder that God counted Abel's unstinted proffer of himself, in faith, an accept-able sacrifice, and received it, as in inter-communion

[1] Gen. 4 : 2–5.   [2] Heb. 11 : 4.   [3] Ruth 1 : 14.

on the basis of inter-union; while Cain's paltry gift,
without any proffer of himself, won no approval from
the Lord.

Then there followed the unhallowed shedding of
Abel's blood by Cain, and the crying out, as it were,
of the spilled life of Abel unto its Divine Author.[1]
"The voice of thy brother's blood crieth unto me from
the ground," said the Lord to the guilty spiller of
blood. "And now cursed art thou from the ground,
which hath opened her mouth to receive thy brother's
blood from thy hand." Here, as elsewhere, the blood
is pre-eminently the life; and even when poured out
on the earth, the blood does not lose its vitality. It
still has its intelligent relations to its Author and
Guardian;[2] as the world has been accustomed to
count a possibility, down to modern times.[3]

After the destruction of mankind by the deluge,
when God would begin anew, as it were, by the re-
vivifying of the world through the vestige of blood—
of life—preserved in the ark,[4] he laid new emphasis
on the sacredness of blood as the representative of

[1] Gen. 4: 10, 11.

[2] "For it must be observed, that by the outpouring of the blood, the
life which was in it was not destroyed, though it was separated from
the organism which before it had quickened: Gen. 4: 10; comp. Heb.
12: 24 (παρὰ τὸν Ἀβελ); Apoc. 6: 10" (Westcott's *Epistles of St.
John*, p. 34).

[3] See pages 143–147, *supra*.   [4] See pages 110–113, *supra*.

that life which is the essence of God himself. Noah's
first act, on coming out from the ark, was to proffer
himself and all living flesh in a fresh blood-covenant
with the Lord. "And Noah builded an altar unto the
Lord ; and took of every clean beast, and of every
clean fowl, and offered burnt offerings on the altar." [1]
From all that we know of the method of the burnt-
offering, either from the Bible-text or from outside
sources, it has, from the beginning, included the preliminary offering of the blood—as the life—to Deity,
by its outpouring, around, or upon, the altar, with or
without the accompaniment of libations of wine ; or,
again, by its sprinkling upon the altar. [2]

It was then, when the spirit of Noah, in this cove-
nant-seeking by blood, was recognized approvingly by
the Lord, that the Lord smelled the sweet savor of
the proffered offering,—" the savor of satisfaction, or de-
lectation," [3] to him, was in it,—and he established a new
covenant with Noah, giving commandment anew concerning the never-failing sacredness of blood: " Every
moving thing that liveth shall be food for you; as [freely
as] the green herb, have I given you all [flesh].   But
flesh with the *life* thereof, which is the *blood* thereof

---

[1] Gen. 8 : 20.

[2] Exod. 24: 5, 6; 29: 15–25; Lev. 1: 1–6, 10–12, 14, 15; 8: 18,
19, etc.   See also pages 102, 106–109, *supra*.

[3] See *Speaker's Commentary*, in loco.

[flesh with the blood in it], shall ye not eat. And surely your blood, the blood of your lives, will I require; at the hand of every beast will I require it: and at the hand of man, even at the hand of every man's brother, will I require the life of man. Whoso sheddeth man's blood, by man shall his blood be shed: for in the image of God made he man."[1] Here, the blood of even those animals whose flesh might be eaten by man is forbidden for food; because it is life itself, and therefore sacred to the Author of life.[2] And the blood of man must not be shed by man,—except where man is made God's minister of justice,—because man is formed in the image of God, and only God has a right to take away—directly or by his minister—the life from one bearing God's likeness.

And this injunction, together with this covenant, preceded the ceremonial law of Moses; and it survived that law as well. When the question came up in the apostolic conference at Jerusalem, on the occasion of the visit of Paul and Barnabas, concerning the duty of Gentile Christians to the Mosaic ceremonial law, the decision was explicit, that, while nothing which was of that ritual alone should be imposed as obligatory on the new believers, those essential ele-

---

[1] Gen. 9 : 3–6.

[2] "A man might not use another's life for the support of his physical life" (Westcott's *Epistles of St. John*, p. 34).

ments of religious observance which were prior to
Moses, and which were not done away with in Christ,
should be emphasized in all the extending domain of
Christianity. Spirituality in worship, personal purity,
and the holding sacred to God all blood—or life—as
the gift of God, and as the means of communion with
God, must never be ignored in the realm of Christian
duty. "Write unto them, that they abstain from the
pollutions of idols, and from fornication, and from
what is strangled, and from blood," [1] said the Apostle
James, in announcing the decision of this conference;
and the circular letter to the Gentile churches was
framed accordingly. Nor does this commandment seem
ever to have been abrogated, in letter or in spirit. However poorly observed by Christians, it stands to-day as it
stood in the days of Paul, and in the days of Noah, a perpetual obligation, with all its manifold teachings of the
blessed benefits of the covenant of blood.[2]

3. THE BLOOD COVENANT IN CIRCUMCISION.

Again the Lord made a new beginning for the race
in his start with Abraham as the father of a chosen

[1] See Acts 15 : 2–29; also 21 : 18–25.

[2] Those, indeed, who would put the dictum of the Church of Rome
above the explicit commands of the Bible, can claim that that Church
has affirmed the mere temporary nature of this obligation, which the
Bible makes perpetual. But apart from this, there seems to be no show
of justification for the abrogation, or the suspension, of the command.

and peculiar people in the world. And again the covenant of blood, or the covenant of strong-friend-ship as it is still called in the East, was the prominent feature in this beginning. The Apostle James says that "Abraham . . . was called the friend of God."[1] God himself, speaking through Isaiah, refers to Abraham, as "Abraham my friend";[2] and Jehosha-phat, in his extremity, calling upon God for help, speaks of "Abraham, thy friend."[3] And this applica-tion of the term "friend" to any human being, in his relations to God, is absolutely unique in the case of Abraham, in all the Old Testament record. Abraham, and only Abraham, was called "the friend of God."[4] Yet the immediate narrative of Abraham's relations to God, makes no specific mention of this unique term "friend," as being then applied to Abraham. It is only as we recognize the primitive rite of blood-friendship in the incidents of that narrative, that we perceive clearly why and how God's covenant with Abraham was pre-eminently a covenant of friendship.

"I will make[5] my covenant between me and thee,

---

[1] James 2 : 23.　　　[2] Isaiah 41 : 8.　　　[3] 2 Chron. 20 : 7.

[4] The only instance in which it might *seem* that there was an excep-tion to this statement, is Exodus 33 : 11, where it is said, "The Lord spake unto Moses face to face, as a man speaketh unto his friend." But here the Hebrew word is *rê'a* (רֵעַ) with the idea of "a compan-ion," or "a neighbor"; while the word applied to Abraham is *ohebh* (אֹהֵב), "a loving one."　　　[5] See Appendix, *infra*, p. 322.

and will multiply thee exceedingly," said the Lord to Abraham.[1]   And again, " I will establish my covenant between me and thee and thy seed after thee throughout their generations for an everlasting covenant, to be a God unto thee; and to thy seed after thee . . . And as for thee, thou shalt keep my covenant, thou, and thy seed after thee throughout their generations."[2]   And then there came the explanation, how Abraham was to enter into the covenant of blood-friendship with the Lord; so that he might be called "the friend of God." "This is my covenant, which ye shall keep, between me and you, and thy seed after thee; every male among you shall be circumcised.   And ye shall be circumcised in the flesh of your foreskin; and it shall be a token of a covenant betwixt me and you."[3]   The blood-covenant of friendship shall be consummated by your giving to me of your personal blood at the very source of paternity—" under your girdle ";[4] thereby pledging yourself to me, and pledging, also, to me, those who shall come after you in the line of natural descent. "And my covenant [this covenant of blood-friendship] shall be in your flesh for an everlasting covenant."[5]

So, "in the selfsame day was Abraham circumcised," and thenceforward he bore in his flesh the evidence

---

[1] Gen. 17: 2.   [2] Gen. 17: 7–9.   [3] Gen. 17: 10, 11.

[4] See page 174 f., *supra.*   [5] Gen. 17: 13.

that he had entered into the blood-covenant of friendship with the Lord.[1]   To this day, indeed, Abraham is designated in all the East, as distinctively, " Khaleel-Allah, "the Friend of God," or " Ibrâheem el-Khaleel," " Abraham the Friend "[2]—the one Friend, of God.

When a Jewish child is circumcised, it is commonly said of him, that he is caused " to enter into the covenant of Abraham"; and, his god-father, or sponsor, is called *Baal-bereeth*,[3] " Master of the covenant." [4]   More-

[1] Bearing in the flesh the marks of one's devotedness to a divinity, is a widely observed custom in the East.   Burton tells of the habit, in Mekkeh, of cutting three parallel gashes down the fleshy cheek of every male child; and of the claim by some that these gashes "were signs that the scarred [one] was the servant of Allah's house " (*Pilgrimage to Mecca and Medinah*, third ed., p. 456).   In India, there are various methods of receiving such flesh-marks of devotedness. "One of the most common consists in stamping upon the shoulders, chest, and other parts of the body, with a red-hot iron, certain marks, to represent the armor [or livery] of their gods; the impressions of which are never effaced, but are accounted sacred, and are ostentatiously displayed as marks of distinctions" (Dubois's *Des. of Man. and Cust. in India*, Part III., chap. 3).   " From henceforth let no man trouble me," says Paul: " for I bear branded on my body the marks of Jesus " (Gal. 6 : 17).   [2] See Price's *Hist. of Arabia*, p. 56.

[3] It is certainly noteworthy, that the Canaanitish god " Baal-bereeth " (see Judges 8 : 33; 9 : 4) seems to have had its centre of worship at, or near, Shechem; and there was where the Canaanites were induced to seek, by circumcision, a part with the house of Jacob in the blood-covenant of Abraham (see Gen. 34 : 1–31).

[4] See Godwyn's *Moses and Aaron*, p. 216 f.

over, even down to modern times, the rite of circumcision has included a recognition, however unconscious,
of the primitive blood-friendship rite, by the custom of
the ecclesiastical operator, as God's representative, receiving into his mouth, and thereby being made a partaker of, the blood mingled with wine, according to the
method described among the Orientals, in the rite of
blood-friendship, from the earliest days of history.[1]

It is a peculiarity of the primitive compact of blood-

---

[1] Buxtorf, who is a recognized authority, in the knowledge of Rabbinical literature and of Jewish customs, says, on this point: "Cum deinde
compater infantulum in sinu habet jacentem, tum Mohel sive circum-
cisor eum è fasciis evolvit, pudendum ejus apprehendit, ejusque anteriorem partem per cuticulam præputii comprehendit, granulumque
pudendi ejus retrorsum premit; quo facto cuticulam præputii fricat, ut illa
per id emortua infantulus cæsuram tanto minus sentiscat.   Deinde cultellum circumcisorium è pueri astantis manu capit, claraque voce, Benedictus
(inquit) esto tu Deus, Domine noster, Rex mundi, qui nos mandatis tuis
sanctificasti, nobisque pactum circumcisionis dedisti.   Interim dum ille
loquitur sic, particulam præputii anteriorem usque eo abscindit, ut capi-
tellum pudendi nudum conspici queat, illamque festinanter in patellam
arena ista plenam conjicit; puero quoque isti, à quo acceperat, cultellum
reddit circumcisorium; ab alio vero poculum vino rubro (ceu dictum fuit)
impletum, capit; haurit ex eo quantum ore continere potest, quod mox
super infantulum expuit, eoque sanguinem ejus abluit: in faciem quoque
infantuli vini aliquid expuit, si eum viribus defici conspexerit.   Mox pudendum puelli ore comprehendit, et sanguinis ex eodem quantumcunque
potest, exugit, ut sanguis idem tanto citius se sistat; sanguinem exuctum
in alterum poculorum vino rubro refertorum, vel in patellam arena abun-
dantem, expuit." (*Synagoga Judaica*, Cap. II.)

friendship, that he who would enter into it must be ready to make a complete surrender of himself, in loving trust, to him with whom he covenants. He must, in fact, so love and trust, as to be willing to merge his separate individuality in the dual personality of which he becomes an integral part. Only he who believes in another unreservedly and fearlessly can take such a step intelligently. The record concerning Abraham stands : " He believed in the Lord ; and He counted it to him for righteousness."[1] The Hebrew word *heëmeen* (הֶאֱמִן), here translated " believed in," carries the idea of an unqualified committal of self to another. It is from the root *aman* (אָמַן) with the two-fold idea of " to be faithful " and " to trust."[2] Its correspondent in the Arabic, (*amana*, امن,) carries the same double idea, of a confident and an entire committal of self to another, in trust and in trustworthiness.[3] Lane's definition[4] of the substantive from this root is : " The becoming true to the trust, with respect to which God has confided in one, by a firm believing of the heart."[5] Abraham so trusted the

---

[1] Gen. 15: 6; Rom. 4: 3; Gal. 3: 6; James 2: 23.

[2] See Fuerst's *Heb. Chald. Lex.*, s. v.

[3] See Freytag's *Lex. Arab. Lat.*, s. v.

[4] See Lane's *Arab. Eng. Lex.*, s. v.

[5] In the Chinese language, likewise, " the word for faithfulness means both to be trustworthy, and also to trust to, and refers chiefly to friendship." (Edkins's *Relig. in China*, p. 118.)

Lord, that he was ready to commit himself to the Lord, as in the rite of blood-friendship. Therefore the Lord counted Abraham's spirit of loving and longing trust, as the equivalent of a spiritual likeness with himself; and the Lord received Abraham, by his circumcision, into the covenant of blood-friendship.[1] Or, as the Apostle James states it: "Abraham believed [in] God, and it was reckoned unto him for righteousness; and he was called the friend of God."[2] Here is the doctrine of "imputation," with real life in it; in lieu of a hard commercial transaction, as some have viewed it.

The recognition of the covenant of blood in the rite of circumcision, throws light on an obscure passage in the life of Moses, as recorded in Exodus 4: 20–26. Moses, himself a child of the covenant, had neglected the circumcision of his own first-born; and so he had been unfaithful to the covenant of Abraham. While on his way from the Wilderness of Sinai to Egypt,

[1] The Rabbis give a pre-eminent place to circumcision as the rite by which Abraham became the Friend of God. They say (see citations from the Talmud, in *Nethivoth Olam*, p. 367): "Abraham was not called perfect before he was circumcised; and because of the merit of circumcision was the covenant made with him concerning the inheritance of the Land. It [circumcision] also saves from the punishment of hell; for our sages have said, that Abraham sits at the gates of hell and suffers no one to enter in there who is circumcised."

[2] James 2: 23.

19*

with a message from God to Pharaoh, concerning the
un-covenanted first-born of the Egyptians,[1] Moses was
met by a startling providence, and came face to face
with death—possibly with a bloody death of some
sort. "The Lord met him, and sought to kill him,"
it is said. It seems to have been perceived, both by
Moses and his wife, that they were being cut off
from a farther share in God's covenant-plans for
the descendants of Abraham, because of their failure
to conform to their obligations in the covenant of
Abraham.

"Then Zipporah took a flint, and cut off the foreskin of her son, and cast it at [made it touch] his
[Moses'] feet; and she said, Surely a bridegroom of
blood [one newly bound through blood], art thou to
me. So He [the Lord] let him [Moses] alone [He
spared him, as one newly true to the covenant of
Abraham, and newly safe within its bounds]. Then
she [Zipporah] said [again], A bridegroom of blood
art thou, because of the circumcision;" or, as the
margin renders it: "A bridegroom of blood [art thou]
in regard of the circumcision."[2]

The Hebrew word *khathan* (חָתָן), here translated
"bridegroom," has, as its root idea, the binding through
severing, the covenanting by blood;[3] an idea that is

---

[1] Exod. 4: 21–23.   [2] Exod. 4: 25, 26.

[3] See Fuerst's *Heb. Chald. Lex.*, s. v.

in the marriage-rite, as the Orientals view it,[1] and that is in the rite of circumcision, also. Indeed, in the Arabic, the corresponding term (*khatan*, خَتَن), is applied interchangeably to one who is a relation by the way of one's wife, and to one who is circumcised.[2] Hence, the words of Zipporah would imply that, by this rite of circumcision, she and her child were brought into blood-covenant relations with the descendants of Abraham, and her husband also was now saved to that covenant; whereas before they were in danger of being covenanted with a bloody death. It is this idea which seems to be in the Targum of Onkelos, where it renders Zipporah's first words: " By the blood of this circumcision, a *khathna* [a blood-won relation] is given to us;" and her second speech: " If the blood of this circumcision had not been given [to us; then we had had] a *khathna* [a blood-won relation] of slaughter [of death]." It is as though Zipporah had said: " We are now newly covenanted to each other, and to God, by blood; whereas, but for this, we should have been covenanted to slaughter [or death] by blood."

[1] See Deut. 22: 13–21. To this day, in the East, an exhibit of bloodstains, as the indubitable proof of a consummated covenant of marriage, is common. See Niebuhr's *Beschreibung von Arabien*, pp. 35–39; Burckhardt's *Arabic Proverbs*, p. 140; Lane's *Mod. Egypt.*, I., 221, note.

[2] See Lane, and Freytag, s. vv., *Khatan, Khatana.*

4. THE BLOOD COVENANT TESTED.

After the formal covenant of blood had been made between Abraham and Jehovah, there was a specific testing of Abraham's fidelity to that covenant, as if in evidence of the fact that it was no empty ceremony on his part, whereby he pledged his blood,—his very life, in its successive generations,—to Jehovah, in the rite of circumcision. The declaration of his " faith," and the promise of his faithfulness, were to be justified, in their manifest sincerity, by his explicit "works" in their direction.

All the world over, men who were in the covenant of blood-friendship were ready—or .were supposed to be ready—to give not only their lives for each other, but even to give, for each other, that which was dearer to them than life itself. And, all the world over, men who pledged their devotedness to their gods were ready to surrender to their gods that which they held as dearest and most precious—even to the extent of their life, and of that which was dearer than life. Would Abraham do as much for his Divine Friend, as men would do for their human friends? Would Abraham surrender to his God all that the worshipers of other gods were willing to surrender in proof of their devotedness? These were questions yet to be answered before the world.

"And it came to pass after these things, that God did prove Abraham [did put him to the test, or the proof, of his friendship], and said unto him, Abraham ; and he said, Here am I. And he said, Take now thy son, thine only son, whom thou lovest, even Isaac, and get thee unto the land of Moriah ; and offer him there for a burnt-offering upon one of the mountains which I will tell thee of."[1] And Abraham rose up instantly to respond to the call of his Divine Friend.

Just here it is important to consider two or three points at which the Western mind has commonly failed to recognize the Oriental thought, in connection with such a transaction as this.

An Oriental father prizes an only son's life far more than he prizes his own. He recognizes it, to be sure, as at his own disposal ; but he would rather surrender any other possession than that. For an Oriental to die without a son, is a terrible thought.[2] His life is a failure. His future is blank. But with a son to take his place, an Oriental is, in a sense, ready to die. When therefore an Oriental has one son, if the choice must be between the cutting short of the father's life, or of the son's, the former would be the lesser surren-

---

[1] Gen. 22 : 1, 2.

[2] " Heaven awaits not one who is destitute of a son," say the Brahmans (See page 194, *supra*). See, also, e. g., Thomson's *Land and Book*, I., 177 ; Roberts's *Orient. Ill.*, p. 53 f., Ginsburg's " Illustrations," in *Bible Educator*, I., 30 ; Lane's *Mod. Egypt.*, I., 68. Livingstone's *Trav. and Res. in So. Af.*, p. 140 ; Pierotti's *Cust. and Trad. of Pal.*, pp. 177 f., 190 f.

der; the latter would be far greater. Pre-eminently did this truth have force in the case of Abraham, whose pilgrim-life had been wholly with reference to the future; and whose earthly-joy and earthly-hopes centered in Isaac, the son of his old age. For Abraham to have surrendered his own toil-worn life, now that a son of promise was born to him, would have been a minor matter, at the call of God. But for Abraham to surrender that son, and so to become again a child-less, hopeless old man, was a very different matter. Only a faith that would neither question nor reason, only a love that would neither fail nor waver, could meet an issue like that. The surrender of an only son by an Oriental was not, therefore, as it is often deemed in the Western mind, a father's selfish yielding of a lesser substitute for himself;[1] but it was the giving of the one thing which he had power to surrender, which was more precious to him than himself. The difference here is as great as that between the enforced sending, by an able-bodied citizen, of a "substitute" defender of the sender's country in a war-time draft, and the willing sending to the front, by an aged father, of his loved and only son, at the first signal of his country's danger. The one case has in it more than a suggestion of cowardly shirking; the other shows only a loyal and self-forgetful love of country.

[1] See illustrations of this error in Tylor's *Prim. Cult.*, II., 403.

Again, we are liable to think of the surrender of a life, as the dooming to death; and of a sacrificial outpouring of blood, as necessarily an expiatory offering. In the case of the only son sent into battle by his patriotic father, death may be an incident to the transaction; but the gift of the son is the gift of his *life*, whether he shall live or die. And although the war itself be caused by sin, and be a result, and so a punishment, of sin, the son is sent into it, not in order that he may bear punishment, but that he may avert its disastrous consequences, even at the cost of his life—with the necessity of his death.

This idea of the surrender of an only son, not in expiation of guilt, but in proof of unselfish and limitless affection, runs down through the ages, apart from any apparent trace of connection with the tradition of Abraham and Isaac. It is seen:—in India, in the story of the sacrifice of Siralen, the only son of Sirutunden and Vanagata-ananga, as a simple proof of their loving devotedness to Vishnoo;[1] in Arabia, in the story of the proffered slaying of the two only children of a king, in order to restore to life by their blood his dearly loved friend and servant, who had been turned to stone;[2] in the Norseland, in the similar story of the king and his friend and servant "Faithful John;"[3] in Great Britain, in

[1] See page 185 f., *supra*.   [2] See page 119 f., *supra*.
[3] See page 120, *supra*.

the story of Amys and Amylion, the one of these friends sacrificing his two only children for the purpose of curing the other friend of the leprosy ;[1] and so in many another guise.[2]   Whatever other value attaches to these legends, they show most clearly, that the conception of such a surrender as that to which Abraham was called in the sacrifice of Isaac, was not a mere outgrowth of the customs of human sacrifices to malignant divinities, in Phoenicia and Moab and the adjoining countries, in the days of Abraham and earlier.[3]   There was a sentiment involved, which is everywhere recognized as the noblest and purest of which humanity is capable.

If, indeed, there were any reluctance to accept this simple explanation of an obvious view of the test of friendship to which God subjected Abraham, because of its possible bearing on the recognized symbolism of the transaction, then it would be sufficient to remember, that one view of such a transaction is not necessarily its only view.   Whatever other view be taken of the fact and the symbolism of God's call on Abraham to surrender to him his only son, it is obvious that, as a fact, God did test, or prove, Abraham his friend, by asking of him the very evidence of his loving and un-selfish devotedness to him, which has been, everywhere

[1] See page 117, *supra*.   [2] See page 118 f., 120 f., *supra*.

[3] See discussions of this point, by Hengstenberg, Kurtz, Oehler, Ewald, Kuenen, Lange, Keil and Delitzsch, Stanley, Mozeley, etc.

and always, reckoned the highest and surest evidence possible of the truest and holiest friendship. And this may well be looked at, also, as a symbol of God's purpose of surrendering *his* only Son, in proof of his fidelity to his blood-covenant of friendship with Abraham and Abraham's true seed forever.

"Greater love [in friendship] hath no man than this, that a man lay down his life for his friends;"[1] and no man, as the Oriental mind views it, can so utterly lay down his life, as when he lays down the larger life of his only son. Abraham showed himself capable of even such friendship as this, in his blood-covenant with Jehovah; and when he had manifested his spirit of devotedness, he was told to stay his hand and spare his son: the will was accepted for the deed. "Yea, he that had gladly received the promises, was offering up his only begotten son; even he of whom it was said, In Isaac shall thy seed be called : accounting that God is able to raise up even from the dead; from whence he did also in a parable receive him back."[2] Then it was, that "the Angel of the Lord called unto Abraham a second time out of heaven and said, By myself have I sworn [by my life], saith the Lord, because thou hast done this thing, and hast not withheld thy son, thine only son: that in blessing I will bless thee, and in multiplying I will multiply thy

[1] John 15: 13.   [2] Heb. 11: 17–19.

20

seed as the stars of the heaven, and as the sand which is upon the seashore; and thy seed shall possess the gate of his enemies; and in thy seed shall all the nations of the earth be blessed: because thou hast [even to this extent] obeyed my voice."[1] The blood-covenant of friendship between Jehovah and Abraham had more meaning in it than ever, through its testing and its triumph, in this transaction.

And it is on this record, and apparently in this view of the record, that the Apostle James says: "Was not Abraham our father justified by works, in that he offered up Isaac his son upon the altar? Thou seest that faith wrought with his works, and by works was faith made perfect [consummated]; and the Scripture was fulfilled which saith, And Abraham believed God, and it was reckoned unto him for righteousness; and he was called the friend of God."

5. THE BLOOD COVENANT AND ITS TOKENS IN THE
PASSOVER.

There came, again, a time when the Lord would give fresh evidence of *his* fidelity to his covenant of blood-friendship with Abraham. Again a new start was to be made in the history of redemption. The seed of Abraham was in Egypt, and the Lord would bring thence that seed, for its promised inheritance in

[1] Gen. 22 : 15–18.　　　　　　　　　[2] James 2 : 21–23.

Canaan. The Egyptians refused to let Israel go, at the call of the Lord. The Lord sent a series of strokes or "plagues" upon the Egyptians, to enforce their obedience to his summons. And first, he turned the waters of Egypt into blood; so that there was nothing for the Egyptians to drink save that which, as the representative of life, was sacred to their gods, and must not be tasted.[1] So on, from "plague" to "plague" —from stroke to stroke; until the Lord's sentence went forth against all the uncovenanted first-born of Egypt. Then it was that the Lord gave another illustration of the binding force of the unfailing covenant of blood.

In the original covenant of blood-friendship between Abraham and the Lord, it was Abraham who gave of his blood in token of the covenant. Now, the Lord was to give of his blood, by substitution, in re-affirmation of that covenant, with the seed of Abraham his friend. So the Lord commanded the choice of a lamb, "without blemish, a male of the first year";[2] typical in its qualities, and representative in its selection. The blood of that lamb was to be put "on the two side posts and on the lintel" of every house of a descendant of Abraham; above and along side of every passer through the doorway.[3] "And the blood shall be to you for a token upon the houses where ye

---

[1] See Exod. 4: 9; 7: 17–21.　　　[2] See Exod. 12: 1–6.

[3] See a reference to a similar custom in China, at page 153, *supra.*

are," said the Lord to this people: "and when I see
the blood [the token of my blood-covenant with Abra-
ham], I will pass over you, and there shall no plague
be upon you to destroy you, when I smite the land of
Egypt." [1]

The flesh of the chosen lamb was to be eaten by
the Israelites, reverently, as an indication of that inter-
communion which the blood-friendship rite secures;
and in accordance with a common custom of the
primitive blood-covenant rite, everywhere.

To this day, as I can testify from personal observation, the Samaritans on Mount Gerizim (where alone
in all the world the passover-blood is now shed, year
by year), bring to mind the blood-covenant aspects of
this rite, by their uses of that sacred blood. The
spurting life-blood of the consecrated lambs is caught
in basins, as it flows from their cut throats; and not
only are all the tents promptly marked with the blood
as a covenant-token, but every child of the covenant
receives also a blood-mark, on his forehead, between
his eyes,[2] in evidence of his relation to God in the
covenant of blood-friendship.

It will be remembered that in the primitive rite of
blood-friendship a blood-stained record of the covenant is preserved in a small leathern case, to be worn
as an amulet upon the arm, or about the neck, by

[1] Exod. 12: 7-13.   [2] See, again, at pages 154, *supra*.

him who has won a friend forever in this sacred rite.[1]
It would even seem that this was the custom in ancient
Egypt, where the red amulet, which represented the
blood of Isis, was worn by those who claimed a blood-
friendship with the gods.[2] It is a noteworthy fact, that
it was in conjunction with the institution of this passover rite of the Lord's blood-friendship with Israel, as
a permanent ceremonial, that the Lord declared of this
rite and its token: "It shall be for a sign upon thine
hand, and for frontlets between thine eyes."[3] And it is
on the strength of this injunction, that the Jews have,
to this day, been accustomed to wear upon their foreheads, and again upon their arm—as a crown and as
an armlet—a small leathern case, as a sacred amulet,
or as a "phylactery"; containing a record of the pass-
over-covenant between the Lord and the seed of Abraham his friend. Not the law itself, but the substance
of the covenant between the Lawgiver and his people,
was the text of this amulet record. It included
Exodus 13: 3–10, 11–16, with its reference to God's
deliverance of his people from bondage, to the institution of the passover feast, and to the consecration of

---

[1] See page 7 f., *supra.*

[2] See page 81 f., *supra.* It is, indeed, by no means improbable, that the
Hebrew word tôtaphôth (טוֹטָפֹת), translated "frontlets," as applied to
the phylacteries was an Egyptian word. Its etymology has been a puzzle to the critics.   [3] See Exod. 13: 11–16.

20*

the redeemed first-born; also Deuteronomy 6: 4–9, 13–22, with its injunction to entire and unswerving fidelity, in the covenant thus memorialized.

The incalculable importance of the symbolism of the phylacteries, in the estimation of the Lord's people, has been recognized, as a fact, by both Jewish and Christian scholars, even after their primary meaning has been lost sight of—through a strange dropping out of sight of the primitive rite of blood-covenanting, so familiar in the land of Egypt and in the earlier and later homes of the Hebrews. The Rabbis even held that God himself, as the other party in this blood-covenant, wore the phylacteries, as its token and memorial.[1] Among other passages in support of this, they cited Isaiah 49: 16: "Behold I have graven thee upon the palms of my hands"; and Isaiah 62: 8: "The Lord hath sworn by his right hand, and by the arm of his strength." Farrar, referring to this claim of the Rabbis, says, "it may have had some mystic meaning";[2] and certainly the claim corresponds singularly with the thought and with the customs of the rite of blood-covenanting. To this day many of the Syrian Arabs swear, as a final and a most sacred oath, by their own blood—as their own

---

[1] See references to *Zohar*, Pt. II., Fol. 2, by Farrar, in Smith-Hackett's *Bible Dictionary*, Art. "Frontlets."

[2] Smith-Hackett's *Bib. Dict.*, Art. "Frontlets."

life;[1] and in making the covenant of blood-friendship they draw the blood from the upper arm, because, as they explain it, the arm is their strength.[2] The cry of the Egyptian soul to his god, in his resting on the covenant of blood, was, " Give me your arm ; I am made as ye." [3] It is not strange, therefore, that those who had the combined traditions of Egypt and of Syria should see a suggestion of the covenant of blood-friendship in the inspired assurance : " The Lord hath sworn by his right hand, and by the arm of his strength." It is by no means improbable, indeed, that the universal custom of lifting up the arm to God in a solemn oath [4] was a suggestion of swear-

---

[1] On this point I have the emphatic testimony of intelligent native Syrians. " As I live, saith the Lord "—or more literally, " I, living, saith the Lord." " For when God made promise to Abraham, since he could swear by no greater, he sware by himself "—by his life. (Comp. Isa. 49 : 18 ; Jer. 22 : 24 ; Ezek. 5 : 11 ; Heb. 6 : 13.)

[2] This also I am assured of, by native Syrians. One who had resided in both Syria and Upper Egypt told me, that in Syria, in the rite of blood-friendship, the blood is taken from the *arm* as the symbol of strength ; while in portions of Africa where the legs are counted stronger than the arms, through the training of the people as runners rather than as burden-bearers, the *leg* supplies the blood for this rite. (See reference to Stanley and Mirambo's celebration of this rite at pages 18–20, *supra.*)   [3] See page 79, *supra.*

[4] See e. g. Gen. 14 : 22 ; Dan. 12 : 7. " It is an interesting fact, that many of the images of the gods of the heathen have the right hand lifted up." (Robert's *Orient. Ill. of Scrip.*, p. 20.)

ing by one's blood, by proffering it in its strength, as in the inviolable covenant of sacred friendship with God. So, again, in the "striking hands" as a form of sacred covenanting[1]; the clasping of hands, in blood.

The Egyptian amulet of blood-friendship was red, as representing the blood of the gods. The Egyptian word for "red," sometimes stood for "blood."[2] The sacred directions in the Book of the Dead were written in red;[3] hence follows our word "rubrics." The Rabbis say that, when persecution forbade the wearing of the phylacteries with safety, a red thread might be substituted for this token of the covenant with the Lord.[4] It was a red thread which Joshua gave to Rahab as a token of her covenant relations with the people of the Lord.[5] The red thread, in China, to-day, as has been already shown, binds the double cup, from which the bride and bridegroom drink their covenant draught of "wedding wine"; as if in symbolism of the covenant of blood.[6] And it is a red thread which in India, to-day, is used to bind a sacred amulet around the arm or the neck.[7] Among the American Indians,

---

[1] See Prov. 6 : 1; 11 : 15 (margin); 22 : 24–26.

[2] See page 47, *supra.*

[3] See Lepsius's exemplar of the *Todtenbuch;* also Birch, in Bunsen's *Egypt's Place*, V., 125.

[4] See Farrar's article on " Frontlets," in Smith-Hackett's *Bib. Dic.*

[5] Joshua 2 : 18–20.   [6] See pages 93 f., *supra.*

[7] See Robert's *Orient. Ill. of Scrip.*, p. 20.

" scarlet, or red," is the color which stands for sacrifices, or for sacrificial blood, in all their picture painting; and the shrine, or *tunkan*, which continues to have its devotees, " is painted red, as a sign of active [or living] worship." [1] The same is true of the shrines in India; [2] the color red shows that worship is still living there; red continues to stand for blood.

The two covenant tokens of blood-friendship with God—circumcision and the phylacteries—are, by the Rabbis, closely linked in their relative importance. " Not every Israelite is a Jew," they say, " except he has two witnesses—the sign of circumcision and phylacteries " ; [3] the sign given to Abraham, and the sign given to Moses.

In the narration of King Saul's death, as given in 2 Samuel 1 : 1–16, the young Amalekite, who reports Saul's death to David, says : " I took the crown that was upon his head, and the bracelet that was on his arm [the emblems of his royalty], and have brought them hither unto my lord." The Rabbis, in their paraphrasing of this passage,[4] claim that it was the phylactery, " the frontlet " (*totephta*) rather than a "bracelet," which was on the arm of King Saul : as if the king of the

[1] Lynd's *Hist. of Dakotas*, p. 81.

[2] Bayard Taylor's *India, China, and Japan*, p. 52.

[3] See *Home and Syn. of Mod. Jew*, p. 5.

[4] See Targum, in Buxtorf's *Biblia Rabbinica*, in loco.

covenant-people of Jehovah would not fail to be without the token of Jehovah's covenant with that people.

So firmly fixed was the idea of the appropriateness and the binding force of these tokens of the covenant, that their use, in one form or another, was continued by Christians, until the custom was denounced by representative theologians and by a Church Council. In the Catacombs of Rome, there have been found " small caskets of gold, or other metal, for containing a portion of the Gospels, generally part of the first chapter of John [with its covenant promises to all who believe on the true Paschal Lamb], which were worn on the neck," as in imitation of the Jewish phylacteries. These covenant tokens were condemned by Irenæus, Augustine, Chrysostom, and by the Council of Laodicea, as a relic of heathenism. [1]

6. THE BLOOD COVENANT AT SINAI.

When rescued Israel had reached Mount Sinai, and a new era for the descendants of Abraham was entered upon, by the issue of the divinely given charter of a separate nationality, the covenant of blood-friendship between the Lord and the seed of the Lord's friend was once more recognized and celebrated. "And Moses came and told the people all the words of the Lord, and all the judgments: and all the peo-

[1] See Jones's *Credulities Past and Present*, p. 188.

ple answered with one voice, and said, All the words
which the Lord hath spoken will we do. And Moses
wrote all the words of the Lord, and rose up early in
the morning [or, 'prepared for a new start' as that
phrase means],[1] and builded an altar under the mount,
and twelve pillars, according to the twelve tribes of
Israel. And he sent young men of the children of
Israel, which offered burnt offerings, and sacrificed
peace offerings of oxen unto the Lord ;"[2] not sin-offer-
ings are named, but burnt-offerings, of consecration, and
peace-offerings, of communion. And now observe the
celebration of the symbolic rite of the blood-covenant
between the Lord and the Lord's people, with the
substitute blood accepted on both sides, and with the
covenant record agreed upon. "And Moses took half
of the blood, and put it in basins ; and half of the
blood he sprinkled on the altar. And he took the
book [the record] of the covenant, and read in the audi-
ence of the people : and they said, All that the Lord
hath spoken will we do, and be obedient. And Moses
took the blood, and sprinkled it on the people [half
of it he sprinkled on the Lord's altar, and half of it
he sprinkled on the Lord's people. The writer of
Hebrews [3] says that Moses sprinkled blood on the
book, also ; thus blood-staining the record of the covenant, according to the custom in the East, to-day],

[1] *Kadesh-Barnea*, p. 382, note.   [2] Exod. 24:3-6.   [3] Heb. 9: 19.

and [Moses] said, Behold the blood of the covenant, which the Lord hath made with you concerning all these words [or, as the margin renders it, ' upon all these conditions,' in the written compact]. Then went up Moses, and Aaron, Nadab, and Abihu, and seventy of the elders of Israel. . . . And they beheld God, and did eat and drink";[1] as in the social inter-communion, which commonly accompanies the rite of blood-friendship.

When Abraham was brought into the covenant of blood-friendship with Jehovah, it was his own blood which Abraham devoted to Jehovah. When Jehovah recognized anew this covenant of blood-friendship in behalf of the seed of his friend, Jehovah provided the substitute blood, for its symbolizing in the passover. When united Israel was to be inducted into the privileges of this covenant of blood-friendship at Mount Sinai, half of the blood came from the one party, and half of the blood came from the other party, to the sacred compact; both portions being supplied from a common and a mutually accepted symbolic substitute.

7. THE BLOOD COVENANT IN THE MOSAIC RITUAL.

With the establishment of the Mosaic law, there was an added emphasis laid on the sacredness of blood, which had been insisted on in the Noachic

[1] See Exod. 24: 1–11.

covenant; and many new illustrations were divinely given of the possibilities of an ultimate union with God through inter-flowing blood, and of present communion with God through the sharing of the substitute flesh of a sacrificial victim.

"Ye shall eat no manner of blood, whether it be of fowl or beast, in any of your dwellings. Whosoever it be that eateth any blood, that soul shall be cut off from his people."[1] "Whatsoever man there be of the house of Israel, or of the strangers that sojourn among them, that eateth any manner of blood; I will set my face against that soul that eateth blood, and will cut him off from among his people. For the life [the soul] of the flesh is in the blood: and I have given it to you upon the altar to make atonement for your souls: for it is the blood that maketh atonement by reason of the life [by reason of its being the life]. Therefore I said unto the children of Israel, No soul of you shall eat blood, neither shall any stranger that is among you eat blood."[2] "For as to the life of all flesh, the blood thereof is all one with the life thereof; therefore I said unto the children of Israel, Ye shall eat the blood of no manner of flesh: for the life of all flesh is the blood thereof: whosoever eateth it shall be cut off."[3]

Because of sin, death has passed upon man. Man

[1] Lev. 7: 26. [2] Lev. 17: 10–12. [3] Lev. 17: 14.

can have new life only from the Author of life. A
transfusion of life is, as it were, a transfusion of blood;
for, " of all flesh, the blood thereof is all one with the
life thereof." If, indeed, the death-possessed man
could enter into a blood-covenant with the Author of
life,—could share the life of him who is Life,—then
the dead might have new life in a new nature; and the
far separated sinner might be brought into oneness
with God; finding atonement in the cleansing flow of
the new blood thus applied. So it pleased God to ap-
point substitute blood upon the altar of witness between
the sinner and Himself, as a symbol of that atonement
whereby the sinner might, through faith, become a
partaker of the divine nature. " The wages of sin is
death; but the free gift of God is eternal life "[1]—in
that foreshadowed divine blood which the blood of
beasts, offered on the altar, can, for a time, typify.
Blood—even the blood of beasts—thus made sacred,
as a holy symbol, must never be counted as a common
thing; but it must be held, ever reverently, as a token
of that life which is the sinner's need; and which is
God's grandest gift and God's highest prerogative.

In the line of this teaching, the command went
forth: "What man soever there be of the house of
Israel, that killeth an ox, or lamb, or goat in the
camp, or that killeth it without the camp, and hath

[1] Rom. 6: 23.

not brought it unto the door of the tent of meeting, to offer it [with its blood] as an oblation unto the Lord before the tabernacle of the Lord: blood shall be imputed unto that man; he hath shed blood [improperly]; and that man shall be cut off from among his people: to the end that the children of Israel may bring their sacrifices, which they sacrifice in the open field, even that they may bring them unto the Lord, unto the door of the tent of meeting, unto the priest, and sacrifice them for sacrifices of peace-offering unto the Lord. And the priest shall sprinkle the blood upon the altar of the Lord at the door of the tent of meeting; and burn the fat for a sweet savour unto the Lord." [1] The children of Israel were, at all times and everywhere, to reach out after communion and union with God, through the surrender of their personal selves in the surrender of their substitute blood—with its divinely appointed symbolism of communion and union with God " in the blood of the eternal covenant " of divine friendship.[2]

And again: " Whatsoever man there be of the children of Israel, or of the strangers that sojourn among them, which taketh in hunting any beast or fowl that may be eaten; he shall pour out the blood thereof, and cover it with the dust." [3] If he be at a distance from the tabernacle, so that he cannot bring

[1] Lev. 17: 3-6.   [2] Comp. Heb. 13: 20.   [3] Lev. 17: 13.

the blood for an oblation at the altar, he must, at all events, reverently pour out the blood as unto God, and cover it as he would a human body in a grave. And to this day this custom prevails widely throughout the East; not among Jews alone, but among Christians and Muhammadans, as also among those of other religions.[1]

Under the Mosaic ritual, the forms and the symbolisms of sacrifice were various. But through them all, where blood was an element,—in the sin-offering, in the trespass-offering, in the burnt-offering, in the peace-offering,—blood always represented life, never death. Death was essential to its securing; but, when secured, blood was life. Death, as the inevitable wages of sin, had already passed unto all men; and "death reigned from Adam to Moses"; but, with the full disclosure of the law, in Moses, which made sin apparent, there came, also, a disclosure of an atonement for sin, and of a cure for its consequences. Death was already here; now came the assurance of an attainable life. The sinner, in the very article of death, was shown that he might turn, in self-surrender and in loving trust, with a proffer of his own

---

[1] A traveler in Mauritius, describing a Hindoo sacrifice there, of a he-goat, in fulfilment of a vow, says: "It was killed on soft ground, where the blood would sink into the earth, and leave no trace" (Pike's *Sub-Tropical Rambles*, p. 223). See also page 109, *supra*.

life, by substitute blood, to God; and that he might reach out hopefully after inter-union with God, by the sharing of the divine-nature in the unfailing covenant of divine-human blood-friendship. Thus "not as the trespass [with its mere justice of punishment; but] so also [and 'much more,' of grace alone,] is the free gift [of life to the justly dead]."[1]

All the detailed requirements of the Mosaic ritual, and all the specific teachings of the Rabbis, as well, go to show the pre-eminence of the *blood* in the sacrificial offerings; go to show, that it is the *life* (which the blood is), and not the *death* (which is merely necessary to the securing of the blood), of the victim, that is the means of atonement; that gives the hope of a sinner's new inter-union with God.

In a commentary on a Talmudic tract, on The Day of Atonement, Rabbi Obadiah of Barttenora, notes the fact,[2] that in the choice by lot of the priests who were to have a part in the daily sacrifice, the priest *first* selected " obtained the right [of priority], and sprinkled the blood upon the altar, after he had received it in the vessel for the purpose; for he who sprinkled the blood [is the one who had] received the blood. The *next* priest to him killed the sacrifice, and this notwith-

---

[1] Rom. 5 : 12–21.

[2] See *Quarterly Statement* of Pales. Expl. Fund, for July, 1885, pp. 197–207.

standing [the fact] that the slaying preceded the receiving of the blood; because *the office of sprinkling
was higher than that of slaying;* for the slaying was law-
ful if done by a stranger; which was not the case with
the sprinkling." The death of the victim was a minor
matter: it was the victim's life,—its blood which was
its life,—that had chief value and sacredness.

On this same point Dr. Edersheim says:[1] "The
Talmud declares the offering of birds, so as to secure
the blood [so as to secure that which was pre-eminently
precious] to have been the most difficult part of a
priest's work. For the *death* of the [victim of the]
sacrifice was only a means towards an end; that end
being the shedding and sprinkling of the *blood*, by
which the atonement was really made. The Rabbis
mention a variety of rules observed by the priest who
caught up the blood—all designed to make the best
provision for its proper sprinkling. Thus, the priest
was to catch up the blood in a silver vessel pointed at
the bottom, so that it could not be put down; and to
keep it constantly stirred, to preserve the fluidity of
the blood. In the sacrifice of the red heifer, however,
the priest caught the blood directly in his left hand,
and sprinkled it with his right towards the Holy
Place: while in that of the leper, one of the two priests
received the blood in the vessel; the other [received

---

[1] *The Temple, Its Ministry and Services,* p. 88, f.

it] in his hand, from which he anointed the purified leper."

Recognizing the truth that in the sacrifices of the Mosaic ritual " consecration by blood is consecration in a living union with Jehovah," Professor W. Robertson Smith observes,[1] that " in the ordinary atoning sacrifices the blood is not applied to the people [it is merely poured out Godward, as if in sign of life surrender]; but in the higher forms, as in the sacrifice for the whole congregation (Lev. 4 : 13 *seq.*), the priest at least dips his hand in it, and so puts the bond of blood between himself, as the people's representative, and the altar, as the point of contact with God."[2] And so, on the basis of the root-idea of the primitive rite of the covenant of blood, an inter-union is symbolized between the returning sinner and his God.

The aim of all the Mosaic sacrifices was, a restored communion with God ; and the hope which runs through them all is of a divine-human inter-union through blood. " The one purpose which is given after every sacrifice in the first chapters of Leviticus,"[3] says Stanley,[4] " is, that it ' shall make a sweet savour unto the Lord'." And Edersheim says,[5] of all the various sacri-

[1] *The Old Test. in the Jewish Church*, Notes on Lect. XII.

[2] See pages 11, 12, *supra.*   [3] Lev. 1: 13, 17 ; 2: 2, 12 ; 3 : 8, 16.

[4] *Christian Institutions*, Chap. 4.

[5] *The Temple, Its Min. and Serv.*, p. 82.

fices of the ritual: " These were, then, either sacrifices
of communion with God, or else [were] intended to restore that communion when it had been disturbed or
dimmed through sin and trespass: sacrifices *in* communion, or [sacrifices] *for* communion, with God. To
the former class belong the burnt and the peace-offerings; to the latter, the sin and the trespass offerings."[1]

The sin-offering of that ritual was, in a sense, the
basis of the whole system of sacrifices. The chief
feature of that offering was the out-flowing of its
blood Godward. The offering itself was a substitute-
offering for an individual or for the entire people. Its
blood was sprinkled upon the horns of the altar of burnt-
offering, or poured out at the base of that altar,[2]—the altar of personal consecration; or, it was sprinkled within
the Holy Place toward the Most Holy Place,[3]—the
symbolic dwelling-place of Jehovah: and again it was
made to touch the horns of the altar of incense, which
sent up its sweet savor to God: in every case, it was
the outreaching of the sinner toward inter-union with
God, in a covenant of blood.

The whole burnt-offering of the Mosaic ritual
symbolized the entire surrender to God, of the individual or of the congregation, in covenant faithfulness;
the giving of one's self in unreserved trust to Him

----

[1] *The Temple, Its Min. and Serv.,* p. 82.

[2] Lev 4: 7, 18, 25, 30, 34.   [3] Lev. 4: 6, 7, 17; 16: 14, 15.

with whom the offerer desired to be in loving oneness.
It was an indication of a readiness to enter fully into
that inter-union which the blood-covenant brought
about between two who had been separated, but who
were henceforth to be as one. This offering also must
be made with blood; for it is blood—which is the
life—that gives the possibility of inter-union. All the
outpoured blood of this offering, however, went directly
to the altar upon which the offering itself was laid;[1] not
toward the Most Holy Place, of the Lord's symbolic
presence. This offering was not, indeed, understood
as in itself compassing inter-union ; it indicated rather
a desire and a readiness for inter-union—anew or
renewed: so both the substitute-body and the substitute-
blood were offered at the altar of typical surrender and
consecration. When other sacrifices were brought, the
burnt-offering followed the sin-offering, but preceded
the peace-offering ;[2] again, it might be offered by itself.
He who was of the blood-covenant stock of Abraham
thereby sought restoration to the full privileges of that
covenant, to which he had not been wholly true ; and
even he who was not of that stock might in this way
show his desire to share in its privileges; "for the burnt
offering was the only sacrifice which non-Israelites were
permitted to bring"[3] to the altar of Jehovah.

[1] Lev. 1: 5, 11, 15.   [2] Lev. 8: 14–22; 9: 8–22; 14: 19, 20; 16: 3–25.

[3] Edersheim's *The Temple, Its Min. and Serv.*, p. 100.

Following the communion-seeking, or the union-seeking, sin-offering (with its connected, or related, trespass-offering, or guilt-offering), and the self-surrendering burnt-offering, there came the joyous communion-symbolizing peace-offering, with its type of completed union,[1] in the sharing, by the sinner and his God, of the flesh of the sacrificial victim at a common feast. And this banquet-sacrifice[2] corresponds with the feast of inter-communion which commonly follows the primitive rite of blood-covenanting, and which marks the completion of the inter-union thereby sought after.

All the other sacrifices of the Mosaic ritual follow in the line of these three classes. Even those which are in themselves offered without blood presuppose the individual's share in the blood-covenant, by the rite of circumcision and through the high priest's sin-offering for the entire congregation. "The Rabbis attach ten comparative degrees of sanctity to sacrifices; and it is interesting to mark, that of these the first belonged to the blood of the sin-offering ; the second to the burnt-offering ; the third to the sin-offering itself; and the fourth to the trespass-offering."[3] The blood which is to secure the covenant-union—anew or re-

---

[1] " From its derivation it might also be rendered, the offering of completion" (Edersheim's *The Temple, Its Min., and Serv.*, p. 106).

[2] See page 149, *supra.*

[3] Edersheim's *The Temple, Its Min. and Serv.*, p. 86.

newed—is of preeminent importance. Then comes the symbol of self-surrendering devotedness. First, the possibility of inter-union; next, the expression of readiness and desire for it. After this, the other sacrifices range themselves according to their signification, until the culmination of the series is reached in the joyous inter-communion feast of the peace-offering.

But, with all the suggestions of the rite of blood-covenanting in the sacrifices of the Mosaic ritual, there were limitations in the correspondences of that rite in those sacrifices, which mark the incompleteness of their symbolism and which point to better things to come. In the primitive blood-covenant rite itself, both parties receive, and partake of, the blood which becomes common to the two. In all the outside religions of the world, where men reach out after a divine-human inter-union through substitute-blood, the offerer drinks of the sacrificial blood, or of something which stands for it; and so he is supposed to share the nature of the God with whom he thus covenants and inter-unites. In the Mosaic ritual, however, all drink-offerings of blood were forbidden to him who would enter into covenant with God; he might not taste of the blood. He might, it is true, look forward, by faith, to an ultimate sharing of the divine nature ; and in anticipation of that inter-union, he could enjoy a symbolic inter-communion with God, by partaking of the peace-offerings at the table of his Lord; but as yet the sacrificial offering which could supply to his death-smitten nature the vivifying blood of an everlasting covenant was not disclosed to him.[1]

Even the substitute blood which he presented at the altar, as he came with his outreaching after a blood-covenant union with the Lord, did not secure to him direct personal access to the symbolic earthly dwelling-place of the Lord. That blood could be poured out at the base of the altar of consecration, or it could be sprinkled upon its horns. That blood could, on occasions be sprinkled before the veil of the Most Holy Place, or could touch the horns of the altar of sweet incense. But that blood could never pass that veil which guarded the place of the Lord's symbolic presence, save once in a year when the high-priest, all by himself, and that not without a show of his own unfitness for the mission, went in thither, to sprinkle the substitute blood before the mercy-seat; "the Holy Ghost this signifying, that the way into the Holy Place hath not yet been manifest[2]"; that the substitute "blood of bulls and of goats"[3] cannot be a means of man's inter-union with God.

Lest, indeed, the Israelite should believe that a blood-covenant union was really secured with God, rather than typified, through these prescribed symbolic sacri-

[1] Psa. 16: 4, 5.   [2] Heb. 9: 8.   [3] Heb. 10: 4.

fices and their sharing, he was repeatedly warned
against that fatal error, and was taught that his true
covenanting must be by a faith-filled recognition of the
symbolism of these substitute agencies ; and by the implicit surrender of himself, in loving trust, to Him who
had ordained them as symbols.   Thus in the Psalms :

> " Hear, O my people, and I will speak ;
> O Israel, and I will testify unto thee :
> I am God, even thy God.
> I will not reprove thee for thy sacrifices ;
> And thy burnt-offerings are continually before me.   .   .   .
> Will I eat the flesh of bulls,
> Or drink the blood of goats ?
> Offer unto God the sacrifice of thanksgiving ;
> And pay thy vows unto the Most High :
> And call upon me in the day of trouble ;
> I will deliver thee, and thou shalt glorify me.

> " But unto the wicked, God saith :
> What hast thou to do to declare my statutes,
> And that thou hast taken my covenant in thy mouth ?
> Seeing thou hatest instruction,
> And castest my words behind thee." [1]

Again, in the prophecy of Isaiah :

> " To what purpose is the multitude of your sacrifices unto me ?
> Saith the Lord :
> I am full of the burnt offerings of rams, and the fat of fed
>   beasts ;
> And I delight not in the blood of bullocks, or of lambs, or
>   of he-goats.

[1] Psa. 50: 7–17.

> When ye come to appear before me,
> Who hath required this at your hand, to tread my courts?
> Bring no more vain oblations;
> Incense is an abomination unto me. . . .
> Wash you, make you clean;
> Put away the evil of your doings from before mine eyes;
> Cease to do evil:
> Learn to do well;
> Seek judgment, relieve the oppressed;
> Judge the fatherless, plead for the widow." [1]

And with this very warning against a false reliance on the symbols themselves, the same prophet gives assurance of better things in store for all those who are in true blood-covenant with God; even though they be not of the peculiar people of Abraham's natural descent. Foretelling the future, when the types of the sacrifice shall be realized, he says:

> "And in this mountain shall the Lord of Hosts make unto
>   all peoples
> A feast of fat things,
> A feast of wine on the lees;
> Of fat things full of marrow,
> Of wines on the lees well refined." [2]

The feast of inter-communion shall be sure, when the blood-covenant of inter-union is complete.

Again, by Jeremiah:

> "Thus saith the Lord of Hosts, the God of Israel:
> Add your burnt-offerings unto your sacrifices, and eat ye flesh.

[1] Isaiah 1 : 11–17.   [2] Isa. 25 : 6.

[But remember that that is not the completion of a covenant with me].

> For I spake not unto your fathers, nor commanded them,
> In the day that I brought them out of the land of Egypt,
> Concerning burnt offerings or sacrifices.

[As if burnt offerings and sacrifices were the all important thing];

> But this thing I commanded them, saying,
> Hearken unto my voice,
> And I will be your God,
> And ye shall be my people;
> And walk ye in all the way that I command you,
> That it may be well with you." [1]

Once more, by Hosea:

> " O Ephraim, what shall I do unto thee?
> O Judah, what shall I do unto thee ?
> For your goodness is as a morning cloud,
> And as the dew that goeth early away.   .   .   .
> For I desire mercy and not sacrifice;
> And the knowledge of God more than burnt-offerings.
> But they like Adam have transgressed the covenant:

[or, as the Revisers' " margin" would render it,

> "But they are as men that have transgressed a covenant" :]
> There have they dealt treacherously against me" [2]

[Therein have they proved unfaithful to the requirements of the blood-covenant on which they assumed to be resting, in their sacrifices].

[1] Jer. 7 : 21–23.   [2] Hosea 6 : 4--7.

And so, all the way along through the prophets, in repeated emphasis of the incompleteness of the blood-covenanting symbols in the ritual sacrifices.

Concerning the very rite of circumcision, which was the token of Abraham's covenant of blood-friendship with the Lord, the Israelites were taught that its spiritual value was not in the formal surrender of a bit of flesh, and a few drops of blood, in ceremonial devotedness to God, but in its symbolism of the implicit surrender of the whole life and being, in hearty covenant with God. " Behold, unto the Lord thy God belongeth the heaven, and the heaven of heavens, the earth with all that therein is. Only the Lord had a delight in thy fathers to love them, and he chose their seed after them, even you above all peoples as at this day. Circumcise therefore the foreskin of your heart, and be no more stiff-necked." [1] "And it shall come to pass, when all these things are come upon thee, the blessings and the curse which I have set before thee, and thou shalt call them to mind among all the nations, whither the Lord thy God hath driven thee, and shalt return unto the Lord thy God, and shalt obey his voice according to all that I command thee this day, thou and thy children, with all thine heart, and with all thy soul ; that then the Lord thy God will turn thy captivity, and have compassion upon thee, and will return and

[1] Deut. 10: 14–16.

gather thee from all the peoples, whither the Lord thy
God hath scattered thee. . . . And the Lord thy
God will circumcise thine heart, and the heart of thy
seed, to love the Lord thy God with all thine heart,
and with all thy soul, that thou mayest live." [1]   And
when this has come to pass, the true seed of Abraham,[2] circumcised in heart,[3] shall be in the covenant
of blood-friendship with God.

So, also, with the phylacteries as the record of the
blood-covenant of the passover, they had a value only
as they represented a heart-remembrance of that covenant, by their wearers.   Says Solomon; in the guise
of Wisdom.

> " My son, forget not my law ;
> But let thine heart keep my commandments. . . .
> Let not mercy and truth forsake thee :
> Bind them about thy neck;
> Write them upon the table of thy heart;
> So shalt thou find favor and good understanding
> In the sight of God and man." [4]

> " Keep my commandments and live;
> And my law as the apple of thine eye.
> Bind them upon thy fingers ;
> Write them upon the table of thine heart." [5]

And the prophet Jeremiah foretells the recognition of
this truth in the coming day of better things:

[1] Deut. 30 : 1–6.   [2] Gal. 3 : 7–9 ; Rom. 4 : 11, 12.
[3] Rom. 2 : 26–29 ; Phil. 3 : 3.   [4] Prov. 3 : 1–4.   [5] Prov. 7 : 2, 3.

" Behold the days come, saith the Lord,
    That I will make a new covenant
    With the house of Israel and with the house of Judah:
    Not according to the covenant that I made with their fathers.
    In the day that I took them by the hand,
    To bring them out of the land of Egypt

[That covenant was the blood-covenant of the passover ; of which the phylacteries were a token.]

Which my covenant they brake,
    Although I was an husband unto them [a lord over them] saith
        the Lord ;
    But this shall be the covenant that I will make with the house of
        Israel,
    After those days, saith the Lord ;
    I will put my law in their inward parts,
    And in their heart will I write it:

[Instead of its being written as now, outside of them, on their hand and on their forehead.]

And I will be their God,
    And they shall be my people.   .   .   .
    For I will forgive their iniquity,
    And their sin will I remember no more." [1]

The blood-covenant symbols of the Mosaic law all pointed to the possibility of a union of man's spiritual nature with God; but they did not in themselves either assure or indicate that union as already accomplished; nor did they point the way to it, as yet made clear. They were only " a shadow of the things to come." [2]

[1] Jer. 31: 31–34.   [2] Col. 2: 17.

Another gleam of the primitive truth, that blood is
life and not death, and that the transference of blood
is the transference of life, is found in the various Mosaic
references to the *goel* (גֹּאֵל), the person who is autho-
rized to obtain blood for blood as an act of justice, in
the East. And another proof of the prevailing error
in the Western mind, through confounding blood with
death, and justice with punishment, is the common
rendering of the term *goel*, as " avenger,"[1] or " revenger,"[2] in our English Bible, wherever that term
applies to the balancing of a blood account; although
the same Hebrew word is in other connections commonly translated " redeemer,"[3] or " ransomer."[4]

Lexicographers are confused over the original import of the word *goel*;[5] all the more, because of this
confusion in their minds over the import of blood in
its relation to death and to justice. But it is agreed
on all hands, that, as a term, the word was, in the East,
applied to that kinsman whose duty it was to secure

---

[1] Num. 35 : 12; Deut. 19 : 6, 12; Josh. 20 : 3, 5, 9.

[2] Num. 35 : 19, 21, 24, 25, 27; 2 Sam. 14 : 11.

[3] Job 19 : 25; Psa. 19 : 14; 78 : 35; Prov. 23 : 11; Isa. 41 : 14;
43 : 14; 44 : 6, 24; 47 : 4; 48 : 17; 49 : 7, 26; 54 : 5, 8; 59 : 20;
60 : 16; 63 : 16; Jer. 50 : 34.

[4] Comp. Isa. 51 : 11; Jer. 31 : 11.

[5] "A term of which the original import is uncertain. The very
obscurity of its etymology testifies to the antiquity of the office which it
denotes." (*Speaker's Com.* at Num. 35 : 12.)

justice to the injured, and to restore, as it were, a normal balance to the disturbed family relations.   Oehler
well defines the goel as " that particular relative whose
special duty it was to restore the violated family integ-
rity, who had to redeem not only landed property that
had been alienated from the family (Lev. 25 : 25 ff.), or a
member of the family that [who] had fallen into slavery
(Lev. 25 : 47 ff.), but also the blood that had been taken
away from the family by murder." [1]   Hence, in the event
of a depletion of the family by the loss of blood—the loss
of a life—the goel had a responsibility of securing to the
family an equivalent of that loss, by other blood, or by
an agreed payment for its value.   His mission was not
vengeance, but equity.   He was not an avenger, but a
redeemer, a restorer, a balancer.   And in that light, and
in that light alone, are all the Oriental customs in connection with blood-cancelling seen to be consistent.

All through the East, there are regularly fixed tariffs
for blood-cancelling; as if in recognition of the relative loss to a family, of one or another of its support-
ing members. [2]   This idea, of the differences in ran-

[1] Cited from Herzog's B. Cycl., in Keil and Delitzsch's *Bib. Com. on
the Pent.*, at Num. 35 : 9–34.

[2] See Niebuhr's *Beschreibung von Arabien*, p. 32 f.; Burckhardt's
Beduinen und Wahaby, pp. 119–127; Lane's *Thousand and One
Nights*, I., 431, note; Pierotti's *Customs and Traditions of Palestine*,
pp. 220–227; Mrs. Finn's "The Fellaheen of Palestine," in *Surv. of
West Pal.*, "Special Papers," pp. 342–346.

soming-value between different members of the family,
is recognized, in the Mosaic standards of ritual-ran-
som;[1] although the accepting of a ransom for the
blood of a blood-spiller was specifically forbidden in
the Mosaic law.[2] This prohibition, in itself, however,
seems to be a limitation of the privileges of the goel,
as before understood in the East. The Qurân, on the
other hand, formally authorizes the settlement of man-
slaughter damages by proper payments.[3]

Throughout Arabia, and Syria, and in various parts
of Africa,[4] the first question to be considered in any
case of unlawful blood-shedding is, whether the lost
life shall be restored—or balanced—by blood, or by
some equivalent of blood. Von Wrede says of the
custom of the Arabs, in concluding a peace, after tribal
hostilities: " If one party has more slain than the other,
the shaykh on whose side the advantage lies, says [to
the other shaykh]: 'Choose between blood and milk'
[between life, and the means of sustaining life]; which
is as much as to say, that he may [either] avenge the
fallen [take life for life]; or accept blood-money." [5]
Mrs. Finn says, similarly, of the close of a combat in

---

[1] Comp. Exod. 21: 18–27; 22: 14–17; Le 27: 1–8.

[2] Num. 35: 30–34.　　　　[3] Sooras, 2 and 17.

[4] Livingstone and Stanley on several occasions made payments, or had
them made, to avoid a conflict on a question of blood. See, e. g. *Trav. and
Res. in So. Africa*, pp. 390, 368–370, 482 f., *The Congo*, I., 520–527.

[5] *Reise in Hadhramaut*, p. 199.

Palestine: "A computation is generally made of the losses on either side by death, wounds, etc., and the balance is paid to the victors."[1]   Burton describes similarly the custom in Arabia.[2]

It is the same in individual cases as in tribal conflicts.   An accepted payment for blood fully restores the balance between the aggrieved parties and the slayer.   As Pierotti says: " This charm will teach the Arab to grasp readily the hands of the slayer of his father or his son, saying, ' Such an one has killed my father, but he has paid me the price of his blood.' "[3] This in itself shows that it is not revenge, but restitution, that is sought after by the goel; that he is not the blood-avenger, but the blood-balancer.

It is true that, still, in some instances, all money payment for blood is refused; but the avowed motive in such a case is the holding of life as above price—the very idea which the Mosaic law emphasized.   Thus Burton tells of the excited Bed'ween mother who dashes the proffered blood-money to the ground, swearing " by Allah, that she will not eat her son's blood."[4]   And even where the blood of the slayer is insisted on, there are often found indications that the purpose of this choice rests on the primitive belief that the lost life is

---

[1] *Surv. of West. Pal.*, "Special Papers," p. 342.

[2] *A Pilgrimage to Mec. and Med.*, 357.

[3] *Cust. and Trad. of Pal.*, p. 221.   [4] *A Pilgrimage*, p. 367.

made good to the depleted family by the newly received blood.[1] Thus, in the region of Abyssinia, the blood of the slayer is drunk by the relatives of the one first slain;[2] and, in Palestine, when the goel has shed the blood of an unlawful slayer, those who were the losers of blood by that slayer dip their handkerchiefs in his blood, and so obtain their portion of his life.[3]

In short, apart from the specific guards thrown around the mission of the goel, in the interests of justice, by the requirements of the Mosaic law, it is evident that the primal idea of the goel's mission was to restore life for life, or to secure the adjusted equivalent of a lost life; not to wreak vengeance, nor yet to mete out punishment. The calling of the goel, in our English Bible, a " revenger" of blood, is a result of the wide-spread and deep-rooted error concerning the primitive and Oriental idea of blood and its value; and that unfortunate translation tends to the perpetuation of this error.

8. THE PRIMITIVE RITE ILLUSTRATED.

Because the primitive rite of blood-covenanting was well known in the Lands of the Bible, at the time of the writing of the Bible, for that very reason we are not to look to the Bible for a specific explanation of

[1] See pages 126–133, *supra.*   [2] See page 132 f., *supra.*

[3] Pierotti's *Cust. and Trad. of Pal.* p. 216.

the rite itself, even where there are incidental references in the Bible to the rite and its observances; but, on the other hand, we are to find an explanation of the biblical illustrations of the primitive rite, in the under-standing of that rite which we gain from outside sources. In this way, we are enabled to see in the Bible much that otherwise would be lost sight of.

The word for "covenant," in the Hebrew, *bereeth* (בְּרִית), is commonly so employed, in the sacred text, as to have the apparent meaning of a thing "cut," as apart from, or as in addition to, its primary meaning of a thing "eaten."[1] This fact has been a source of confusion to lexicographers.[2] But when we consider that the primitive rite of blood-covenanting was by cutting into the flesh in order to the tasting of the blood, and that a feast was always an accompaniment of the rite, if, indeed, it were not an integral portion of it, the two-fold meaning of "cutting" and "eating" attaches obviously to the term "covenant"; as the terms "carving," and "giving to eat," are often used interchangeably, with reference to dining; or as we speak of a "cut of beef" as the portion for a table.

The earliest Bible reference to a specific covenant between individuals, is in the mention, at Genesis 14 : 13, of Mamre, Eshcol, and Aner, the Amorites,

---

[1] Comp. Gen. 15 : 18; Jer. 34 : 18; 2 Sam. 12 : 17.

[2] See Gesenius, Fuerst, Cocceius, s. v.

who were in covenant with—literally, were " masters
of the covenant of "—" Abram the Hebrew." After
this, comes the record of a covenant between Abraham
and Abimelech, at the wells of Beer-sheba. Abimelech sought that covenant ; he sought it because of his
faith in Abraham's God. "God is with thee in all that
thou doest," he said : " Now, therefore, swear unto me
here by God, that thou wilt not deal falsely with me,
nor with my son, nor with my son's son : but according to the kindness that I have done unto thee, thou
shalt do unto me, and to the land wherein thou hast
sojourned. And Abraham said, I will swear."[1] Then
came the giving of gifts by Abraham, according to the
practice which seems universal in connection with this
rite, in our own day.[2] "And Abraham took sheep
and oxen, and gave them unto Abimelech." And they
two " made a covenant,"—or, as the Hebrew is, " they
two cut a covenant." This covenant, thus cut between
Abraham and Abimelech—patriarchs and sovereigns as
they were—was for themselves and for their posterity.
As to the manner of its making, we have a right to
infer, from all that we know of the manner of such
covenant-making among the people of their part of the
world, in the earliest days of recorded history.

Herodotus, who goes back well-nigh two-thirds of
the way to Abraham, says, that when the Arabians

[1] Gen. 21 : 22–24.   [2] See pages 14, 16, 20, 22, 25, 27, etc., *supra.*

23

would covenant together, a third man, standing between the two, cuts, with a sharp stone, the inside of
the hands of both, and lets the blood therefrom drop
on seven stones which are between the two parties.[1]
Phicol, the captain of Abimelech's host, was present,
as a third man, when the covenant was cut between
Abimelech and Abraham; at Beer-sheba—the Well
of the Seven, or the Well of the Oath.[2] Instead of
seven stones as a "heap of witness"[3] between the two
in this covenanting, "seven ewe lambs" were set apart
by Abraham, that they might "be a witness"[4]—a symbolic witness to this transaction.

In the primitive rite of blood-covenanting, as it is
practised in some parts of the East, to the present
time, in addition to other symbolic witnesses of the
rite, a *tree* is planted by the covenanting parties, "which
remains and grows as a witness of their contract."[5] So
it was, in the days of Abraham. "And Abraham
planted a tamarisk tree in Beer-sheba, and called
there on the name of the Everlasting God. And
Abraham sojourned [was a sojourner] in the land of
the Philistines many days"[6]—while that tree, doubtless, remained and grew as a witness of his blood-
covenant compact with Abimelech the ruler of the

[1] See page 47, *supra.*   [2] Gen. 21 : 31.

[3] Comp. Gen. 31 : 44–47.   [4] Gen. 21 : 30.

[5] See page 53, *supra.*   [6] Gen. 21 : 33.

Philistines.[1] Abimelech was, as it were, the first-fruits
of the " nations "[2] who were to have a blessing through
the covenanted friend of God.

It is a noteworthy fact, that when Herodotus describes the Scythians' mode of drinking each other's
mingled blood, in their covenanting, he tells of their
" cutting covenant" by " striking the body " of the covenanting party. In this case, he employs the words
tamnomenon (ταμνομένων) " cutting," and *tupsantes* (τύ-
ψαντες) " striking," which are the correspondents, on
the one hand of the Hebrew *karath* (כָּרַת) " to cut,"
and on the other hand of the Latin *ferire*, " to strike;"
as applied to covenant making.[3] And this would
seem to make a tri-lingual " Rosetta Stone " of this
statement by Herodotus, as showing that the Hebrew
" cutting " of the covenant, and the Latin " striking "
of the covenant, is the Greek, the Arabian, the
Scythian, and the universal primitive, method of covenanting, by cutting into, or by striking, the flesh of a
person covenanting; in order that another may become
a possessor of his blood, and a partaker of his life.

Yet later, at the same Well of the Seven, another
Abimelech came down from Gerar, with " Ahuzzath
his friend, and Phicol the captain of his host," and,

prompted by faith, sought a renewal of the covenant with the house of Abraham.[1] It is not specifically declared that Abimelech and Isaac *cut* a covenant together; but it is said that "they did eat and drink" in token of their covenant relations, and that they "sware one to another."[2] Apparently they either cut a new covenant, or they confirmed one which their fathers had cut.[3]

When Jacob and Laban covenanted together, in "the mountain [the hill-country] of Gilead," before their final separation, they had their stone-heap of witness between them ; such as Herodotus says the Arabs were accustomed to anoint with their own blood, in their covenanting by blood, in his day ;[3] for Jacob, perhaps, had more tolerance than Abraham, for perverted religious symbols.[4] "And now let us cut a covenant, I and thou," said Laban ; "and let it be for a witness between me and thee. And Jacob took a stone, and set it up for a pillar [a pillar instead of a tree]. And Jacob said unto his brethren, Gather stones ; and they took stones, and made an heap : and they did eat there on the heap [the Revisers have translated this, *by* the heap"].[5] And Laban called it Jegar-sahadutha: but

---

[1] Gen. 26 : 25-29.   [2] Gen. 26 : 30, 31.   [3] See page 62, *supra.*

[4] Comp. Gen. 12 : 6-8 ; 28 : 18-22 ; 31 : 19-36.

[5] Mr. Forbes tells of a custom, in Sumatra, of taking a binding oath above the grave of the original patriarch of the Passumah. An animal

Jacob called it Gilead. And Laban said, This heap is witness between me and thee this day. . . . God is witness betwixt me and thee. . . . The God of Abraham and the God of Nahor, the God of their father, judge betwixt us. And Jacob sware by the Fear of his father Isaac. And Jacob offered a sacrifice in the mountain, and called his brethren to eat bread: and they did eat bread."[1] Here, again, the cutting of the covenant and the sharing of a feast in connection with the rite—the "cutting" and the "eating"—are in accordance with all that we know of the primitive rite of blood-covenanting in the East, in earlier and in later times.

Yet more explicit is the description of the blood-covenanting which brought into loving unity David and Jonathan. It was when the faith-filled heroism of the stripling shepherd-boy was thrilling all Israel with grateful admiration that David was brought into the royal presence of Saul, and of Saul's more than royal hero-son, Jonathan, to receive the thanks of the

is sacrificed, cut into small pieces, and cooked in a pot. "Then he who is to take the oath, holding his hand, or a long kriss of the finest sort, over the grave-stone, and over the cooked animal, says: 'If such and such be not the case, may I be afflicted with the worst evils.' The whole of the company then partake of the food" (*A Naturalist's Wanderings*, p. 198 f.). This seems to be a vestige of the primitive custom of eating on the witness-heap of an oath.

[1] Gen. 31 : 44–54.

23*

king for the rescue of the tarnished honor of the
Israelitish host. Modestly, David gave answer to the
question of the king. "And it came to pass, when he
had made an end of speaking unto Saul, that the soul
of Jonathan was knit with the soul of David, and
Jonathan loved him as his own soul." "Then Jonathan and David cut a covenant, because he [Jonathan]
loved him [David] as his own soul [as his own life, his
own blood]."[1] Then followed that gift of raiment and
of arms which was a frequent accompaniment of blood-
covenanting.[2] "And Jonathan stripped himself of the
robe that was upon him, and gave it to David, and his
apparel, even to his sword, and to his bow, and to his
girdle."[3] From that hour the hearts of David and
Jonathan were as one. Jonathan could turn away from
father and mother, and could repress all personal ambi-
tion, and all purely selfish longings, in proof of his
loving fidelity to him who was dear to him as his own
blood.[4] His love for David was "wonderful, passing
the love of women."[5]

Nor was this loving compact between Jonathan and
David for themselves alone. It was for their posterity
as well.[6] "The Lord be with thee, as he hath been
with my father," said Jonathan. "And thou shalt

[1] I Sam. 18 : 1–3.   [2] See pages 14, 24, 28, 35 f., 62, *supra.*

[3] I Sam. 18 : 4 ; 20 : 1–13.   [4] I Sam. 19 : 1–7.

[5] 2 Sam. 1 : 26.   [6] See pages 10, 53, *supra.*

not only while yet I live shew me the kindness of the Lord, that I die not: but also thou shalt not cut off thy kindness from my house for ever: no, not [even] when the Lord hath cut off the enemies of David every one from the face of the earth. So Jonathan cut a covenant with the house of David, saying [as in the imprecations of a blood-covenant], And the Lord shall require it [fidelity to this covenant] at the hand of David's enemies. And Jonathan caused David to swear again, for the love he had to him: for he loved him as he loved his own soul [his own life, his own blood]."[1] And years afterward, when the Lord had given David rest from all his enemies around about him, the memory of that blood-covenant pledge came back to him; "and David said, Is there yet any that is left of the house of Saul, that I may shew him kindness for Jonathan's sake?"[2] The seating of lame Mephibosheth at David's royal table[3] was an illustration of the unfailing obligation of the primitive covenant of blood—which had bound together David and Jonathan, for themselves and for theirs forever.

9. THE BLOOD COVENANT IN THE GOSPELS.

And now from David to David's greater Son; from type to anti-type; from symbol and prophecy to reality and fruition.

[1] 1 Sam. 20: 13-17.   [2] 2 Sam. 7: 1; 9: 1.   [3] 2 Sam. 9: 2-13.

Death had passed upon all men. Yet in the hearts of the death-smitten there was still a longing for life. Sin-leprous souls yearned for that in-flow of new being which could come only through inter-union with the divine nature, in oneness of life with the Author and Source of all life. Revelation and prophecy had assured the possibility and the hope of such inter-union. Rite and ceremony and symbol, the wide world over, signified man's desire, and man's expectation, of covenanted access to God, through personal surrender, and through life-giving, life-representing blood.

But where men yielded up unauthorized offerings, even of their own blood, or of the very lives of their first-born, they confessed themselves unsatisfied with their attitude God-ward; and, where men followed a divinely prescribed ritual, they were taught by that very ritual itself that the outpoured blood and the partaken flesh of the sacrifices were, at the best, but mere shadows of good things to come.[1] The whole creation was groaning and travailing in pain together, until the birth of the world's promised redemption.[2]

The symbolic covenant of blood-friendship was between God and Abraham's seed; and in that seed were all the nations of the earth to have a blessing. God had called on Abraham to surrender to him his only

---

[1] Heb. 10: 1–4.

[2] Rom. 8: 22.

son, in proof of his unfailing love ; and, when Abraham
had stood that test of his faith, God had spared to him
the proffered offering. It now remained for God to
transcend Abraham's proof of friendship, and to spare
not his own and only Son,[1] but to make him a sacrificial offering, by means of which the covenant of
blood-friendship, between God and the true seed of
Abraham, might become a reality instead of a symbol.
Abraham had given to God of his own blood, by the
rite of circumcision, in token of his desire for inter-
union with God. God was now to give of his blood,
in the blood of his Son, for the re-vivifying of the sons
of Abraham in " the blood of the eternal covenant."[2]

Then, in the fullness of time, there came down into
this world He who from the beginning was one with
God, and who now became one with man. Becoming
a sharer of the nature of those who were subject to
death, and who longed for life, Jesus Christ was here
among men as the fulfillment of type and prophecy ;
to meet and to satisfy the holiest and the uttermost
yearnings of the human soul after eternal life, in communion and union with God. " And the Word became
flesh, and dwelt among us, . . . full of grace and
truth." " In him was life [life that death could not
destroy; life that could destroy death], and the life
[which was in him] was the light [the guide and the

---

[1] Rom. 8: 32.   [2] Heb. 13: 20.

hope] of men." " He came unto his own, and they
that were [called] his own received him not.   But as
many as received him [whether, before, they had been
called his own, or not] to them gave he the right to
become children of God [by becoming partakers of his
life], even to them that believe on his name: which
were [through faith] begotten, not of bloods [not by
ordinary generation], nor of the will of the flesh, nor
of the will of man, but of God."[1]   Having in his own
blood the life of God and the life of man, Jesus Christ
could make men sharers of the divine nature by
making them sharers of his own nature ; and this was
the truth of truths which he declared to those whom
he instructed.

In the primitive rite of blood-covenanting, men
drank of each other's blood, in order that they might
have a common life ; and they ate together of a
mutually prepared feast, in order that they might
evidence and nourish that common life.   In the outreaching of men Godward, for the privileges of a
divine-human inter-union, they poured out the substitute blood of a chosen victim in sacrifice, and they
partook of the flesh of that sacrificial victim, in symbolism of sharing the life and the nourishment of
Deity.   This symbolism was made a reality in Jesus
Christ.   He was the Seed of Abraham ; the fulfillment

[1] Comp. John 1: 1–14; Heb. 1: 1–3; 2: 14–16.

of the promise, " In Isaac shall thy Seed be called." [1]
He was the true Paschal Lamb; the " Lamb without
blemish and without spot "; [2] "the Lamb that hath
been slain from the foundation of the world." [3] The
blood which he yielded, was Life itself. The body
which he laid on the altar was the Peace Offering of
Completion. [4]

"Wherefore, when he cometh into the world, he saith:

Sacrifice and offering thou wouldest not,
But a body didst thou prepare for me;
In whole burnt offerings and sacrifices for sin thou hadst no pleasure:
Then said I, Lo, I am come
(In the roll of the book it is written of me)
To do thy will, O God.

Saying above, [He here says.] Sacrifices and offerings
and whole burnt offerings and sacrifices for sin thou
wouldest not, neither hadst pleasure therein [as if in
themselves sufficient] (the which are offered according
to the Law); then [also] hath he said, Lo I am come to
do thy will. He taketh away the first [the symbolic],
that he may establish the second [the real]." [5]

He was here, in the body of his blood and flesh, for
the yielding of his blood and the sharing of his flesh,
in order to make partakers of his nature whosoever
would seek a divine-human inter-union and a divine-

[1] Gen. 21: 12; Heb. 11: 18.　　　[2] 1 Pet. 1: 19.
[3] Rev. 13: 8.　　[4] See page 250, *supra*, note.　　[5] Heb. 10: 5-9.

human inter-communion, through the sacrifice made by him, " once for all."

" Jesus therefore said unto them, Verily, verily, I say unto you, Except ye eat the flesh of the Son of man and drink his blood, ye have not life in your-selves. He that eateth my flesh and drinketh my blood hath eternal life; and I will raise him up at the last day. For my flesh is meat indeed [is true meat], and my blood [my life] is drink indeed [is true drink]. He that eateth my flesh and drinketh my blood abideth in me, and I in him [Herein is communion through union]. As the living Father sent me, and I live because of the Father; so he that eateth me, he also shall live because of me. This is the bread which came down out of heaven: not as the fathers did eat, and died: he that eateth this bread shall live forever." [1]

" These things said he in the synagogue, as he taught in Capernaum "—toward the close of the second year of his public ministry. The fact that he did speak thus, so long before he had instituted the Memorial Supper, has been a puzzle to many com-mentators who were unfamiliar with the primitive rite of blood-covenanting, and with the world-wide series of substitute sacrifices and substitute forms of com-munion which had grown out of the suggestions, and

[1] John 6: 53-58.

out of the perversions, of the root symbolisms of that
rite. But, in the light of all these customs, the words
of Jesus have a clearer meaning. It was as though
he had said: "Men everywhere long for life. They
seek a share in the life of God. They give of their
own blood, or of substitute blood, and they taste of
substitute blood, or they receive its touch, in evidence
of their desire for oneness of nature with God. They
crave communion with God, and they eat of the flesh
of their sacrifices accordingly. All that they thus
reach out after, I supply. In me is life. If they will
become partakers of my life, of my nature, they shall
be sharers of the life of God." Then he added, in
assurance of the fact that it was a profound spiritual
truth which he was enunciating: "It is the spirit that
quickeneth; the flesh profiteth nothing: the words
that I have spoken unto you are spirit, and are life."[1]
The divine-human inter-union and the divine-human
inter-communion are spiritual, and they are spiritually
wrought; or they are nothing.

The words of Jesus on this subject were not understood by those who heard him. "The Jews therefore
strove one with another, saying, How can this man
give us his flesh to eat?"[2] But this was not because
the Jews had never heard of eating the flesh of a sacrificial victim, and of drinking blood in a sacred covenant:

[1] John 6: 63. [2] John 6: 60.

24

it was, rather, because they did not realize that Jesus was to be the crowning sacrifice for the human race; nor did they comprehend his right and power to make those who were one with him through faith thereby one with God in spiritual nature. " Many," even "of his disciples, when they heard" these words of his, "said, This is a hard saying; who can hear it?"[1] Nor are questioners at this point lacking among his disciples to-day.

Before Jesus Christ was formally made an offering in sacrifice, as a means of man's inter-union and inter-communion with God, there were two illustrations of his mission, in the giving of his blood for the bringing of man into right relations with God. These were, his circumcision, and his agony in Gethsemane.

By his circumcision, Jesus brought his humanity into the blood-covenant which was between God and the seed of God's friend, Abraham, of whose nature, according to the flesh, Jesus had become a partaker;[2] Jesus thereby pledged his own blood in fidelity to that covenant; so that all who should thereafter become his by their faith, might, through him, be heirs of faithful Abraham.[3]   The sweet singer of the Christian Year[4] seems to find this thought in this incident in the life of the Holy Child:

[1] John 6: 60.   [2] Heb. 1: 14-16.
[3] Gal. 3: 6-9, 16, 29.   [4] Keble.

"Like sacrificial wine
　　Poured on a victim's head,
　Are those few precious drops of thine,
　　Now first to offering led.

"They are the pledge and seal
　　Of Christ's unswerving faith,
　Given to his Sire, our souls to heal,
　　Although it cost his death.

"They, to his Church of old,
　　To each true Jewish heart,
　In gospel graces manifold,
　　Communion blest impart."

In Gethsemane, the sins and the needs of humanity so pressed upon the burdened soul of Jesus that his very life was forced out, as it were, from his aching, breaking heart, in his boundless sympathy with his loved ones, and in his infinite longings for their union with God, through their union with himself, in the covenant of blood he was consummating in their behalf.[1] "And being in an agony, he prayed more earn-

[1] " In the garden of Gethsemane, Christ endured mental agony so intense that, had it not been limited by divine interposition, it would probably have destroyed his life without the aid of any other sufferings; but having been thus mitigated, its effects were confined to violent palpitation of the heart accompanied with bloody sweat. . . . Dr. Millingen's explanation of bloody sweat . . . is judicious. 'It is probable,' says he, 'that this strange disorder arises from a violent commotion of the nervous system, turning the streams of blood out of their natural course, and forcing the red particles into the cutaneous excretories.'" (Stroud's *Physical Cause of the Death of Christ*, pp. 74, 380).

estly: and his sweat became as it were great drops of blood falling down to the ground."[1]

Because of his God-ward purpose of bringing men into a loving covenant with God, Jesus gave of his blood in the covenant-rite of circumcision. Because of his man-ward sympathy with the needs and the trials of those whom he had come to save, and because of the crushing burden of their death-bringing sins, Jesus gave of his blood in an agony of intercessory suffering. Therefore it is that the Litany cry of the ages goes up to him in fulness of meaning: " By the mystery of thy holy incarnation; by thy holy nativity and circumcision; . . . by thine agony and bloody sweat, . . . Good Lord, deliver us."

In process of time, the hour drew nigh that the true covenant of blood between God and man should be consummated finally, in its perfectness. The period chosen was the passover-feast—the feast observed by the Jews in commemoration of that blood-covenanting occasion in Egypt when God evidenced anew his fidelity to his promises to the seed of Abraham, his blood-covenanted friend. " Now before the feast of the passover, Jesus knowing that his hour was come that he should depart out of this world to the Father, having loved his own which were in the world, he loved them unto the end."[2] "And when the hour

[1] Luke 22: 44.

[2] John 13: 1.

was come, he sat down, and the apostles with him. And he said unto them, With desire I have desired to eat this passover with you before I suffer."[1]   Whether he actually partook of the passover meal at that time or not is a point still in dispute;[2] but as to that which follows there is no question.

"As they were eating, Jesus took bread, and blessed, and brake it; and he gave to the disciples, and said, Take, eat; this is my body."[3]   "This do in remembrance of me.   And the cup in like manner after supper;"[4] "and when he had given thanks, he gave [it] to them,"[5] " saying, Drink ye all of it; for this is my blood of the covenant,"[6] or, as another Evangelist records, " this cup is the new covenant in my blood,"[7] "which is shed for many unto remission of sins"[8] [unto the putting away of sins].   " This do, as oft as ye drink it, in remembrance of me."[9]   "And they all drank of it."[10]

Here was the covenant of blood; here was the communion feast, in partaking of the flesh of the fitting and accepted sacrifice;—toward which all rite and symbol, and all heart yearning and inspired

[1] Luke 22: 14, 15.

[2] As to the points in this dispute, see Andrews's *Life of our Lord*, pp. 425–460, and Farrar's *Life of Christ*, Excursus X., Appendix.

[3] Matt. 26: 26.   [4] Luke 22: 19, 20.   [5] Mark 14: 23.

[6] Matt. 26: 27, 28.   [7] Luke 22: 20.   [8] Matt. 26: 28.

[9] 1 Cor. 11: 25.   [10] Mark 14: 23.

24*

prophecy, had pointed, in all the ages. Here was the realization of promise and hope and longing, in man's possibility of inter-union with God through a common life—which is oneness of blood; and in man's inter-communion with God, through participation in the blessings of a common table. He who could speak for God here proffered of his own blood, to make those whom he loved of the same nature with himself, and so of the same nature with his God; to bring them into blood-friendship with their God; and he proffered of his own body, to supply them with soul nourishment, in that Bread which came down from God.

Then it was, while they were there together in that upper room, for the consummating of that blood-covenant of friendship, that Jesus said to his disciples: " Greater love hath no man than this, that a man lay down his life for his friends. Ye are my friends, if ye do the things which I command you. No longer do I call you servants; for the servant knoweth not what his lord doeth: but I have called you friends [friends in the covenant of blood-friendship now]; for all things that I heard from my Father, I have made known unto you." [1] A common life, through oneness of blood, secures an absolute unreserve of intimacy; so that neither friend has aught to conceal from his other self. "Abide in me, and I in you; . . . for

[1] John 15: 13–15.

apart from me ye can do nothing," was the injunction
of Jesus to his blood-covenant friends, at this hour of
his covenant pledging. "If ye abide in me, and my
words abide in you, ask whatsoever ye will, and it
shall be done unto you."[1]

Then it was, also, that the prayer of Jesus for his
new blood-covenant friends went up: "Father, the
hour is come; glorify thy Son, that the Son may
glorify thee: even as thou gavest him authority over
all flesh, that whatsoever [whomsoever] thou hast
given him, to them he should give eternal life [in an
eternal covenant of blood]. And this is life eternal,
that they should know thee the only true God, and
him whom thou didst send [as the means of life], even
Jesus Christ. . . . Holy Father, keep them in thy
name which thou hast given me, that they may be one,
even as we are: . . . Neither for these [here pres-
ent] only do I pray, but for them also that believe on me
through their word; that they may all be one; even
as thou, Father, art in me, and I in thee, that they
also may be in us: that the world may believe that
thou didst send me. And the glory which thou hast
given me I have given unto them; that they may be
one, even as we are one; I in them, and thou in me,
that they may be perfected into one; that the world
may know that thou didst send me, and lovedst them,

[1] John 15: 4-7.

even as thou lovedst me."[1]   Here was declared the scope of this blood-covenant, and here was unfolded its doctrine.

It was not an utterly new symbolism that Jesus was introducing into the religious thought of the world : it was rather a new meaning that he was introducing into, or that he was disclosing in, an already widely recognized symbolism.   The world was familiar with the shadow of truth ; Jesus now made clear to the world the truth's substance.   Man's longing to be a partaker of the divine nature had manifested itself through all the ages and everywhere.   Jesus now showed how that longing of death-smitten man could be realized.   " The appearing of our Saviour Jesus Christ . . . abolished death, and brought life and immortality to light through the gospel "[2] of his blood-covenant.

But a covenant of blood, a covenant to give one's blood, one's life, for the saving of another, cannot be consummated without the death of the covenanter. " For where [such] a covenant is, there must of necessity be [be brought] the death of him that made it. For [such] a covenant is of force [becomes a reality] where there hath been death [or, over the dead] : for doth it [such a covenant] ever avail [can it be efficient] while he that made it liveth ? "[3]   Jesus had said,

[1] John 17 : 1-24.   [2] 2 Tim. 1 : 10.   [3] Heb. 9 : 16, 17.

" Greater love hath no man than this, that a man lay down his life for his friends." [1] Of his readiness to show this measure of love for those who were as the sheep of his fold, he had declared : " I came that they may have life, and may have it abundantly. . . . I lay down my life for the sheep. . . . Therefore doth my Father love me, because I lay down my life, that I may take it again. No one taketh it away from me, but I lay it down of myself." [2] And again : " I am the living bread which came down out of heaven : if any man eat of this bread, he shall live for ever : yea, and the bread which I will give is my flesh, for the life of the world." [3] " For my flesh is meat indeed, and my blood is drink indeed." [4] Such a covenant as this could be of force only through the death of him who pledges it.

The promise of the covenanting-cup, at the covenanting-feast, was made good on Calvary. [5] The pierced hands and feet of the Divine Friend yielded their life-giving streams. Then, with the final cry, " It is finished," the very heart of the self-surrendered sacrificial victim was broken, [6] and the life of the Son of God and of the

---

[1] John 15 : 13. [2] John 10 : 10, 18. [3] John 6: 51. [4] John 6: 55.

[5] See Matt. 27 : 33–54; Mark 15 : 22–39; Luke 23 : 33–47 ; John 19 : 17–37.

[6] " He was ultimately ' slain,' not by the effects of the anguish of his corporeal frame, but by the effects of the mightier anguish of his mind;

Seed of Abraham was poured out unto death,[1] in order
that all who would, might become sharers in its re-vivifying and saving power.   He who was without sin had
received the wages of sin ; because, that, only through
dying was it possible for him to supply that life which
would redeem from the penalty of sin those who had
earned death, as sin's wages.[2]   He who, in himself, had
life, had laid down his life, so that those who were without life might become its partakers, through faith, in the
bonds and blessings of an everlasting covenant.   So
the long symbolized covenant of blood was made a
reality.   "And the witness is this, that God gave unto
us eternal life, and this life is in his Son.   He that hath
the Son hath the life; he that hath not the Son of God
hath not the life." [3]

10. THE BLOOD COVENANT APPLIED.

Under the symbolic sacrifices of the Old Covenant,
it was the *blood* which made atonement for the soul.
It was not the death of the victim, nor yet its broken
body, but it was the blood, the life, the soul, that was

the fleshy walls of his heart—like the veil, as it were, in the temple of
his human body—becoming rent and riven, as, for us, ' he poured out
his soul unto death.' " (Sir James Y. Simpson, cited in Appendix to
Stroud's *Physical Cause of Death of Christ*.)

[1] Isa. 53 : 12.   [2] Comp. Rom. 6 : 23 ; 1 Pet. 3 : 18 ; Isa. 53 : 4–6.

[3] 1 John 5 : 11, 12.

made the means of a soul's ransom, of its rescue, of its
redemption. "The life [the soul] of the flesh is in the
blood," said the Lord: "and I have given it to you
upon the altar to make atonement [to be a cover, to
be a propitiation] for your souls [for your lives]: for it
is the blood that maketh atonement by reason [of its
being] the life [the soul]."[1] "For as to the life [the
soul] of all flesh, the blood thereof is all one with the
life [the soul] thereof."[2] And so all through the
record of the Old Covenant.

It is the same in the New Covenant as it was in the
Old. Atonement, salvation, rescue, redemption, is by
the blood, the life, of Christ; not by his death as such;
not by his broken body in itself; but by that blood
which was given at the inevitable cost of his broken
body and of his death. The figure of leprosy and its
attempted cure by blood may tend to make this truth
the clearer. In the leper, the very blood itself—the
life—was death smitten. The only hope of a cure was
by purging out the old blood, by means of an inflowing current of new blood—which was new life.[3] To
give this blood, the giver himself must die; but it was
his blood, his life, not his death, which was to be the
means of cure. So, also, with the sin-leprous nature.
The old life must be purged out, by the incoming of a
new life; of such a life as only the Son of God can supply.

[1] Lev. 17: 11.   [2] Lev. 17: 14.   [3] See pages 116–125.

In order to supply that blood, its Giver must himself die, and so be a sharer of the punishment of sin, although he was himself without sin. Thus was the new life made a possibility to all, by faith.

So it is that " we have redemption [rescue from death] through [by means of] his blood";[1] and that "the blood of Jesus . . . cleanseth us [by its purging inflow] from all sin."[2] So it is that he "loosed us [freed us] from our sins by his [cleansing, his re-vivifying] blood."[3] So it is that " if any man is in Christ [is one in nature with Christ, through sharing, by faith, the blood of Christ], he is a new creature [Of course he is]: the old things are passed away; behold they are become new."[4] So it is, also, that it can be said of those whose old lives were purged away by the inflowing redeeming life of Christ: " Ye died, and your life is hid with Christ in God."[5] And "this is the true God and eternal life."[6]

"These things have I written unto you," says the best loved of the disciples of Jesus, "that ye may know that ye have eternal life; even unto you that believe on the name of the Son of God";[7] "that ye may believe that Jésus is the Christ, the Son of God; and that, believing, ye may have life in his name."[8] For "God commendeth his own love toward us, in that, while we

[1] Eph. 1 : 7.   [2] 1 John 1 : 7.   [3] Rev. 1 : 5.   [4] 2 Cor. 5 : 17.
[5] Col. 3 : 3.   [6] 1 John 5 : 20.   [7] 1 John 5 : 13.   [8] John 20 : 31.

were yet sinners, Christ died for us [while we were separated from God by sin, God yielded his only Son, to give his blood, at the cost of his death, as a means of our inter-union with God]. Much more then, being now justified by [or, in] his blood [being brought into inter-union with God by that blood], shall we be saved from the wrath of God [against sin] through him [in whom we have life]. For if, while we were enemies, we were reconciled to God [restored to union with God] through the [blood-giving] death of his Son, much more, being [thus] reconciled, shall we be saved by [or, in] his life."[1]

All who will, may, now, "be partakers of the divine nature,"[2] through becoming one with Christ, by sharing his blood, and by being nourished with his body. Entering into the divine-human covenant of blood-friendship, which Christ's death has made possible, the believer can be so incorporated with Christ, by faith, as to identify himself with the experience and the hopes of the world's Redeemer ; and even to say, in all confidence : "I have been crucified with Christ ; yet I live ; and yet no longer I, but Christ liveth in me ; and that life which I now live in the flesh, I live in faith, the faith which is in [which centres in] the Son of God, who loved me and gave himself up for me."[3] "For as the Father hath life in himself, even so gave

[1] Rom. 5 : 8–12.   [2] 2 Pet. 1 : 4.   [3] Gal. 2 : 20.

he to the Son also to have life in himself." [1]   And " it was the good pleasure of the Father that in him [the Son] should all the fulness dwell; and through him to reconcile all things unto himself, having made peace [having completed union] through the blood of his cross " [2]—in the bonds of an everlasting covenant —between those who before were separated by sin.

" Remember, that aforetime ye, the Gentiles in the flesh, who are called Uncircumcision by that [people] which is called Circumcision, in the flesh, made by hands,—that ye were at that time separate from Christ, alienated from the commonwealth of Israel, and strangers from the covenants of the promise, having no hope and without God in the world.   But now in Christ Jesus ye that once were far off are made nigh in the blood of Christ.   For he is our peace, who made both [Jew and Gentile] one, and broke down the middle wall of partition, having abolished in his flesh the enmity, even the law of commandments contained in ordinances; that he might create in himself of the twain one new man, so making peace; and might reconcile them both in one body unto God through the cross, having slain the enmity thereby: and he came and preached peace to you that were far off, and peace to them that were nigh : for through them we both have our access in one Spirit unto the Father " [3]

[1] John 5: 26.   [2] Col. 1 : 19, 20.   [3] Eph. 2 : 11–16.

" For in him [Christ] dwelleth all the fulness of the
Godhead bodily, and in him ye are made full, who is
the head of all principality and power : in whom ye
were also circumcised with a circumcision not made
with hands, in the putting off of the body of the flesh,
in the circumcision of Christ." [1] " For ye all are one
man in Christ Jesus. And if ye are Christ's, then are
ye Abraham's seed, heirs according to promise " [2]—
inheritors of the blood-covenant promises of God to
Abraham his friend.

No longer is there a barrier between the yearning,
loving, trusting heart, and the mercy-seat of reconciliation in the very presence of God. We who share the
body and the blood of Christ, by faith, are one with
him in all the privileges of his Sonship. " For by one
offering he hath perfected [hath completed in their
right to be sharers with him] for ever them that are
sanctified [that are devoted, that are consecrated, to
him]. And the Holy Ghost also beareth witness to
us : for after he hath said,

> This is the covenant that I will make with them
> After those days, saith the Lord ;
> I will put my laws on their heart,
> And upon their mind also will I write them ;

then saith he,

> And their sins and their iniquities will I remember no more.

[1] Col. 2 : 9–11.　　　　　[2] Gal. 3 : 28, 29.

Now where remission of these [of sins and iniquities] is, there is no more offering [no more need of offering] for sin. Having, therefore, brethren, boldness [the right of boldness] to enter into the Holy Place [the Holy of Holies] by the blood of Jesus, by the way which he dedicated for us, a new and living way, through the veil, that is to say his flesh ; and having a Great Priest over the house of God ; let us draw near with a true heart in fulness of faith, having our hearts sprinkled from an evil conscience, and our body washed with pure water [there being no longer need of blood-sprinkling or blood-laving, to those who are sharers of the divine nature—the divine blood]."[1]

No more an altar of sacrifice, but a table of communion,[2] is where we share the presence of Him in whom we have life, by the blood of the everlasting covenant. To question the sufficiency of the " one sacrifice " which Christ made, " once for all,"[3] of his body and his blood, as a means of the believer's inter-union with God, is to count the blood of the covenant an unholy, or a common, thing, and is to do despite unto the Spirit of grace.[4] "Wherefore, my beloved, flee from idolatry. I speak as to wise men ; judge ye what I say. The cup of blessing which we bless, is it not a communion of the blood of Christ? The bread which we

[1] Heb. 10: 14–22.   [2] See page 167 ff., *supra*.
[3] Comp. Heb. 9: 24–28; 10: 10.   [4] Heb. 10: 28, 29.

break, is it not a communion of the body of Christ?[1]
Seeing that we [believers together in Christ], who are
many, are one bread, one body: for we all partake of
the one bread."[2]

"Now the God of peace, who brought again from
the dead the great Shepherd of the sheep with [or, by;
or, by means of] the blood of the eternal covenant,
even our Lord Jesus, make you perfect [complete] to
do his will, working in us that which is well pleasing
in his sight, through Jesus Christ; to whom be the
glory for ever and ever. Amen."[3]

[1] The Covenant of Bread and the Covenant of Blood are two distinct
covenants, in Oriental practice as well as in biblical teaching; although
this difference has been strangely overlooked by biblical students in the
realm of Orientalisms. The Covenant of Bread is temporary; the
Covenant of Blood is permanent. The one secures a truce; the other
secures a vital union. Symbolically, the one gives nourishment, the
other gives life. The Covenant of Bread is an exhibit and a pledge of
hospitality, and it brings one into family or tribal relations with those
proffering it. The Covenant of Blood is immediately personal and
individual. There seems to be an unconscious trace of this distinction
in the refusal of the Romish Church to include the laity in the symbolizing of the Covenant of Blood, at the Lord's table.

[2] I Cor. 10: 14–17.   [3] Heb. 13: 20, 21.

APPENDIX.

APPENDIX.

IT seems strange that a primitive rite like the blood-covenant, with its world-wide sweep, and its manifold applications to the history of sacrifice, should have received so little attention from students of the latter theme. Nor has it been entirely ignored by them; although its illustrations have, in this connection, been drawn almost entirely from the field of the classic writers, where its religious aspects have a minor prominence; and, as a result, the suggestion of any real importance in the religious symbolism of this rite has been, generally, brushed aside without its receiving due consideration.

Thus, in The Speaker's Commentary,—which is one of the more recent, and more valuable, scholarly and sensible compends of sound and thorough biblical criticism,—there are references to the rite of human blood-covenanting in its possible bearing on the blood-covenanting of God with Israel before Mount Sinai,[1] after this sort: "The instances from classical antiquity, adduced, as parallels to this sacrifice of Moses, by Bähr, Knobel, and Kalisch, in which animals were slaughtered on the making of covenants, are either: those in which the animal was slain to signify the punishment due to the party that might break the covenant (Hom. *Il.*, III., 298; XIX., 252; Liv. *Hist.*, I., 24; XXI., 45); those in which confederates dipped their hands, or their weapons, in the same blood (Æsch. *Sept. c. Theb.*, 43; Xenoph. *Anab.*, II., 2, § 9); or those in which the contracting parties tasted

[1] See pages 238-240, *supra*.

each other's blood (Herodot. [*Hist.*] I., 74; IV., 74; Tac. *Annal.*, XII., 47). All these usages are based upon ideas which are but very superficially related to the subject; they have indeed no true connection whatever with the idea of sacrifice as the seal of a covenant between God and man."[1]

When the entire history of man's outreaching after an inter-union of natures with his fellow-man and with his God is fairly studied, in the light thrown on it by the teachings of the divine-human Being, who gave of his own blood for the consummation of the longed-for divine-human inter-union, it will be more clearly seen, whether it were the relation of the primitive rite itself to the idea of sacrifice, or the study of that relation, which was "very superficial," as a cause of its popular overlooking.

The closest and most sacred form of covenant ever known in the primitive world, was that whereby two persons covenanted to become one, through being partakers of the same blood. At Sinai, when Jehovah would covenant with Israel, a common supply of substitute blood —proffered by Israel and accepted by Jehovah—was taken; and one-half of it was cast upon the altar, Godward, while the other half of it was cast Israelward, upon the people.[2] The declaration of Moses to Israel, then, was: "Behold the blood of the covenant, which the Lord hath made with you;" or, as that declaration is repeated, in Hebrews: "This is the blood of the covenant which God covenanted to you-ward."[3] And from that time forward, the most sacred possession of Israel,—above which hovered the visible sign of the presence of Jehovah,—was the casket which contained the record of that blood-made covenant; and it was toward the mercy-seat cover of that Covenant Casket, that House of the Covenant, that the symbolic blood of atonement through new life was sprinkled, in the supreme renewals of that covenant by Israel's representative year by year.

Even the Speaker's Commentary says, of this mutual blood-sharing by Israel and Jehovah at Sinai: "The blood thus divided between the

[1] *Speaker's Comm.*, at Exod. 24: 8.   [2] Exod. 24: 3-8.   [3] Heb. 9: 20.

two parties to the covenant signified the sacramental union between the Lord and his people." [1] Of the blood which was to be poured out on Calvary, Jesus said : " This is my blood of the [new] covenant, which is shed for many." [2] And of the sacramental union which could be secured, between his trustful disciples and himself, by tasting his blood, and by being nourished on his flesh, he said : " Except ye eat the flesh of the Son of man and drink his blood, ye have not life in yourselves. He that eateth my flesh and drinketh my blood hath eternal life." [3] It really looks as if there were more than a superficial relation between the fact of an absolute inter-union of two natures through an inter-flow of a common life, in the rite of blood-covenanting, and the sacramental union between the Lord and his people, which was typified in the blood-covenant at Sinai, and which was consummated in the blood-covenant at Calvary.

Herbert Spencer, indeed, seems to have a clearer conception than the Speaker's Commentary, of the relation of human blood-covenanting, to the inter-union of those in the flesh, with spiritual beings. He perceives that the primitive offerings of blood over the dead, from the living person, are, in some cases, " explicable as arising from the practice of establishing a sacred bond between living persons by partaking of each other's blood : the derived conception being, that those who give some of their blood to the ghost of a man just dead and lingering near [and of course, the principle is the same when the offering of blood is to the gods, thereby] effect with it a union, which on the one side implies submission, and on the other side friendliness." [4] This admission by Mr. Spencer covers the essential point in the argument of this entire volume.

LIFE IN THE BLOOD, IN THE HEART, IN THE LIVER.

Among all primitive peoples, the blood has been deemed the representative of life. The giving of blood has been counted the giving of

[1] *Speaker's Com.*, at Exod. 24 : 8.   [2] Mark 14 : 24.

[3] John 6 : 53, 54.   [4] *Principles of Sociology*, II., § 364.

life. The receiving of blood has been counted the receiving of life. The sharing of blood has been counted the sharing of life. Hence, the blood has always been counted the chief thing in any sacrificial victim proffered to the gods; and whatever was sought through sacrifice, was to be obtained by means of the blood of the offering. Even though no specific reference to the blood be found in the preserved descriptions of one of the earlier sacrifices,—as, for example, the Akkadian sacrifice of the first-born (page 166, *supra*), the very fact that the offering made was of a *life*, and that *blood* was recognized as life, is in itself the proof that it was the blood which gave the offering its value.

Sir Gardiner Wilkinson, who was thoroughly familiar with both Egyptian and biblical antiquities, was impressed by the "striking resemblance" of many of the religious rites of the Jews to those of Egypt, "particularly the manner in which the sacrifices were performed;"[1] and he points out the Egyptian method of so slaying the sacrificial ox, that its blood should be fully discharged from the body; a point which was deemed of such importance in the Jewish ritual.[2] Of the illustration of this ceremony given by Wilkinson from an ancient Egyptian painting,[3] the Speaker's Commentary says: "There is no reason to doubt that this picture accurately represents the mode pursued in the court of the [Jewish] Tabernacle."[4]

Almost as universal as the recognition of the life in the blood has been the identification of the heart as the blood-centre and the blood-fountain, and so as the epitome of the life itself. Says Pierret,[5] the French Egyptologist, concerning the pre-eminence given to the heart by the ancient Egyptians: "The heart was embalmed separately in a vase placed under the guardianship of the genius Duaoumautew [rather, Tuau-mut-ef, or, Reverencer of his Mother. 'My heart was my mother.' See page 99, *supra*] without doubt because this organ,

---

[1] *Anc. Egypt.*, III., 411. [2] See pages 245 f., *supra*.
[3] *Anc. Egypt.*, II., 32. [4] Note on Lev. chap. 17.
[5] *Dictionnaire d'Archéologie Égyptienne*, s. v. "Coeur."

indispensable to the resurrection, could not be replaced in the body of a man, until it had been weighed in the scale of the balance of the Osirian judgment (*Todtenbuch* cxxv.); where representing the acts of the dead, it ought to make equilibrium with the statue of the goddess Truth [Maat]. (See the framed papyri in the funereal hall of the Museum of the Louvre.) Indeed the favorable sentence is thus formulated: 'It is permitted that his heart be in its place.' It is said to Setee I., in the temple of Abydos: 'I bring thee thy heart to thy breast; I put it in its place.' The heart, principle of existence and of regeneration, was symbolized by the scarabæus: it is for this reason that the texts relative to the heart were inscribed upon the funereal scarabæuses, which at a certain epoch were introduced into the body of the mummy itself, to replace the absent organ."

The idea that the heart is in itself life, and that it can even live apart from the body, is found all the world over. References to it in ancient Egypt, in India, and in primitive America, have already been pointed out (pages 100–110, *supra*). It shows itself, likewise, in the folk-lore of the Arctic regions, and of South Africa, as well as of the Norseland. In a Samoyed tale, "seven brothers are in the habit of taking out their hearts and sleeping without them. A captive damsel, whose mother they have killed, receives the extracted hearts, and hangs them on the tent-pole, where they remain till the following morning. One night her brother contrives to get the hearts into his possession. Next morning, he takes them into the tent, where he finds the brothers at the point of death. In vain do they beg for their hearts, which he flings on the floor. 'And as he flings down the hearts, the brothers die.'"[1] According to a Hottentot story, "the heart of a girl, whom a lion has killed and eaten, is extracted from the lion, and placed in a calabash filled with milk [the 'heart' and 'milk'; or blood and bread, life and its nourishment (See pages 10–12, 261 f., *supra*)]. 'The cala-

[1] In substance from Castren's *Ethnologische Vorlesungen über die Altaischen Völker*, p. 174, as cited in Ralston's *Russian Folk Tales*, p. 122.

bash increased in size; and, in proportion to this, the girl grew again inside [of] it.'"[1] "In a Norse story, a giant's heart lies in an egg, inside a duck, which swims in a well, in a church, on an island;"[2] and this story is found in variations in other lands.[3] So, again, in a "Russian story, a prince is grievously tormented by a witch who has got hold of his heart, and keeps it perpetually seething in a magic cauldron."[4]

This same idea is found in the nomenclature of the Bible, and in the every-day speech of the civilized world of the present age. In more than nine hundred instances, in our common English Bible, the Hebrew or the Greek word for "heart," as a physical organ, is applied to man's personality; as if it were, in a sense, synonymous with his life, his self, his soul, his nature. In every phase of man's character, of man's needs, or of man's experiences, "heart" is employed by us as significant of his innermost and realest self. He is "hard-hearted," "tender-hearted," "warm-hearted," "cold-hearted," "hearty," or "heartless." His words and his conduct are "heart-touching," "heart-cheering," "heart-searching," "heart-piercing," "heart-thrilling," "heart-soothing," or "heart-rending;" and they are a cause, in others, of "heart-burning," "heart-aching," "heart-easing," or "heart-expanding." At times, his "heart is set upon" an object of longing, or again "his heart is in his mouth" because of his excited anxiety. It may be, that he shows that "his heart is in the right place," or that "his heart is at rest" at all times. The truest union of two young lives, is where "the heart goes with the hand" in the marriage covenant.

And so, all the world over, from the beginning, primitive man, in the lowest state of savagery and in the highest stage of civilization, has

[1] From Bleek's *Reynard the Fox in South Africa*, p. 55; as cited *Ibid.*, p. 123, note.

[2] From *Asbjornsen and Moe*, No. 36, Dasent, No. 9, p. 71, as cited *Ibid.*, p. 120.

[3] See references to Köhler's *Orient und Occident*, II., 99–103, *Ibid.*, p. 123, note.

[4] From Khudyakof, No. 110, as cited *Ibid.*, p. 124.

been accustomed to recognize the truth, and to employ the symbolisms of speech, which are in accordance with the latest advances of physiological and psychological science, and with the highest spiritual conceptions of biblical truth, in our nineteenth Christian century, concerning the mental, the moral, and the religious needs and possibilities of the human race. Man as he is needs a " new heart," a new nature, a new life; and that need can be supplied by the Author of life, through that regeneration which is indicated, and which, in a sense, is realized in new blood which is pure at the start, and which purifies by its purging inflow. The recognition of this truth, and the outreaching of man in its direction, are at the basis of all forms of sacrifice in all the ages. And this wonderful attainment of primitive man everywhere, we are asked to accept as man's mere natural inheritance from the sensory quiverings of his ancestral tadpole!

" The knowledge of the ancients on the subject [of blood as the synonym of life] may, indeed, have been based on the mere observation that an animal loses its life when it loses its blood," says the Speaker's Commentary. But it does seem a little strange, that none of the ancients ever observed that man is very liable to lose his life when he loses his *brains,* and that few animals are actively efficient for practical service without a *head;* whereas both man and the lower animals do lose *blood* freely without death resulting.

It is true that in many parts of the world the *liver* was made prominent as seemingly a synonym of life ; but this was obviously because of the popular belief that the liver was itself a mass of coagulated blood. The idea seems to have been that, as the heart was the blood-fountain, the liver was the blood-cistern ; and that, as the source of life (or of blood, which life is,) was at the heart, so the great receptacle of life, or of blood, was the liver. Thus, in the classic myth of Prometheus, the avenging eagle of Jupiter is not permitted to gnaw upon the life-giving heart itself of the tortured victim, but upon the compacted body of life in the captive's liver; the fountain of life is not to be destroyed, but the cistern of life is to be emptied daily of all that it had received from the out-flowing heart during the preceding' night. And in the symbolism of these two organs, the ancients seem to have been agreed, that " The heart is the seat of the soul [thumos ($\theta\nu\mu\delta\varsigma$) the nobler passions] ; the liver [is the seat], of desire ; " [1] or, as again it is phrased, "The seat of the soul is unquestionably the heart, even as the liver is the seat of emotion." [2]

Burton has called attention to the fact that among the Arabs "the liver and the spleen are both supposed to be ' congealed blood,' " and that the Bed'ween of the Hejaz justify their eating of locusts, which belong to an " unclean " class of animals, and of liver which represents forbidden blood, by this couplet :

> " We are allowed two carrions, and two bloods,
>   The fish and locust, the liver and the spleen." [3]

He has also noted that the American Indian partakes of the liver, as well as of the heart of a fallen enemy, in order to the assimilating of the enemy's life ; [4] and he finds many correspondences between the desert dwellers of America and of Arabia. " The [American] ' brave,' " he says, " stamps a red hand upon his mouth to show that he has drunk the blood of a foe. Of the Utaybah ' Harami,' it is similarly related, that, after mortal combat, he tastes the dead man's gore." [5]

Even in modern English, the word " liver " has been thought by many to represent " life " or " blood." Thus, in one of our dictionaries we are told that the word is derived from the Anglo-Saxon and the Scandinavian verb "to live," "because [the liver is] of so great import-ance to *life*, or animal vitality." [6] In another, its derivation is ascribed

---

[1] Timæus of Locri, cited in Liddell and Scott's *Greek Eng. Lex.*, s. v. " Hepar." See also page 108 f., *supra*.

[2] Pollux's *Onomasticon*, II., 4, 226.   [3] *Pilgrim. to Mec. and Med.*, p. 376.

[4] See page 128, *supra*.

[5] *Pilgrim. to Mec. and Med.*, p. 378. See also page 129 f., *supra*.

[6] Richardson's *Eng. Dict.*, s. v. " Liver."

to *lopper*, and *lapper*, "to coagulate," "from its resemblance to a mass of clotted blood." [1]

Among the aborigines of America the prominence given to the blood and to the heart was as great, and as distinctly marked, as among the peoples of ancient Egypt, or any other portion of the far East. This truth has been brought out most fully by the valuable personal researches of Mr. Frank H. Cushing, of the Smithsonian Institution, into the mythology and sociology of the Zuñis of New Mexico. From his reports it would appear that, according to the priests of that people, "all true fetiches [or, material symbols of spiritual existences] are either actual petrifactions of the animals they represent, or were such originally"—according as the present form of the fetish is natural, or is mechanically fashioned. These rude stone images of the animals of prey, "which are of course mere concretions or strangely eroded rock forms," are supposed to be the shriveled and distorted remains of beings which were long ago turned to stone. Within these fetishes the *heart* of the original animal still exists; ("his heart still lives, even though his person be changed to stone";) and it needs for its sustenance the blood, or the "life fluid," of the game which was, from the beginning, the ordinary prey of that animal. Hence each fetish is pleased to hear the prayers and to give success to the hunting of its present possessor, in order to the obtaining of the life fluid which is essential to its nourishing.

These prey fetishes of the Zuñis belong to the Prey-God Brotherhood, and when not in use they are guarded by the "Keeper of the Medicine of the Deer." Before they are employed in a hunt, there is an assembly for their worship; and, after ceremonial prayer to them for their assistance, they are taken out for service by members of the Brotherhood to which they belong. "The fetich is then placed in a little crescent-shaped bag of buckskin which the hunter wears suspended over the left breast (or, heart) by a buckskin thong, which is tied above the right shoulder." When the trail of the animal hunted is discovered by the hunter, he finds a place where the animal has lain down, and there he makes an oblation by depositing his offering "in exactly the spot over which the heart of the animal is supposed to have rested." Then he brings out his fetish and with certain ceremonies and invocations he puts it on the track of the prey.

"As soon as the animal is dead, he [the hunter] lays open its viscera, cuts through the diaphragm, and makes an incision in the aorta, or in the sac which incloses the heart. He then takes out [of its bag] the prey fetich, breathes on it, and addresses it thus :   .   .   .   'Si! My father, this day of the blood [literally of the 'life fluid'] of a game-being, thou shalt drink ([shalt] water thyself). With it thou shalt enlarge (add unto) thy heart.' He then dips the fetich into the blood which the sac still contains, continuing meanwhile the prayer, as follows: .   .   . Likewise, I, a "done" being [a living human being], with the blood [the "life-fluid," which is] the flesh of a raw being (game animal), shall enlarge (add unto) my heart.' Which [prayer] finished, he scoops up, with his hand, some of the blood and sips it; then tearing forth the *liver*, ravenously devours a part of it [as the blood-flesh, or, the blood which is the flesh], and exclaims, '*É-lah-kwá !*' (Thanks)." After all this, he deposits a portion of the clot of blood from within the· heart, commingled with various articles, in a grave digged on the spot where the animal has died; repeating, as he does this, a prayer which seems to show his belief that the slain animal still lives in this buried heart-blood. Again, when the game is at the hunter's home, the women "lay on either side of its body, next to the heart, an ear of corn (significant of renewed life), and say prayers" over it. Finally "the fetich is returned to the Keeper of the Deer Medicine, with thanksgiving and a prayer, not unlike that uttered on taking it forth." [1]

In these ceremonies, it is evident that the Zuñis, like the Orientals,

[1] See Cushing's paper on "Zuñi Fetiches," in *Second Annual Report of the Bureau of Ethnology*, pp. 3–43.

recognize the blood as the life, the heart as the epitome of life, the liver as a congealed mass of blood, and the transference of blood as the transference of life. Moreover, there is here a trace of that idea of the revivifying, by blood-bathing, of a being that had turned into stone, which is found in the legends of Arabia, and of the Norseland (See page 119 f., *supra*). Is there not, indeed, a reference to this world-wide figure of the living stone, in the Apostle's suggestion, that those who were counted as worthless stones by an ignorant world are vivified by the renewing blood of Christ, and so are shown to be a holy people? "As new born babes [renewed by the blood of Christ] long for the spiritual milk [the means of sacred nourishment] which is without guile, that ye may grow thereby unto salvation; if ye have tasted that the Lord is gracious [if, indeed, ye have been made alive by the touch of his blood] : unto whom coming, [unto Him who is] a Living Stone rejected indeed of men, but with God [who knows the possibilities of that Stone] elect, precious,—ye also, as living stones [as new.blood-vivified petrifactions], are built up a spiritual house, to be a holy priesthood, to offer up spiritual sacrifices, acceptable to God through Jesus Christ." [1]

There is another gleam of this idea of the stones vivified by blood, in a custom reported from among the Indians of British Columbia, in a private letter written by a careful observer of Indian habits and ceremonies. When the Indian girls arrived at the years of womanhood they were accustomed, there as in many other parts of the world, to pass through a formal initiation into a new stage of existence. Going apart by themselves, at some distance from their settlements, they would remain for three days and nights, while they rubbed their naked bodies with loose stones until the blood came, and then laid the blood-stained stones in a double row as a memorial. She who could cover the largest number of stones with her blood, had the fairest prospect in life, in the line of a woman's peculiar mission. This certainly would be a not unnatural thought as an outgrowth of the belief that stones

[1] 1 Peter 2 : 2-5.

anointed with freely surrendered blood, can be made to have life in themselves.

It is much the same in war as in the hunt, among the Zuñis. "As with the hunter, so with the warrior; the fetich is fed on the life-blood of the slain."[1] And here, again, is a link of connection between cannibalism and religious worship. Another illustration of the pre-eminence given to the heart, as the epitome of the very being itself, is the fact that the animals pictured on the pottery of these people, and of neighboring peoples, commonly had the rude conventional figure of a heart represented in its place on each animal; as if to show that the animal was living, and that it had a living soul.[2]

At the other side of the world, as it were, in Borneo, there is given similar pre-eminence, as among the Zuñis, to the blood as the life, to the liver as a representative of blood, and to the heart as the epitome of the life. "The principal sacrifice of the Sakarang Dayaks," says Mr. St. John, "is killing a pig and examining its *heart*, which is supposed to foretell events with the utmost certainty." This custom seems to have grown out of the idea that the heart of any God-devoted organism, as the embodiment of its life is closely linked with the Author of all life, who is the Disposer of all events. A human heart is naturally deemed preferable to a pig's; but the latter is the common substitute for the former. Yet, "not many years ago," one of the Sakarang chiefs put to death a lad "of his own race," remarking, as he did so: "It has been our custom heretofore to examine the heart of a pig, but now we will examine a human one."[3] The Kayans, again, examine "the *heart* and *liver*," as preliminary to covenant-making.[4] Among the Dayaks, the blood of a fowl sacrificed by one who is supposed to be in

[1] Cushing's "Zuñi Fetiches," p. 43.

[2] See "Illustrated Catalogue of Collections. from Indians of New Mexico and Arizona," 1879, in *Second Annual Report of Bureau of Ethnology*, Figures 361–387; 421–430.

[3] St. John's *Life in Far East*, I., 74 f.   [4] *Ibid.*, I., 115 f.

favor with the gods, has peculiar potency when sprinkled upon " the lintels of the doors." [1]   And a house will be deserted by its Dayak inhabitants, " if a drop of blood be seen sprinkled on the floor, unless they can prove whence it came." [2]

An incidental connection of this recognition of the blood as the life, with the primitive rite of blood covenanting, is seen in one form of the marriage rite among the Dayaks.[3]—In the rite of blood-covenanting itself, as consummated between Mr. St. John and Siñgauding, a cigarette stained with the blood of the covenanting parties was smoked by them mutually (See page 51, *supra*).   In the marriage covenant, a cigar and betel leaf prepared with the areca nut are put first into the mouth of the bride by the bridegroom, and then into the mouth of the bridegroom by the bride; while two fowls are waved over their heads by a priest, and then killed; their blood being " caught in two cups " for examination, instead of for drinking.[4]

So, whether it be the heart as the primal fountain of blood, or the liver as the great receptacle of blood, or the blood itself in its supposed outflowing from the heart through the liver, that is made prominent in the rites and teachings of primitive peoples, the root-idea is still the same,—that " as to the life of all flesh, the blood thereof is all one with the life thereof;" [5] and that as a man is in his blood, so he is in his nature ; that his " good blood " or "his bad blood," his " hot blood " or his "cold blood," will be evidenced in his daily walk ; for that which shows out in his outer life is " in the blood " which is his inner life ; and that in order to a change of his nature there must in some way be a change of his blood.   Hence, the universal outreaching of the race after new blood which is new life. Hence, the provisions of God for new life through that blood which is the Life.

[1] St. John's *Life in Far East*, I., 160.   [2] *Ibid.*, I., 187.

[3] This is a different form from that reported at page 192 f., *supra*.

[4] St. John's *Life in Far East*, I., 61.   [5] Lev. 17 : 14.

TRANSMIGRATION OF SOULS.

A belief in the transmigration of souls, from man to the lower animals, and *vice versâ*, has been found among various peoples, in all the historic ages. The origin of this belief has been a puzzling question to rationalistic myth-students. Starting out, as do most of these students, with the rigid theory that man worked himself slowly upward from the lowest savagery, without any external revelation, they are confronted with primitive customs on every side which go to show a popular belief in soul-transmigration, and which they must try to account for within the limits of their unproven theory. The result is, that they first pre-suppose some conception in the primitive man's mind of spiritual things, and then they conveniently refer all confusing facts to that pre-supposed conception. "Animism" is one of the pet names for this re-solvent of grave difficulties. And when "Animism" is supplemented by "Fetishism," "Zoolatry," and "Totemism," the requisite number of changes is secured for the meeting of any number of perplexing facts in the religious belief of primitive man everywhere.

As a matter of simple fact, man's conception of spiritual existences is not accounted for by the "scientists." And the claim that such a conception was innate in primitive man, or that it was a natural growth in man's unaided progress, is at the best but an unproved theory. In the early part of this century, there were thousands of deaf-mutes in the United States, who had never been educated by the system which is now so effective for that class in the community. This gave a rare opportunity of learning the normal spiritual attainments of unsophisticated man; of man uninfluenced by external revelation or traditions. Nor was this opportunity unimproved for a good purpose. When the Rev. Thomas H. Gallaudet (himself a philosophical scientist) introduced the system of deaf-mute instruction into this country, he made a careful examination into the intelligence of all the deaf mutes brought under his care, on this point of spiritual conceptions. His declaration was, that he never found a person who, prior to specific instruction, had any conception of the nature or the existence of God. A single illustration of Mr. Gallaudet's experiences in this line will suffice for the entire series of them. A young girl of sixteen years of age, or so, who proved to be of far more than ordinary intelligence and mental capacity, had been brought up in a New England Christian home. She had been accustomed to bow her head when grace was said at the daily meals, to kneel in family prayer, and to attend church regularly, from early childhood; yet she had no idea of God, no thought of spiritual existences of any sort whatsoever, until she was instructed in those things, in the line of her new education.[1] A writer on this subject, who differed with Mr. Gallaudet in his conclusions from these facts, added: "This testimony is confirmed by that of all the teachers of the deaf and dumb, and the fact must be admitted." [2] Until some human being can be found with a conception of spiritual existences, without his having received instruction on that point from those who went before him, the claim—in the face of such facts as these—that primitive man ever obtained his spiritual knowledge or his spiritual conceptions from within himself alone, or without an external revelation to him, is an unscientific assumption, in the investigation of the origin of religions in the world.

But, with man's conception of spiritual things already existing[3] (however he came by it), and with the existing belief that the blood is the life, or the soul, or the nature, of an organism, the idea of the transmigration of souls as identical with the transference of blood, is a very natural corollary. The blood being the life, or the soul, of man and of

---

[1] As to this specific instance, I can bear personal testimony, from my frequent communications on the subject with the person whose experience is here recited.

[2] *Am. Annals of Deaf and Dumb*, Vol. VI., p. 134

[3] Paul's claim, in Romans 1 : 18–23, is not that man knows God intuitively; but that, having the knowledge of God, which he does have by tradition, man ought not to liken God to "four-footed beasts and creeping things."

beast, if the blood of man passes into the body of a beast, or the blood of a beast passes into the body of a man, why should it not be inferred that the soul of the man, or of the beast, transmigrated accordingly? If the Hindoo, believing that the blood of man is the soul of man, sees the blood of a man drunk up by a tiger, is it strange that he should look upon that tiger as having within him the soul of the Hindoo, which has been thus appropriated? If the South African supposes that, by his drinking the blood or eating the heart of a lion, he appropriates the lion's courage,[1] is it to be wondered at that when he sees a lion licking the blood and eating the heart of a South African, he should infer that the lion is thereby the possessor of whatever was distinctive in the Zulu, or the Hottentot, personality?

Indeed, as has been already stated, in the body of this work, there is still a question among physiologists, how far the transference of *blood* from one organism to another carries a transmigration of *soul* (of the *psyche*, not of the *pneuma*).[2] However this may be, the popular belief in such transmigration is fully accounted for, by the recognized conviction that the blood is the soul.

In this view of the case, there is an added force in the Mosaic prohibition—repeated as it is in the Apostolic Encyclical—of the eating, or drinking, of the blood of the lower animals; with the possibility of thereby being made a partaker of the lower animal nature. And what fresh potency is given to Elijah's prophecy against Ahab and Jezebel, by this conception of the transference of nature by the transference of blood! " Thus saith the Lord [to Ahab], Hast thou killed [Hast thou taken the blood of Naboth?], and also taken possession [of Naboth's vineyard]? . . . Thus saith the Lord, In the place where dogs licked the blood of Naboth, shall dogs lick thy blood, even thine. . . . And of Jezebel also spake the Lord, saying, The dogs shall eat Jezebel by the ramparts of Jezreel." The blood, the life, the soul of royalty, shall become a portion of the very life of the prowl-

---

[1] See page 136, *supra.* [2] See page 133 f., *supra.*

ing scavenger dogs of the royal city. And it came to pass accordingly, to both Ahab and Jezebel.[1]

THE BLOOD-RITE IN BURMAH.

Mention is made, in the text of this volume,[2] of the fact that the primitive rite of blood-covenanting is in practice all along the Chinese border of the Burman Empire. In illustration of this truth, the following description of the rite and its linkings, is given by the Rev. R. M. Luther, of Philadelphia, formerly a missionary among the Karens, in Burmah. This interesting sketch was received, in its present form, at too late a date for insertion in its place in the text; hence its appearance here.

" The blood-covenant is well known, and commonly practised among the Karens of Burmah. There are three methods of making brotherhood, or truce, between members of one tribe and those of another.

" The first is the common method of eating together. This, however, is of but little binding force, being a mere agreement to refrain from hostilities for a limited time, and the truce thus made is liable to be broken at the briefest notice.

" The second method is that of planting a tree. The parties to this covenant select a young and vigorous sapling, plant it with certain ceremonies, and covenant with each other to keep peace so long as the tree lives. A covenant thus made is regarded as of greater force than that effected or sealed by the first method.

" The third method is that of the blood-covenant, properly so called. In this covenant the chief stands as the representative of the tribe, if it be a tribal agreement; or the father as the representative of the family, if it be a more limited covenant. The ceremonies are public and solemn. The most important act is, of course, the mingling of the blood. Blood is drawn from the thigh of each of the covenanting parties, and mingled together. Then each dips his finger into the blood and applies it to his lips. In some cases, it is said that the blood is

[1] I Kings 21 : 17–23 ; 22 : 35–38 ; 2 Kings 9 : 30–37.　　　[2] At page 44, *supra*.

actually drunk; but the more common method is that of touching the lips with the blood-stained finger.[1]

" This covenant is of the utmost force. It covers not merely an agreement of peace, or truce, but also a promise of mutual assistance in peace and in war. It also conveys to the covenanting parties mutual tribal rites. If they are chiefs, the covenant embraces their entire tribes. If one is a private individual, his immediate family and direct descendants are included in the agreement.

" I never heard of the blood-covenant being broken. I do not remember to have inquired particularly on this point, because the way in which the blood-covenant was spoken of, always implied that its rupture was an unheard-of thing. It is regarded as a perfectly valid excuse for any amount of reckless devotion, or of unreasoning sacrifice on behalf of another, for a Karen to say: ' *Thui p'aw th'coh li;* ' literally, ' The blood,—we have drunk it together.' An appeal for help on the basis of the blood-covenant is never disregarded.

" A few of our missionaries have entered into the blood-covenant with Karen tribes; though most have been deterred, either from never having visited the ' debatable land ' where the strong arm of British rule does not reach, or else, as in most instances, from a repugnance to the act by which the covenant is sealed. In one instance, at least, where a missionary did enter into covenant with one of these tribes, the agreement has been interpreted as covering not only his children, but one who was so happy as to marry his daughter. In an enforced absence of fifteen years from the scene of his early missionary labors nothing has been at once so touching and so painful to the writer as the frequent messages and letters asking ' When will you come back to *your people ?* ' Yet, mine is only the inherited right above mentioned.

" The blood-covenant gives even a foreigner every right which he would have if born a member of the tribe. As an instance, the writer once shot a hawk in a Karen village, just as it was swooping down

[1] See page 154, *supra.*

upon a chicken. He was surprised to find, half an hour afterward, that his personal attendant, a straightforward Mountain Karen, had gone through the village and 'collected' a fat hen from each house. When remonstrated with, the mountaineer replied, 'Why, Teacher, it is your right,—that is our custom,—you are one of us. These people wouldn't understand it if I did not ask for a chicken from each house, when you killed the hawk.'

" In the wilder Karen regions, it is almost impossible to travel unless one is in blood-covenant with the chiefs, while on the other hand one is perfectly safe, if in that covenant. The disregard of this fact has cost valuable lives. When a stranger enters Karen territory, the chiefs order the paths closed. This is done by tying the long elephant grass across the paths. On reaching such a signal, the usual inquiry in the traveling party is, ' Who is in blood-covenant with this tribe ? ' If one is found, even among the lowest servants, his covenant covers the party, on the way, as far as to the principal village or hill fortress. The party goes into camp, and sends this man on as an ambassador. Usually, guides are sent back to conduct the party at once to the chief's house. If no one is in covenant with the tribe, and the wisp of grass is broken and the party passes on, the lives of the trespassers are forfeited. A sudden attack in some defile, or a night surprise, scatters the party and drives the survivors back the way they came.

" Notwithstanding the widespread prevalence of the blood-covenant, the ceremonies attendant upon its celebration, and even the existence of such a custom, are shrouded with a certain degree of secrecy, at least from outside nations. The writer has been surprised to find, on some occasions, those longer resident in Burmah than himself in total ignorance of the existence of such a custom ; and even the Karens themselves would probably deny its existence to a casual inquirer. Apropos of this, the writer did not know of such a custom in any other country until his attention was called to the fact by Dr. Trumbull, while this treatise was in preparation."

Another account of the blood-covenant rite in Burmah is kindly furnished to me by the Rev. Dr. M. H. Bixby, of Providence, Rhode Island, who was also for some years a missionary among the Karens. He says:

"In my first journey over the mountains of Burmah, into Shanland, toward Western China, I passed through several tribes of wild Karens among whom the practice of 'covenanting by blood' prevailed.

"'If you mean what you say,' said the old chief of the Gecho tribe to me, referring to my professions of friendship, 'you will drink truth with me.' 'Well, what is drinking truth?' I said. In reply, he said: 'This is our custom. Each chief pierces his arm—draws blood—mingles it in a vessel with whisky, and drinks of it; both promising to be true and faithful to each other, down to the seventh generation.'

"After the chiefs had drunk of the mingled blood and whisky, each one of their followers drunk of it also, and were thereby included in the covenant of friendship.

"A company of Shans laid a plot to kill me and my company in Shanland, for the purpose of plunder. They entered into covenant with each other by drinking the blood of their leader mingled with whisky, or a kind of beer made from rice.

"Those wild mountain tribes have strange traditions which indicate that they once had the Old Testament Scriptures, although now they have no written language. Some of the Karen tribes have a written language, given them by the missionaries.

"The covenant, also, exists in modified forms, in which the blood is omitted."

BLOOD-STAINED TREE OF THE COVENANT.

In various parts of the East, a *tree* is given prominence in the rite of blood-covenanting. In Burmah, as above shown, one mode of covenanting is by the mutual planting of a tree.[1] In Timor, a newly planted

[1] See page 313, *supra.*

fig-tree is made to bear a portion of the blood of the covenant, and to remain as a witness to the sacred rite itself.[1] In one portion of Central Africa, a forked palm branch is held by the two parties, at their entering into blood-friendship;[2] and, in another region, the ashes of a burned tree and the blood of the covenanting brothers are brought into combination, in the use of a knotted palm branch which the brothers together hold.[3] And, again, in Canaan, in the days of Abraham, the planting of a tree was an element in covenant making ; as shown in the narrative of the covenant which Abraham cut with Abimelech, at Beer-sheba.[4]

It may, indeed, be fair to suppose that the trees at Hebron, which marked the dwelling-place of Abraham were covenant-trees, witnessing the covenant between Abraham and the three Amorite chiefs ; and that therefore they have prominence in the sacred story. " Now he [Abram] dwelt by [or, in : Hebrew, *beëlonay* (בְּאֵלֹנֵי)] the [four] oaks [or, terebinths] of Mamre, the Amorite, brother of Eschol, and brother of Aner; and these [three it was who] were confederate [literally, were masters of the covenant] with [the fourth one] Abram."[5] This rendering certainly gives a reason for the prominent mention of the trees at Hebron, in conjunction with Abram's covenant with Amorite chieftains ; and it accords with Oriental customs of former days, and until to-day. So, also, it would seem that the tree which witnessed[6] the confirmation, or the recognition, of the covenant between another Abimelech and the men of Shechem and the men of Beth-millo, by the pillar (the symbol of Baal-bereeth)[7] in Shechem,[8] was a covenant-tree, after the Oriental custom in sacred covenanting.

There is apparently a trace of the blood-covenanting and tree-planting rite of primitive times in the blood-stained " Fiery Cross " of the

---

[1] See page 53, *supra.*   [2] See page 35, *supra.*   [3] See page 37, *supra.*

[4] Gen. 21 : 33.   [5] See Gen. 13: 18 ; 14: 13 ; 18: 1.

[6] The covenant was " with " [Hebrew, עִם *'im*, not " with " as an instrument, but " with " as in the presence of, as accompanied by] the tree at Shechem.

[7] See page 218, *supra*, note.   [8] Judges 9 : 1–6.

Scottish Highlands, with its correspondent Arabian symbol of tribal covenant-duties in the hour of battle. Von Wrede, describing his travels in the south-eastern part of Arabia, tells of the use of this symbol as he saw it employed as preliminary to a tribal warfare. A war-council had decided on conflict. Then, "the fire which had burned in the midst of the circle was newly kindled with a great heap of wood, and the up-leaping flames were greeted with loud rejoicing. The green branch of a nŭbk tree [sometimes called the ' lote-tree,' and again known as the ' dôm,' although it is not the dôm palm] [1] was then brought, and also a sheep, whose feet were at once tied by the oldest shaykh. After these preparations, the latter seized the branch, spoke a prayer over it, and committed it to the flames. As soon as every trace of green had disappeared, he snatched it from the fire, again said a short prayer, and cut with his *jembeeyeh* [his short sword] the throat of the sheep, with whose blood the yet burning branch was quenched. He then tore a number of little twigs from the burnt branch, and gave them to as many Bed′ween, who hastened off with them in various directions. The black bloody branch was then planted in the earth. . . . The little twigs, which the shaykh cut off and gave to the Bed′ween, serve as alarm signals, with which the messengers hasten from valley to valley, calling the sons of the tribe to the impending war [by this blood-stained symbol of the sacred covenant which binds them in brotherhood]. None dare remain behind, without loss of honor, when the chosen [covenant] sign appears at his encampment, and the voice of its bearer calls to the war. . . . At the conclusion of the war [thus inaugurated], the shaykhs of the propitiated tribe return the branches to the fire, and let them burn to ashes." [2]

How strikingly this parallels the use and the symbolism of the Fiery Cross, in the Scottish Highlands, as portrayed in The Lady of the Lake. Sir Roderick Dhu would summon Clan Alpine against the King.

---

[1] Robinson's *Biblical Researches*, II., 210 f., note.
[2] Von Wrede's *Reise in Hadhramaut*, p. 197 f.

" A heap of withered boughs was piled,
  Of juniper and rowan wild,
  Mingled with shivers from the oak,
  Rent by the lightning's recent stroke.
  Brian the Hermit by it stood,
  Barefooted, in his frock and coat.
  .   .   .   .
  'Twas all prepared ;—and from the rock
  A goat, the patriarch of the flock,
  Before the kindling fire was laid,
  And pierced by Roderick's ready blade.
  Patient the sickening victim eyed
  The life-blood ebb in crimson tide
  Down his clogged beard and shaggy limb,
  Till darkness glazed his eyeballs dim.
  The grisly priest, with murmuring prayer,
  A slender crosslet framed with care,
  A cubit's length in measure due ;
  The shaft and limbs were rods of yew,
  Whose parents in Inch-Cailliach wave
  Their shadows o'er Clan Alpine's grave."

Lifting up this fragment of the tree from the grave of the patriarch of
the Clan,[1] the old priest sounded anathemas against those who should
be untrue to their covenant obligations as clansmen, when they recognized this symbol of their common brotherhood.

" Burst with loud roar their answer hoarse,
     ' Woe to the traitor, woe ! '
  Ben-an's gray scalps the accents knew,
  The joyous wolf from covert drew,
  The exulting eagle screamed afar,—
  They knew the voice of Alpine's war.

" The shout was hushed on lake and fell,
  The monk resumed his muttered spell :
  Dismal and low its accents came,
  The while he scathed the cross with flame.

[1] See reference (in note at page 268 f. *supra*) to the custom in Sumatra, of taking
an oath over the " grave of the original patriarch of the Passumah."

. . . .
The crosslet's points of sparkling wood
He quenched among the bubbling blood,
And, as again the sign he reared,
Hollow and hoarse his voice was heard :
' When flits this cross from man to man,
Vich-Alpine's summons to his clan,
Burst be the ear that fails to heed !
Palsied the foot that shuns to speed !
. . . .
Then Roderick with impatient look
From Brian's hand the symbol took :
' Speed, Malise, speed !' he said, and gave
The crosslet to his henchman brave.
' The muster-place be Lanrick mead—
Instant the time—Speed, Malise, speed ! ' " [1]

" At sight of the Fiery Cross," says Scott, " every man, from sixteen years old to sixty, capable of bearing arms, was obliged instantly to repair, in his best arms and accoutrements, to the place of rendezvous. . . . During the civil war of 1745–6, the Fiery Cross often made its circuit ; and upon one occasion it passed through the whole district of Breadalbane, a tract of thirty-two miles, in three hours." [2]

BLOOD-DRINKING.

Another item of evidence that the blood-covenant in its primitive form was a well-known rite in primitive Europe, is a citation by Athenæus from Poseidonios to this effect : " Concerning the Germans, Poseidonios says, that they, embracing each other in their banquets, open the veins upon their foreheads,[3] and mixing the flowing blood with their drink, they present it to each other ; esteeming it the farthest attainment of friendship to taste each other's blood." [4] As Poseidonios was earlier than our Christian era, this testimony shows that the custom with our ancestors was in no sense an outgrowth, nor yet a perversion, of Christian practices.

[1] *Lady of the Lake*, Canto III.   [2] *Ibid.*, note.
[3] See pages 13, 86 f., *supra*.   [4] Athenæus's *Deipnosophistæ*, II., 24 (45).

In Moore's Lalla Rookh, the young maiden, Zelica, being induced by Mokanna, the Veiled Prophet of Khorassan, to accompany him to the charnel-house, pledged herself to him, body and soul, in a draught of blood.

> " There in that awful place, when each had quaffed
> And pledged in silence such a fearful draught,
> Such—oh ! the look and taste of that red bowl
> Will haunt her till she dies—he bound her soul
> By a dark oath, in hell's own language fram'd.''

It was after this that he reminded her of the binding force of this blood-covenant :

> " That cup—thou shudderest, Lady—was it sweet ?
> That cup we pledg'd, the charnel's choicest wine,
> Hath bound thee—aye—body and soul all mine.''

And her bitter memory of that covenant-scene, in the presence of the " bloodless ghosts," was :

> " The dead stood round us, while I spoke that vow,
> Their blue lips echo'd it. I hear them now !
> Their eyes glared on me, while I pledged that bowl,
> 'Twas burning blood—I feel it in my soul ! ''

Although this is Western poetry, it had a basis of careful Oriental study in its preparation ; and the blood-draught of the covenant is known to Persian story and tradition.

One of the indications of the world-wide belief in the custom of covenanting, and again of life seeking, by blood-drinking, is the fact that both Jews and Christians have often been falsely charged with drinking the blood of little children at their religious feasts. This was one of the frequent accusations against the early Christians (See Justin Martyr's *Apol.*, I., 26; Tertullian's *Apol.*, VIII., IX.) And it has been repeated against the Jews, from the days of Apion down to the present decade. Such a baseless charge could not have gained credence but for the traditional understanding that men were wont to pledge each other to a close covenant by mutual blood-drinking.

COVENANT-CUTTING.

It is worthy of note that when the Lord enters into covenant with
Abraham by means of a prescribed sacrifice (Gen. 15 : 7–18), it is said
that the Lord " cut a covenant with Abram " ; but when the Lord calls
on Abraham to cut a covenant of blood-friendship, by the rite of circumcision (Gen. 17 : 1–12), the Lord says, for himself, " I will make
[or I will fix] my covenant between me and thee." In the one case,
the Hebrew word is *karath* (כָּרַת) " to cut " ; in the other, it is *nathan*
(נָתַן) " to give," or " to fix." This change goes to show that the idea of
cutting a covenant includes the act of a cutting—of a cutting of one's
person or the cutting of the substitute victim—as an integral part of the
covenant itself ; that a covenant may be made, or fixed, without a cutting,
but that the term " cutting " involves the act of cutting.

Thus, again, in Jeremiah 34 : 18, there is a two-fold reference to
covenant-cutting ; where the Lord reproaches his people for their faith-
lessness to their covenant. " And I will give [to destruction] the men
that have transgressed my covenant, which have not performed the
words of the covenant which they made [literally, ' cut '] before me [in
my sight] when they cut the calf in twain, and passed between the parts
thereof." In this instance, there is in the Hebrew, a pun, as it were, to
give added force to the accusation and reproach. The same word *'abhar*
(עָבַר) means both " to transgress " and " to pass over " [or, " between "],
so that, freely rendered, the charge here made, is, that they went through
the covenant when they had gone through the calf ; which is another way
of saying that they cut their duty when they claimed to cut a covenant.

The correspondence of cutting the victim of sacrifice, and of cutting
into the flesh of the covenanting parties, in the ceremony of making
blood-brotherhood, or blood-friendship, is well illustrated in the inter-
changing of these methods in the primitive customs of Borneo.[1] The
pig is the more commonly prized victim of sacrifice in Borneo. It

[1] St. John's *Life in Far East*, Comp. I., 38, 46, 56, 74–76, 115, 117, 185.

seems, indeed, to be there valued only next after a human victim. In some cases, blood-brotherhood is made, in Borneo, by "imbibing each other's blood." In other cases, "a pig is brought and placed between the two [friends] who are to be joined in brotherhood. A chief addresses an invocation to the gods, and marks with a lighted brand [1] the pig's shoulder. The beast is then killed, and after an exchange of jackets,[2] a sword is thrust into the wound, and the two [friends] are marked with the blood of the pig." On one occasion, when two hostile tribes came together to make a formal covenant of brotherhood, "the ceremony of killing a pig for each tribe" was the central feature of the compact; as in the case of two Kayans becoming one by interchanging their own blood, actually or by a substitute pig. And it is said of the tribal act of cutting the covenant by cutting the pig, that "it is thought more fortunate if the animal be severed in two by one stroke of the parang (half sword, half chopper)." In another instance, where two tribes entered into a covenant, "a pig was placed between the representatives of [the] two tribes; who, after calling down the vengeance of the spirits on those who broke the treaty, plunged their spears into the animal ['cutting a covenant' in that way], and then exchanged weapons.[2] Drawing their krises, they each bit the blade of the other [as if 'drinking the covenant'],[3] and so completed the affair." So, again, "if two men who have been at deadly feud, meet in a house [where the obligations of hospitality restrain them], they refuse to cast their eyes upon each other till a fowl has been killed, and the blood sprinkled over them."

In every case, it is the *blood* that seals the mutual covenant, and the "cutting of the covenant" is that cutting which secures the covenanting, or the inter-uniting, blood. The cutting may be in the flesh of the covenanting parties; or, again it may be in the flesh of the substitute victim which is sacrificed.

[1] A trace of the burnt branch of the covenant-tree.

[2] See page 270, *supra.*   [3] See pages 9, 154, *supra.*

BLOOD-BATHING.

In the Midrash Rabboth (*Shemoth*, Beth, 92, col. 2) there is this comment by the Rabbis on Exodus 2 : 23 : "'And the king of Egypt died.' He was smitten with leprosy. . . . 'And the children of Israel sighed.' Wherefore did they sigh? Because the magicians of Egypt said : 'There is no healing for thee save by the slaying of the little children of the Israelites. Slay them in the morning, and slay them in the evening ; and bathe in their blood twice a day.' As soon as the children of Israel heard the cruel decree, they poured forth great sighings and wailings." That comment gives a new point, in the rabbinical mind, to the first plague, whereby the waters of the Nile, in which royalty bathed (Exod. 2 : 5), were turned into blood, because of the bondage of the children of Israel.

A survival of the blood-baths of ancient Egypt, as a means of re-vivifying the death-smitten, would seem to exist in the medical practices of the Bechuana tribes of Africa ; as so many of the customs of ancient Egypt still survive among the African races (See page 15, *supra*). Thus, Moffat reports (*Missionary Labours*, p. 277) a method employed by native physicians, of killing a goat "over the sick person, allowing the blood to run down the body."

BLOOD-RANSOMING.

Among other Bible indications that the custom of balancing, or canceling, a blood account by a payment in money, was well known in ancient Palestine, appears the record of David's conference with the Gibeonites, concerning their claim for blood against the house of Saul, in 2 Samuel 21 : 1–9. When it was found that the famine in Israel was because of Saul's having taken blood—or life—unjustly from the Gibeonites, David essayed to balance that unsettled account. "And the Gibeonites said unto him, It is no matter of silver or gold between us and Saul, or his house ; neither is it for us to put any man to death in

Israel;" which was equivalent to saying: "Money for blood we will not take. Blood for blood we have no power to obtain." Then said David, "What ye shall say, that will I do for you." At this, the Gibeonites demanded, and obtained, the lives of the seven sons of Saul. The blood account must be balanced. In this case, as by the Mosaic law, it could only be by life for life.

In some parts of Arabia, if a Muhammadan slays a person of another religion, the relatives of the latter are not allowed to insist on blood for blood, but must accept an equivalent in money. The claim for the spilled blood is recognized, but a Muhammadan's blood is too precious for its payment. (See Wellsted's *Travels in Arabia*, I., 19.)

It is much the same in the far West as in the far East, as to this canceling of a blood-debt by blood or by other gifts. Parkman (*Jesuits in No. Am.*, pp. lxi.–lxiii.; 354–360) says of the custom among the Hurons and the Iroquois, that in case of bloodshed the chief effort of all concerned was to effect a settlement by contributions to the amount of the regular tariff rates of a human life.

Another indication that the mission of the goel was to cancel the loss of a life rather than to avenge it, is found in the primitive customs of the New World. "Even in so rude a tribe as the Brazilian Topanazes," says Farrer (citing Eschwege, in *Prim. Man. and Cust.*, p. 164), " a murderer of a fellow tribesman would be conducted by his relations to those of the deceased, to be by them forthwith strangled and buried [with his forfeited blood in him], in satisfaction of their rights; the two families eating together for several days after the event as though for the purpose of [or, as in evidence of] reconciliation,"—not of satisfied revenge.

Yet more convincing than all, in the line of such proofs that it is restitution, and not vengeance, that is sought by the pursuit of blood in the mission of the goel, is the fact that in various countries, when a man has died a natural death, it is the custom to seek blood, or life, from those immediately about him; as if to restore, or to equalize, the family loss. Thus, in New South Wales, " when any one of the tribe dies a natural

28

death, it is usual to avenge [not to avenge, but to meet] the loss of the
deceased by taking blood from one or other of his friends," and it is said
that death sometimes results from this endeavor (Angas's *Sav. Life*, II.,
227). In this fact, there is added light on the almost universal custom
of blood-giving to, or over, the dead. (See, *e. g.* Ellis's *Land of Fetish*,
pp. 59, 64; Stanley's *The Congo*, II., 180–182; Angas's *Sav. Life*, I.,
98, 331; II., 84, 89 f.; Ellis's *Polyn. Res.*, I., 527–529; Dodge's *Our
Wild Indians*, p. 172 f.; *First An. Rep. of Bureau of Ethn.*, pp. 109,
112, 159 f., 164, 183, 190.)

THE COVENANT-REMINDER.

It has already been shown that the blood-stained record of the covenant of blood, shielded in a leathern case, is proudly worn as an
armlet or as a necklace by the Oriental who has been fortunate enough
to become a sharer in such a covenant; and that there is reason for
believing that there are traces of this custom in the necklaces, the
armlets, the rings, and the frontlets, which have been worn as the
tokens of a sacred covenant, in well-nigh all lands, from the earliest
days of Chaldea and Egypt down to the present time. There is a confirmation of this idea in the primitive customs of the North American
Indians, which ought not to be overlooked.

The distinctive method by which these Indians were accustomed to
confirm and signalize a formal covenant, or a treaty, was the exchange
of belts of wampum; and that these wampum belts were not merely
conventional gifts, but were actual records, tokens, and reminders, of
the covenant itself, there is abundant evidence. In a careful paper on the
" Art in Shell of the Ancient Americans," in one of the reports of the
Bureau of Ethnology, of the Smithsonian Institution, the writer [1] says :
" One of the most remarkable customs practiced by the Americans is
found in the mnemonic use of wampum. . . . It does not seem
probable . . . that a custom so unique and so widespread could

[1] W. H. Holmes, in *Second Annual Report of Bureau of Ethnol.*, pp. 240–254.

have grown up within the historic period, nor is it probable that a practice foreign to the genius of tradition-loving races could have become so well established and so dear to their hearts in a few generations. . . . The mnemonic use of wampum is one which, I imagine, might readily develop from the practice of gift giving and the exchange of tokens of friendship, such mementoes being preserved for future reference as reminders of promises of assistance or protection. . . . The wampum records of the Iroquois [and the same is found to be true in many other tribes] were generally in the form of belts [as an encircling and binding token of a covenant], the beads being strung or woven into patterns formed by the use of different colors." Illustrations, by the score, of this mnemonic use of the covenant-confirming belts, or " necklaces," [1] as they are sometimes called, are given, or are referred to, in this interesting article.

In the narrative of a council held by the " Five Nations," at Onondaga, nearly two hundred years ago, a Seneca sachem is said to have presented a proposed treaty between the Wagunhas and the Senecas, with the words : " We come to join the two bodies into one " ; and he evidenced his good faith in this endeavor, by the presentation of the mnemonic belts of wampum. " The belts were accepted by the Five Nations, and their acceptance was a ratification of the treaty." [2] Lafitau, writing of the Canadian Indians, in the early years of the eighteenth century, says : " They do not believe that any transaction can be concluded without these belts ; " and he mentions, that according to Indian custom these belts were to be exchanged in covenant making ; " that is to say, for one belt [received] one must give another [belt]." [3] And a historian of the Moravian Missions says : " Everything of moment transacted at solemn councils, either between the Indians themselves, or with Europeans, is ratified and made valid by strings and belts of wam-

---

[1] W. H. Holmes, in *Second Annual Report of Bureau of Ethnol.*, p. 243.

[2] *Events in Indian History*, p. 143 ; cited *Ibid.*, p. 242 f.

[3] *Moeurs des Sauvages Ameriq.*, tom. II., pp. 502–507 ; cited *Ibid.*, p. 243 ff.

pum." [1] "The strings," according to Lafitau, "are used for affairs of little consequence, or as a preparation for other more considerable presents "; but the binding "belts" were as the bond of the covenant itself.

These covenant belts often bore, interwoven with different colored wampum beads, symbolic figures ; such as two hands clasped in friendship, or two figures with hands joined. As the belts commonly signalized tribal covenants, they were not worn by a single individual, but were sacredly guarded in some tribal depository ; yet their form and their designation indicate the origin of their idea.

There is still preserved, in the Historical Society of Pennsylvania, the wampum belt which is supposed to have sealed the treaty of peace and friendship between William Penn and the Indians. It contains two figures, wrought in dark colored beads, representing "an Indian grasping with the hand of friendship the hand of a man evidently intended to be represented in the European costume, wearing a hat." [2]

Still more explicit in its symbolism is the royal belt of the primitive kings of Tahiti. Throughout Polynesia, red feathers, which had been inclosed in a hollow image of a god, were considered not only as emblematic of the deities, but as actually representing them in their personality (Ellis's *Polyn. Res..* I., 79, 211, 314, 316; II., 204; *Tour thro' Hawaii*, p. 121). "The inauguration ceremony [of the Tahitian king], answering to coronation among other nations, consisted in girding the king with the *maro ura*, or sacred girdle of red feathers; which not only raised him to the highest earthly station, but *identified him with their gods* [as by oneness of blood]. The *maro*, or girdle, was made with the beaten fibres of the ava ; with these a number of *ura*, red feathers, taken from the images of their deities [where they had, seemingly, represented the blood, or the life, of the image], were interwoven; . . . the feathers [as the blood] being supposed to retain all the

---

[1] Loskiel's *Missions of the United Brethren*, Trans. by La Trobe, Bk. I., p. 26; cited in *Ibid.*, p. 245 f.

[2] *Ibid.*, p. 253 f.

dreadful attributes of vengeance which the idols possessed, and with which it was designed to endow the king." In lieu of the king's own blood, in this symbolic ceremony of inter-union, a human victim was sacrificed, for the "fastening on of the sacred maro." "Sometimes a human victim was offered for every fresh piece added to the girdle [blood for blood, between the king and the god]; . . . and the girdle was considered as consecrated by the blood of those victims." The chief priest of the god Oro formally invested the king with this "sacred girdle, which, the [blood-representing] feathers from the idol being interwoven in it, was supposed to impart to the king a power equal to that possessed by Oro." After this, the king was supposed to be a sharer of the divine nature of Oro, with whom he had entered into a covenant of blood-union (Ellis's *Polyn. Res.*, II., 354–360).

Thus it seems that a band, as a bond, of a sacred covenant, is treasured reverently in the New World; as a similar token, of one kind or another, was treasured, for the same reason, in the Old World. And it is in view of these recognized facts that one school of criticism assumes that the Jewish phylacteries were a survival of the superstitious idea of a pagan amulet. Yet, on the other hand, another school of criticism is equally confident in ascribing the idea of the pagan amulet itself to a perversion of that common primitive idea of the binding bond of a sacred covenant which shows itself in the blood-friendship record of Syria, in the red covenant-cord of China and India, in the divine-human covenant token of ancient Egypt, in the red-feather belt of divine-royal union in the Pacific Islands, in the wampum belt of America, and in the evolved wedding-covenant ring, or amulet, of a large portion of the civilized world. Here is where a difference in processes of reasoning is inevitable, according to the different hypotheses as to primitive man's original state. The one school assumes that man started with no well-defined religious ideas, and gradually acquired them; the other school assumes that man originally had a revelation from God, and gradually lost its distinct features through sinning.

Yet another indication that the binding circlet of the covenant-token stands, among primitive peoples, as also among cultivated ones, as the representative, or proof, of this very covenant itself, is found in a method of divorce prevailing among the Balau Dayaks, of Borneo. It has already been shown (page 73, *supra*) that a ring of blood is a binding symbol in the marriage covenant in some parts of Borneo. It seems, also, that when a divorce has been agreed on by a Balau couple, "it is neces- sary for the offended husband to send a ring to his wife, before the marriage can be considered as finally dissolved; without which, should they marry again, they would be liable to be punished for infidelity." [1] This practice seems to have grown out of the old custom already referred to (page 73 f.), of the bride giving to the bridegroom a blood- representing ring in the marriage cup. Until that symbolic ring is re- turned to her by the bridegroom, it remains as the proof of her cove- nant with him.

This connection of the encircling ring with the heart's blood is of very ancient origin, and of general, if not of universal, application. Wilkinson (*Anc. Egypt.*, III., 420) cites Macrobius as saying, that "those Egyptian priests who were called prophets, when engaged in the temple near the altars of the gods, moistened [anointed] the ring-finger of the left hand (which was that next to the smallest) with various sweet ointments, in the belief that a certain nerve communicated with it from the heart." He also says, that among the Egyptian women, many finger rings were worn, and that "the left was considered the hand peculiarly privileged to wear these ornaments; and it is remarkable that its third finger [next to the little finger] was considered by them, as by us, *par excellence* the ring finger; though there is no evidence [to his knowledge] of its having been so honored at the marriage ceremony." Birch adds (*Ibid.*, II., 340) that "it is very difficult to distinguish between the ring worn for mere ornament, and the signet [standing for the wearer's very life] em- ployed to seal [and to sign] epistles and other things." The evidence

[1] St. John's *Life in the Far East*. I., 67

is, in fact, ample, that the ring, in ancient Egypt, as elsewhere, was not a mere ornament, nor yet a superstitious amulet, but represented one's heart, or one's life, as a symbol and pledge of personal fidelity.

In South Australia, the rite of circumcision is one of the steps by which a lad enters into the sphere of manhood. This involves his covenanting with his new god-father, and with his new fellows in the sphere of his entering. In this ceremony, the very ring of flesh itself is placed " on the third finger of the boy's left hand " (Angas's *Sav. Life*, I., 99). What clearer indication than this is needed, that the finger-ring is a vestige of the primitive blood-covenant token?

An instance of the use of a large ring, or bracelet, encircling the two hands of persons joining in the marriage covenant, is reported to me from the North of Ireland, in the present century. It was in the county Donegal. The Roman Catholic priest was a French exile. In marrying the people of the poorer class, who could not afford to purchase a ring, he " would take the large ring from his old-fashioned double-cased watch, and hold it on the hands, or the thumbs, of the contracting parties, while he blessed their union."

Yet another illustration of the universal symbolism of the ring, as a token of sacred covenant, is its common use as a pledge of friendship, even unto death. The ring given by Queen Elizabeth to the unfortunate Earl of Essex is an instance in point. Had that covenant-token reached her, her covenant promises would have been redeemed.

There is an old Scottish ballad, " Hynd Horn,"—perhaps having a common origin with the Bohemian lay on which Scott based The Noble Moringer,[1]—which brings out the idea of a covenant-ring having the power to indicate to its wearer the fidelity of its giver; corresponding with the popular belief to that effect, suggested by Bacon.[2] Hynd Horn has won the heart of the king's daughter, and the king sends him over the sea, as a means of breaking up the match. As he sets out Hynd Horn carries with him a symbol of his lady-love's troth.

[1] See page 73, *supra*.   [2] See page 75, *supra*

" O his love gave him a gay gold ring,
　　With a hey lillelu, and a how lo lan ;
　With three shining diamonds set therein,
　　And the birk and the broom blooms bonnie.

" As long as these diamonds keep their hue,
　　With a hey lillelu, and a how lo lan,
　Ye'll know that I'm a lover true,
　　And the birk and the broom blooms bonnie.

" But when your ring turns pale and wan,
　　With a hey lillelu, and a how lo lan,
　Then I'm in love with another man,
　　And the birk and the broom blooms bonnie." [1]

Seven years went by, and then the ring-gems grew "pale and wan."
Hynd Horn hastened back, entered the wedding-hall disguised as a
beggar, sent the covenant-ring to the bride in a glass of wine; and the
sequel was the same as in The Noble Moringer.

At a Brahman wedding, in India, described by Miss H. G. Brittan (in
" The Missionary Link," for October, 1864; cited in *Women of the
Orient,* pp. 176–179) a silver dish, filled with water, (probably with water
colored with saffron, or with turmeric, according to the common custom in
India,) " also containing a very handsome ruby ring, and a thin iron bracelet," was set before the father of the bride, during the marriage ceremony.
At the covenanting of the young couple, " the ring was given to the
groom; the bracelet to the bride; then some of the [blood-colored ?]
water was sprinkled on them [See page 194, *supra*], and some flowers
[were] thrown at them." Here seem to be combined the symbolisms
of the ring, the bracelet, and the·blood, ın a sacred covenanting.

HINTS OF BLOOD-UNION.

From the very fact that so little attention has been given to the primitive rite of blood-covenanting, in the studies of modern scholars, there
is reason for supposing that the rite ıtself has very often been unnoticed

---

[1] Allingham's *Ballad Book,* p. 6 f.

by travelers and missionaries in regions where it was practiced almost under their eyes. Indeed, there is proof of this to be obtained, by comparing the facts recorded in this volume with the writings of visitors to the lands here reported from. Hence it is fair to infer that more or less of the brotherhoods or friendships noted among primitive peoples, without any description of the methods of their consummating, are either directly based on the rite of blood-covenanting, or are outgrowths and variations of that rite ; as, for example, in Borneo, blood-tasting is sometimes deemed essential to the rite, and again it is omitted. It may be well, therefore, to look at some of the hints of blood-union among primitive peoples, in relationships and in customs where not all the facts and processes involved are known to us.

Peculiarly is it true, that wherever we find the idea of an absolute merging of two natures into one, or of an inter-union or an inter-changing of two personalities in loving relation, there is reason for suspecting a connection with the primitive rite of inter-union through a common blood flow. And there are illustrations of this idea in the Old World and in the New, all along the ages.

It has already been mentioned (page 109, *supra*) that, in India, the possibility of an inter-union of two natures, and of their inter-merging into one, is recognized in the statement that "the heart of Vishnu is Sivâ, and the heart of Sivâ is Vishnu " ; and it is a well-known philosophical fact that man must have an actual basis of human experience for the symbolic language with which he illustrates the nature and characteristics of Deity.

In the most ancient portion of the ancient Egyptian Book of the Dead,[1] there is a description of the inter-union of Osiris and Râ, not unlike that above quoted concerning Sivâ and Vishnoo. It says that "Osiris came to Tattu (Mendes) and found the soul of Râ there; each embraced the other, and became as one soul in two souls"[2]—as one life in two lives; or, as it would be phrased concerning two human

[1] *Todtenbuch*, xvii., 42, 43.   [2] Renouf's *The Relig. of Anc. Egypt*, p. 107.

beings united in blood-friendship, "one soul in two bodies"; a common life in two personalities. Again it is said in an Egyptian sacred text, "Râ is the soul of Osiris, and Osiris is the soul of Râ." [1]

An exchange of names, as if in exchange of personalities, in connection with a covenant of friendship, is a custom in widely diverse countries; and this custom seems to have grown out of the idea of an inter-union of natures by an inter-union of blood, even if it be not actually an accompaniment of that rite in every instance. It is common in the Society Islands,[2] as an element in the adoption of a "tayo," or a personal friend and companion (See page 56, *supra*). It is to be found in various South Sea islands, and on the American continent.

Among the Araucanians, of South America, the custom of making brothers, or brother-friends, is called *Lacu*. It includes the killing of a lamb and dividing it—"cutting" it—between the two covenanting parties; and each party must eat his half of the lamb—either by himself or by such assistance as he chooses to call in. None of it must be left uneaten. Gifts also pass between the parties; and the two friends exchange names. "The giving [the exchanging] of a name [with this people] establishes between the namesakes a species of relationship which is considered almost as sacred as that of blood, and obliges them to render to each other certain services, and that consideration which naturally belongs to relatives." [3]

It is related of Tolo, a chief of the Shastika Indians, on the Pacific coast, that when he made a treaty with Col. McKee, an American soldier, in 1852, for the cession of certain tribal rights, he was anxious for some ceremony of brotherhood that should give binding sacredness to the mutual covenant. After some parleying, he proposed the formal exchange of names, and this was agreed to. Thenceforward he desired

---

[1] Renouf's *The Relig. of Anc. Egypt*, p. 107.

[2] *Miss. Voyage to So. Pacif. Ocean*, p. 65.

[3] See E. R. Smith's *The Araucanians*, p 262.

to be known as " McKee." The American colonel was now " Tolo."
But after a while the Indian found that, as in too many other instances,
the terms of the treaty were not adhered to by the authorities making
it. Then he discarded his new name, " McKee," and refused to re-
sume his former name, " Tolo." He would not answer to either, and
to the day of his death he insisted that his name, his identity, was
" lost." [1]—There is a profound sentiment underneath such a course, and
such a custom, as that.

So fully is the identity of one's name and one's life recognized by
primitive peoples, that to call on the name of a dead person is generally
supposed to summon the spirit of that person to the caller's service.
Hence, among the American Indians, if one calls the dead by name, he
must answer to the dead man's goel. He must surrender his own blood,
or pay blood-money, in restitution of the life—of the dead—taken by
him. (*First An. Rep. of Bureau of Ethnol.*, p. 200.)

Even Herbert Spencer sees the correspondence of the blood-covenant
and the exchange of names. He says: " By absorbing each other's
blood, men are supposed to establish actual community of nature.
Similarly with the ceremony of exchanging names. . . . This,
which is a widely-diffused practice, arises from the belief that the name
is vitally connected with its owner. . . . To exchange names,
therefore, is to establish some participation in one another's being." [2]
Hence, as we may suppose, came the well-nigh universal Oriental practice of inter-weaving the name of one's Deity with one's name, as a
symbolic evidence of one's covenant-union with the Deity. The blood-
covenant, or the blood-union, idea is at the bottom of this.

Another custom, having a peculiar bearing upon this thought of a
new name, or a new identity, through new blood, is the rite of initiation into manhood, by the native Australians. During childhood the
Australian boys are under the care of their mothers, and they bear

---

[1] Power's Tribes of California," in *Contrib. to No. Am. Ethnol.*, III., 247.
[2] *Principles of Sociology*, II., 21.

names which designate the place and circumstances of their birth. But when the time comes for them to put away childish things,[1] they are subjected to a series of severe and painful tests, to prove their powers of physical and mental endurance, preparatory to their reception of a new name, as indicative of a new life. A rite resembling circumcision is one step in their progress. During these ceremonies, there is selected for each lad a sponsor (or godfather) who is a representative of that higher life into which the lad seeks an entrance. One of the latest steps in the long series of ceremonies, is the choosing and conferring, by the sponsor, of the lad's new name, which he is to retain thenceforward during his life. With a stone-knife, the sponsor opens a vein in his own arm, and causes the lad to drink his warm-flowing blood. After this, the lad drops forward on his hands and knees, and the sponsor's blood is permitted to form a pool on his back, and to coagulate there. Then the sponsor cuts, with his stone-knife, broad gashes in the lad's back, and pulls open the gaping wounds with the fingers. The scars of these gashes remain as permanent signs of the covenant ceremony.[2] And encircling tokens of the covenant[3] are bound around the neck, each arm, and the waist, of the young man; who is now reckoned a new creature[4] in the life represented by that godfather, who has given him his new name, and has imparted to him of his blood.[5]

That the transfusion of blood in this ceremony is the making of a covenant between the youth and his sponsor, and not the giving him blood in vivification, is indicated in another form of the same rite of manhood-initiation, as practised in New South Wales. There, the youth is seated upon the shoulders of his sponsor, while one of his teeth is knocked out. The blood that flows from the boy's lacerated gum in this ceremony is not wiped away, but is suffered to run down upon his breast, and thence upon the head of his sponsor, whose name he takes. This blood, which secures, by its absorption, a common life between the two, who have now

[1] 1 Cor. 13: 11.   [2] See note at page 218, *supra.*   [3] See pages 65-77, *supra.*
[4] 2 Cor. 5: 17; Eph. 4: 24; Col. 3: 9, 10.   [5] Angas's *Savage Life*, I., 114-116.

a common name, is permitted to dry upon the head of the man and upon the breast of the boy, and to remain there untouched for several days.

In this New South Wales ceremonial, there is another feature, which seems to suggest that remarkable connection of life with a stone, which has been already referred to (page 307, *supra*) ; and yet again to suggest the giving of a new name as the token of a new life. A white stone, or a quartz crystal, called *mundie*, is given to each novitiate in manhood. at the time he receives his new name. This stone is counted a gift from deity, and is held peculiarly sacred. A test of the young man's moral stamina is made by the old men's trying, by all sorts of persuasion, to induce him to surrender this possession, when first he has received it. This accompaniment of a new name " is worn concealed in the hair, tied up in a packet, and is never shown to the women, who are forbidden to look at it under pain of death." The youths receiving and retaining these white stones, with their new names, are termed " *Kebarrah*, from *keba*, a rock, or stone." (Angas's *Savage Life*, II., 221.) That the idea of a sacred covenant, a covenant of brotherhood and friendship, is underneath these ceremonies, is indicated by the fact, that when the rites of Kebarrah are celebrated, even " hostile tribes meet in peace ; all animosity between them being laid aside during the performance of these ceremonies." "To him that overcometh, [saith the Spirit,] . . . I will give him a white stone, and upon the stone a new name written, which no one knoweth but he that receiveth it" (Rev. 2: 17). The Rabbis recommend the giving secretly of a new name, as a means of new life, to him who is in danger of dying. (See *Seph. Hakhkhay.*, p. 37 f. and note.)

Again, in a form of marriage ceremony in Tahiti, there is a hint of this universal idea of inter-union by blood. An observer of this ceremony, in describing it says : " The female relatives cut their faces and brows [1] with the instrument set with shark's teeth,[2] received the flowing blood on a piece of native cloth, and deposited the cloth,

---

[1] See references to drawing blood from the forehead, at page 86 ff., *supra*.

[2] See pages 85–88, *supra*.

sprinkled with the mingled blood of *the mothers* of the married pair, at
the feet of the bride. By the latter parts of the ceremony, any inferiority
of rank that might have existed was removed, and they were [now]
considered as equal. The two families, also, to which they respectively
belonged, were ever afterwards regarded as one [through this new blood-
union]." [1] Had these mothers mingled and interchanged their own
blood before the births of their children, the children—as children of
a common blood—would have been debarred from marriage; but now
that the two children were covenanting to be one, their mothers might
interchange their blood, that the young couple might have an absolute
equality of family nature.

There are frequent references by travelers to the rite of brotherhood,
or of close friendship, in one part of the world or another, with or without a description of its methods. Thus of one of the tribes in Central
Africa it is said: " The Wanyamuezi have a way of making brotherhood, similar to that which has already been described, except that
instead of drinking each other's blood, the newly made brothers mix it
[their blood] with butter on a leaf, and exchange leaves. The butter is
then rubbed into the incisions, so that it acts as a healing ointment at
the same time that blood is exchanged.[2] The ceremony is concluded
by tearing the leaves to pieces and showering the fragments on the heads
of the brothers." [3] The Australians, again, are said to have "the custom
of making ' *Kotaiga*,' or brotherhood, with strangers. When Europeans
visit their districts, and behave as they ought to do, the natives generally
unite themselves in bonds of fellowship with the strangers; each selecting one of them as his Kotaiga. The new relations are then considered
as having mutual responsibilities, each being bound to forward the welfare of the other." [4] Once more, in Feejee, two warriors sometimes bind
themselves to each other by a formal ceremony, and although its details

---

[1] Ellis's *Polynesian Researches*, II., 569 f.   [2] See Prov. 27 : 9.

[3] Cited from Capt. Grant's description ; in Wood's *Unciv. Races*, I., 440.

[4] *Ibid.*, II., 81.

are not described, a missionary writer says of it: "The manner in which they do this is singular, and wears the appearance of a marriage contract; and the two men entering into it are spoken of as man and wife, to indicate the closeness of their military union. By this mutual bond, the two men pledge themselves to oneness of purpose and effort, to stand by each other in every danger, defending each other to the death, and if needful to die together." [1]

With the American Indians, there are various traces of the blood-brotherhood idea. Says Captain Clark, in his work on the Indian Sign Language: "Among many tribes there are brothers by adoption, and the tie seems to be held about as sacredly as though created by nature." [2] Stephen Powell, writing of the Pacific Coast Indians, gives this tie of brotherhood-adoption yet more prominence, than does Clark. He says: "There is an interesting institution found among the Wyandots, as among some other of our North American tribes, namely, that of fellowship. Two young men agree to be perpetual friends to each other, or *more than brothers*. Each reveals to the other the secrets of his life, and counsels with him on matters of importance, and defends him from wrong and violence, and at his death is chief mourner." [3] This certainly suggests the relation of blood-brotherhood; whether blood be intermingled in the consummation of the rite, or not.

Colonel Dodge tells of a ceremony of Indian-brotherhood, which includes a bloody rite, worthy of notice in this connection. He says: "A strong flavor of religious superstition attaches to a scalp, and many solemn contracts and binding obligations can only be made over or by means of a scalp;" for is it not the representative of a life? In illustration of this, he gives an incident which followed an Indian battle, in which the Pawnees had borne a part with the whites against the Northern Cheyennes. Colonel Dodge was sitting in his tent, when "the

---

[1] Williams and Calvert's *Fiji and Fijians*, p. 35.

[2] *Indian Sign Language*, s. v. "Brother."

[3] *Contributions to No. Am. Ethnology*, Vol. III., p. 68.

acting head-chief of the Pawnees stalked in gravely, and without a word." The Colonel continues : " We had long been friends, and had on several occasions been in tight places together. He sat down on the side of my bed, looked at me kindly, but solemnly, and began in a low tone to mutter in his own language, half chant, half recitative. Know-ing that he was making ‘ medicine ’ [that he was engaged in a religious exercise] of some kind, I looked on without comment. After some moments, he stood erect, and stretched out his hand to me. I gave him my hand. He pulled me into a standing position, embraced me, passed his hands lightly over my head, face, arms, body, and legs to my feet, muttering all the while ; embraced me again, then turned his back upon me, and with his face toward heaven, appeared to make adoration. He then turned to embrace and manipulate me again. After some five minutes of this performance, he drew from his wallet a package, and unrolling it, disclosed a freshly taken [and therefore still bloody] scalp of an Indian. Touching me with this [blood-vehicle] in various places and ways, he finally drew out his knife, [and ‘ cutting the covenant ’ in this way, he] divided the scalp carefully along the part [the seam] of the hair, and handing me one half, embraced me again, kissing me on the forehead. ‘ Now,’ said he in English, ‘ you are my brother.’ He subsequently informed me that this ceremony could not have been per-formed without this scalp." [1]

Here seems to be an illustration of cutting the covenant of blood-brotherhood, by sharing the life of a substitute human victim. It is much the same in the wild West as in the primitive East.

So simple a matter as the clasping of hands in token of covenant fidelity, is explicable, in its universality, only as a vestige of the primitive custom of joining pierced hands in the covenant of blood-friendship. Hand-clasping is not, by any means, a universal, nor is it even the com-monest, mode of friendly and fraternal salutation among primitive peoples. Prostrations, embracings, kissings, nose-rubbings, slappings of one's own

[1] Dodge's *Our Wild Indians*, page 514 f.

body, jumpings up and down, the snapping of one's fingers, the blowing of one's breath, and even the rolling upon one's back, are all among the many methods of primitive man's salutations and obeisances (See, e. g., Spencer's *Principles of Sociology*, II., 16–19). But, even where hand clasping is unknown in salutation, it is recognized as a symbol of the closest friendship. Thus, for example, among tribes of North American Indians where nose-rubbing is the mode of salutation, there is, in their widely diffused sign language, the sign of clasped, or inter-locked, hands, as indicative of friendship and union. (*First An. Rep. of Bureau of Ethnol.*, pp. 385 f., 521, 534 f.) So again, similarly, in Australia (*Ibid.*, citation from Smith's *Aborigines of Victoria*, II., 308). In the Society Islands, the clasping of hands marks the marriage union, and marks a loving union between two brothers in arms; although it has no place in ordinary greetings (Ellis's *Polyn. Res.*, II., II., 11, 492, 569). And so, again, in other primitive lands.

There seems, indeed, to be a gleam of this thought in Job 17 : 3 :

> " Give now a pledge, be surety for me with thyself;
> Who is there that will strike hands with me?"

The Hebrew word *taq'a* (תָּקַע)[1] here translated "strike," has also the meaning "to pierce" (Judg. 4: 21) and "to blow through," or "to drive through" (Num. 10: 3); and Job's question might be freely rendered: Who is there that will pierce [or that will clasp pierced] hands with me, in blood-friendship? Thus, suretyship grew out of blood-covenanting.

Again, in Zechariah 13 : 6, where the prophet foretells the moral reformation of Judah, there is a seeming reference to the pierced hands of blood-friendship. When one is suspected of being a professional prophet, by certain marks of cuttings between his hands, he declares that these are marks of his blood-covenant with his friends. "And one shall say unto him, What are these wounds [these cuttings] between thine hands? Then he shall answer, [They are] these [cuttings] with which

[1] Is there any correspondence between this word, *taq'a*, and the Hindoo word *tika* (the blood-mark on the Rajput chief), referred to at page 137, *supra?*

29*

I was wounded [or stricken, or pierced] in the house of my friends [in the covenant of friendship]." If, indeed, the translation of the Revisers, "between thine arms," were justified, the cuttings would still seem to be the cuttings of the blood-covenant (See pages 13, 45, *supra*).

It is a noteworthy fact, that among the Jews in Tunis, near the old Phœnician settlement of Carthage, the sign of a bleeding hand is still an honored and a sacred symbol, as if in recognition of the covenant-bond of their brotherhood and friendship. "What struck me most in all the houses," says a traveler (Chevalier de Hesse-Wartegg) among these Jews, "was the impression of an open bleeding hand, on every wall of each floor. However white the walls, this repulsive [yet suggestive] sign was to be seen everywhere."

How many times, in the New Testament epistles, does the idea show itself, of an inter-union of lives, between Christ and his disciples, and between these disciples and each other. "We, who are many, are one body in Christ, and severally members one of another" (Rom. 12: 5). "We are members of his body" (Eph. 5: 30). "We are members one of another" (Eph. 4: 25). "Know ye not that your bodies are members of Christ?" (1 Cor. 6: 15). "Ye are the body of Christ, and severally [are] members thereof" (1 Cor. 12: 27).

It is in this truth of truths, concerning the possibility of an inter-union of the human life with the divine, through a common inter-bloodflow, that there is found a satisfying of the noblest heart yearnings of primitive man everywhere, and of the uttermost spiritual longings of the most advanced Christian believer, in the highest grade of intellectual and moral enlightenment. No attainment of evolution, or of development, has brought man's latest soul-cry beyond the intimations of his earliest soul-outreaching.

> " Take, dearest Lord, this crushed and bleeding heart,
>   And lay it in thine hand, thy piercèd hand ;
>   That thine atoning blood may mix with mine,
>   *Till I and my Beloved are all one.*"

SUPPLEMENT TO SECOND EDITION.

SUPPLEMENT TO SECOND EDITION.

THE reception accorded to the first edition of this work was unexpectedly gratifying. Both the freshness and the importance of its field of research were cordially recognized by biblical scholars on both sides of the water; and a readiness to accept more or less of the main outline of its hypothesis of symbolisms in their application to biblical theology, was shown by exegetes and theologians to an extent quite unanticipated. Of course, there have been questionings of its positions, at one point or another; and it is in view of some of the more prominent criticisms that a few supplemental facts are now given—in addition to fresh material on the general subject of the volume.

Perhaps the most important exceptions taken to the proffered proofs of the linkings of the primitive blood-covenant with the sacrifices of the Old Testament, and of the New, are: (1) "That there is a wide step between a union made by the inter-transfusion of blood, and the union made by substitute blood, whether sprinkled on both parties, as at Sinai, or poured in the sacrifice of a victim whose flesh is eaten as a symbol of sharing the life and the nourishment of Deity;" (2) That "the covenant union in sacrifice was represented by eating the flesh of the victim, not by sprinkling the blood;" (3) "That in the heathen world there is no satisfactory evidence that the desire to participate in the divine nature lay at the basis of animal sacrifice." [1] To the meeting of these exceptions a portion of this supplementary matter is addressed.

[1] These three points of exception are taken by three prominent members of the American Company of Old Testament Revisers, and therefore are worthy of special attention.

345

VITAL UNION BY SUBSTITUTE BLOOD.

It would appear that the more primitive form of blood-covenanting is by the intermingling, or the inter-drinking, of the blood of the two parties making the covenant. It would also appear that time and circumstances have, in many cases, so modified this primitive mode, as to admit of the use of *substitute* blood as the means of inter-union; and of a mutual blood-*anointing* or blood-*sprinkling* as a symbolic—if not indeed a realistic—equivalent of blood-*mingling*. Illustrations of this gradation, all the way along, have been given in the preceding pages; [1] but if proof at any point be still counted lacking, there is ample material for its supply.

For example, in portions of Madagascar the same people solemnize the rite of blood-covenanting, at one time by drinking the mingled blood of the two parties to the covenant, and at another time by the two parties drinking in common the fresh blood of a substitute animal; the compact and the bond of union being counted the same, whether wrought by substitute or by personal blood. Of this fact, the Rev. James Sibree, Jr., of the London Missionary Society, an exceptionally careful and scholarly observer, bears abundant testimony. [2] Ordinarily "the ceremony consists in taking a small portion of blood from the breast or side," which "is mixed with other ingredients," the mixture being "stirred up with a spear-point, and then a small portion swallowed by each of the contracting parties." The relation thus formed is termed by the Malagasy *Fàto-dra*, [3] or "bound by blood," and Mr. Sibree designates it "Brotherhood by Blood Covenant." Partaking of each other's blood, he says, "they thus become of one blood." But in some cases, as he illustrates by the record of "the French traveler, M. Grandidier," who "became a brother

---

[1] Compare the accounts of the rite in China, in India, in Borneo, and among the American Indians, at pp. 52, 137 f., 154, 323, 339, etc.

[2] See Sibree's *The Great African Island*, pp. 223–226.

[3] This seems to be the word which Ellis (*Hist. of Mad.*, I., 187, cited at page 44 *supra*) mistook for *Fatrida* or "Dead Blood."

by blood with Zoména, a chief of the Tanòsy, in the southwest of Madagascar," the unifying blood is from a substitute animal. " In this case
[of Grandidier and Zoména] the blood was not taken from the contracting
parties, but from an ox sacrificed for the purpose." The rite, as
described by M. Grandidier,[1] was similar to that described by Ellis, in
his History of Madagascar,[2] and it included the drinking by Grandidier
and Zoména of the blood of the substitute ox.

It is to be borne in mind that among the Malagasy, as among the
Aryans, and the proto-Semites, the ox has a semi-sacred character, and
is looked upon as in a peculiar sense belonging to or representing Deity.[3]
Hence, for the two covenanting parties to partake together of the blood,
which is the life, of a sacred ox, is to bring them into a common higher
life through their sharing a new and a diviner nature.

Again, in a work on the family ties in Early Arabia, by Professor W. Robertson Smith, issued a little later than the first edition
of The Blood Covenant, there is evidence of a corresponding use of
substitute blood as a means of inter-union of life among the Semites.[4]
Showing that the closest and most sacred of alliances in Arabia were
based on the idea of "unity of blood," Professor Smith says that a
primitive " covenant in which two groups promised to stand by each
other to the death (ta'âçadû 'ala 'l-maut), that is, took upon them the
duties of common blood-feud (Ibn Hishâm, I., 125), was originally
accompanied by a sacramental ceremony, the meaning of which was that
the parties commingled their blood. . . . A covenant of alliance
and protection was based upon an oath. Such an oath was necessarily
a religious act; it is called casâma (Diw. Hodh., lxxxvii, cxxviii), a
word which almost certainly implies that there was a reference to the
god at the sanctuary before the alliance was sealed, and that he was made

---

1 In *Bull. de la Soc. de Géog.*, Fev. 1872, p. 144; cited in Sibree's *The Great
African Island*, p. 223 f.

2 Cited at pp. 44-48, *supra*. 3 See Sibree's *The Great Afr. Island*, pp. 271-274.

4 *Kinship and Marriage in Early Arabia*, pp. 47-50.

a party to the act. . . . At Mecca, within historical times, such a life and death covenant was formed between the group of clans subsequently known as ' blood-lickers' (*la 'acat al-dam*).[1] The form of the oath was that each party dipped their hands in a pan of blood and tasted the contents."

He refers to certain other forms of covenanting at Mekkeh, as " by taking zemzem water [water taken from the sacred well] and washing the corners of the Ka'ba [the holy shrine] with it, after which it was drunk by the [covenanting] parties ; " and, again, as by two parties " dipping their hands in a pan of perfume or unguent, and then wiping them on the Ka'ba, whereby the god himself became a party to the compact " ; and of these forms he says : " All these covenants are Meccan and were made about the same period, so that it is hardly credible that there was any fundamental difference in the praxis. We must rather hold that they are all types of one and the same rite, imperfectly related and probably softened by the narrator. The form in which *blood* is used is plainly the more primitive or the more exactly related, but the account of it must be filled up by the addition of the feature that the blood was also applied to the sacred stones or fetishes at the corners of the Ka'ba. And now we can connect the rite with that described in Herodotus iii. 8, where the contracting parties draw each other's blood and smear it on seven stones set up in the midst.[2] Comparing this with the later rite we see that they are really one, and that Herodotus has got the thing in its earliest form, but has omitted one trait necessary to the understanding of the symbolism, and preserved in the Meccan tradition. *The later Arabs had substituted the blood of a victim* [a beast] *for human blood,* but they retained a feature which Herodotus had missed : they licked the blood as well as smeared it on the sacred stones.[3] Originally therefore the ceremony was that known in so many parts of the world, in

---

[1] See p. 11, *supra.*   [2] Cited at p. 62 f., *supra.*

[3] Elsewhere Herodotus (IV., 70) describes the method of covenanting among the Scythians, by the drinking of each other's blood. See p. 61 f., supra.

which the contracting parties became one by actually drinking or tasting one another's blood. The seven stones in Herodotus are of course sacred stones, the Arabic *ansâb*, Hebrew *massêbôth*, which, like the sacred stones at the Ka'ba were originally Baetylia, Bethels or god boxes. So we find in *Tâj.* iii. 560, a verse of Rashêd ibn Ramêd of the tribe of 'Anaza, ' I swear by the flowing blood round 'Aud, and by the sacred stones which we left beside So'air.' So'air is the god of the 'Anaza (*Yacût* iii. 94) and 'Aud [is the god] of their allies and near kinsmen Bakr-Wâil (*Bakri* p. 55). We see then that two groups might make themselves of one blood by a process of which the essence was that they commingled their blood [or a substitute therefor], at the same time applying the blood to the god or fetish so as to make him a party to the covenant also. Quite similar is the ritual in Exod. xxiv., where blood [the blood of the ox] is applied to the people of Israel and to the altar."

In added illustration of the gradations of substitution in the symbolism of blood-covenanting, Professor Smith shows, by various citations, that among the early Arabians fruit-juice and wine-dregs were sometimes " taken to imitate blood." [1] This is an incidental verification of the position taken in this volume (at pages 191-202) concerning " symbolic substitutes for blood ; " a position which finds added proof in Plutarch's *De Iside* (6).

Is it, indeed, really true that " there is a wide step between a union made by the inter-transfusion of blood and the union made by substitute blood, whether [in the case of the blood of the substitute ox in Madagascar, of the substitute sheep or goat in Arabia, or of the substitute ox] sprinkled on both parties, as at Sinai [or by which they are anointed as in China and Borneo], or poured in the sacrifice of a victim whose flesh is eaten as a symbol of sharing the life and the nourishment of Deity [as in India, in Assyria, in Arabia, in Egypt, in Europe, and in America]"? Or, however wide this step may be, is it not shown to have been taken so early in the history of the race as to

[1] *Kinship and Marriage in Early Arabia*, note 5, at p. 260 ff.

30

have left its traces in the terminology of the Bible—written in the light of these primitive customs ?

BLOOD MAKES UNITY : EATING SHOWS UNION.

It is having a common blood, not partaking of food in common, that makes unity of life between two parties who are brought together in covenant. Yet the sharing of food is often a proof of agreement, or even of agreed union; and all the world over and always the act of eating together accompanies, or rather follows, the rite of covenanting by blood.[1] Never, however, is the mere eating in common supposed to perfect a vital union, or an organic unity, between the parties to a mutual feast; while the sharing a common blood, or an accepted substitute for blood, through its tasting or by being touched with it, is supposed to perfect such a unity. So far biblical and extra-biblical symbolisms agree.

A "covenant union in sacrifice"[2] is an indefinite and ambiguous term. It may mean a covenant union wrought by sacrifice, or a covenant union accompanied by sacrifice, or a covenant union exhibited in sacrifice. But, in whatever sense it is employed, the fact remains true, that, wherever a bloody offering is made in connection with sacrifice and with covenanting, it is the blood-drinking, the blood-pouring, or the blood-touching, that represents the covenant-making; while eating the flesh of the victim, or of the feast otherwise provided, represents the covenant-ratifying, or the covenant-showing.[3]

Thus at Sinai the formal covenanting of the Lord with his people was accompanied by sacrificing.[4] Representatives of the people of Israel " offered burnt-offerings, and sacrificed peace-offerings of oxen unto the Lord." Nothing is here said of the technical sin-offering, but the whole burnt-offering and the peace-offering are included. The blood-outpouring and the blood-sprinkling preceded any feasting. And as if to make it clear that " by sprinkling the blood " and *not* " by eating the flesh of

[1] See pp. 41, 148–190, 240, 268 f.   [2] See p. 345, *supra.*
[3] See pp. 147–190.   [4] Exod. 24 : 1–11.

the victim," the " covenant union in [this] sacrifice was represented," Moses took a portion of the blood and "sprinkled [it] on the altar," and another portion "and sprinkled it on the people," saying as he did so, " Behold *the blood of the covenant,* which the Lord hath made with you." It was not until after this covenanting by blood, that the people of Israel, by their representatives, " did eat and drink " in ratification, or in proof, or in exhibit, of the covenant thus wrought by blood.

The Babylonian Talmud finds in the prohibitions of blood-eating, in Leviticus 17 : 3–14, a command " not to eat any portion of a sacrifice before its blood is sprinkled upon the altar." [1] Professor Robertson Smith shows from Arabic authorities that of old in Arabia "it required a *casâ-ma* [or a covenanting sacred rite] to enable two tribes to eat and drink together." [2] And this *casâma* he shows to have included ordinarily among Arabians a common blood-drinking or blood-sprinkling, similar to that described at Mount Sinai.[3] This custom indeed would seem to have a trace in the common Oriental mode of hastening to kill a lamb, or a calf, as the first act in receiving a guest; [4] pouring out the covenanting blood and then sharing the flesh of the peace-offering. Any one familiar with Oriental customs can testify to the prevalence of this method of receiving a guest. Thus with Arabs, as with Hebrews, the real covenant-union in sacrifice was *represented* by the blood-sharing, and was *celebrated* by the feast-partaking.

Maimonides calls attention to the fact that in the Mishnah there is a suggestion of a commingling of two bloods in a covenant-rite between the Lord and his people, at the time of the exodus. This is quite in accord with the suggestion in this volume that in the rite of circumcision it was Abraham and his descendants who supplied the blood of the covenant, while in the passover-sacrifice it was the Lord who commanded the substitute blood in token of his blood-covenanting. Refer-

---

[1] Cited in Friedländer's *Guide of the Perplexed of Maimonides*, note at p. 233.

[2] *Kinship and Marriage in Early Arabia*, note at p. 262.

[3] *Ibid.*, pp. 48–50.   [4] See Gen. 18 : 1–8 ; 1 Sam. 28 : 21–24.

ring to the command, in Exodus 12 : 44–48, for the circumcision of the Israelites as precedent to their partaking of the passover (the covenanting by blood to precede the exhibit of the covenant in sharing the flesh of the sacrifice), Maimonides says of the Mishnah teachings : " The number of the circumcised being large, the blood of the Passover and that of the circumcision flowed together [thus perfecting a blood-covenant]. The Prophet Ezekiel (16 : 6), referring to this event, says, ' When I saw thee sprinkled with thine own blood, I said unto thee, Live because of thy blood,' *i. e.*, because of the blood of the Passover and that of the circumcision [thus commingled]." [1] The question of the correctness of this exegesis of Ezekiel's words is, of course, unimportant as affecting the proof here given of the rabbinical recognition of the blood-covenanting idea in the Exodus narrative.

Another Jewish teacher, cited by Cudworth,[2] said of the influence of the Old Testament sacrifices, that "the *blood* of beasts offered up in sacrifice had an attractive power to draw down Divinity, and unite it to the Jews." Yet again, Hamburger, one of the foremost rabbinical authorities of the present day, insists that the very word for " atonement," in the Hebrew, commonly taken to mean " a cover," or "a covering," has in it more properly the idea of a compassed union, or an " at-one-ment." He says : [3] " I hold the word *kaphar*, in the sense ' to pitch ' [to overlay with pitch, Gen. 6 : 14] ' to fill up the seam ' [' to close up the chasm '], as a symbolic expression for the *reunion* of the sinner with God." And it is not the *flesh* of the sacrifice, but the *blood*, that God counts the atonement, or the means of at-one-ment between the sinner and himself.[4]

That " sprinkling the blood " toward the altar in the Jewish sacrifices as preliminary to " eating the flesh of the victim," represented the idea

[1] Friedländer's *Guide*, p. 232. See, also, Lightfoot's *Hor. Heb.*, IV., 241.

[2] See citation from " that learned Hebrew book Cozri," in Cudworth's *Intellectual System of the Universe*, Am. Ed., II., 537.

[3] Hamburger's *Real Encyclopädie f. Bibel u. Talmud*, I., 804, note.

[4] See Lev. 17 : 11.

of *blood-drinking*, as in the primitive mode of blood-covenanting, would seem to be indicated by the words of the Lord in Psalm 50: 12, 13:—

> "If I were hungry, I would not tell thee:
> For the world is mine, and the fulness thereof.
> Will I eat the flesh of bulls,
> Or drink the blood of goats?"

"For though it be here denied," says Cudworth,[1] "that God did really feed upon the sacrifices, yet it is implied that there was some such allusive signification in them" in the minds of their offerers; and that the blood-sprinkling represented the covenant blood-drinking, as surely as the flesh-sharing represented the covenant-celebrating. Why should the Lord say that he does not care to drink the blood of goats, if no one of his worshipers ever thought of his doing so?

Every gleam of the old religions goes to show that it was blood-sharing, and not food-sharing, that made a vital union—for the life that is or for the life that is to come. Thus "for the significance which the Arabs down to the time of Mohammed attached to the tasting of another man's living blood, there is an instructive evidence in Ibn Hishâm, p. 572. Of Malik, who sucked the prophet's wound at Ohod and swallowed the blood, Mohammed said, ' He whose blood has touched mine cannot be reached by hell-fire.' "[2] Not he who shared a meal with the prophet, but he who had become a partaker of his blood, which was his life, was in vital union with the prophet—so that not even death could finally separate the two.

Whether all bloody sacrifices included the idea of covenant-union as immediately accomplished, or whether, again, they sometimes merely looked toward covenant-union through atonement as their ultimate fruition, may indeed be a point in question; but that "covenant-union in [bloody] sacrifice" as finally accomplished was represented in its accomplishing not by the *flesh*, but by the *blood*, would seem to be a fact

[1] *Intellect. Syst.*, II., 537.

[2] W. Robertson Smith's *Kinship and Marriage in Early Arabia*, p. 50.

30*

beyond fair question. On this point Bähr, out of his world-wide outlook over religious symbols, says : [1] " Everywhere, from China to Iceland, the blood is the chief element, the kernel, and the central point, of sacrifice. In blood lies its [i. e. sacrifice's] peculiar efficacy ; through blood is its peculiar action; blood is synonymous with sacrifice ; it *is* the sacrifice in the narrower sense. . . . In this point the Mosaic sacrifice harmonizes perfectly with the heathen. . . . To sacrifice is to proffer and to receive *life*. When the blood is shed and it streams forth, a life is given to the divinity to which the sacrifice is dedicated. This giving is at the same time the taking (the receiving) of a life from the divinity ; and the sacrifice looks also, in general, to a binding together of life, or to a communion of life between those offering and the divinity. In so far as this communion is the end and object of all religion, every cult concentrates finally in sacrifice [and 'blood is synonymous with sacrifice ; it *is* the sacrifice in the narrower sense ']."

This view of blood-union in, or through, typical sacrifices, thus found to be held by Jewish rabbis and by later Arabians, as well as by adherents of the ethnic religions, shows itself more or less clearly in writings of the Christian Fathers, in their explanation of the covenant relation between Christ, as the Antitype of all bloody sacrifice, and his trustful people. For example, Ignatius says : [2] " I desire the drink of God, his blood, which is love incorruptible and life eternal ; " and again : [3] " Being kindled to new life in the blood of God, [4] ye have accomplished wholly the work of that relationship." [5] Says Clement of Alexandria : [6] " In all respects, therefore, and in all things, we are brought into union with Christ, into relationship through his blood, by which we are redeemed ; " and again : [7] " To drink the blood of Jesus, is to become

---

[1] *Symbolik*, II., 262 f.   [2] *Ad Romanos*, 7.   [3] *Ad Ephesios*, 1.

[4] The old Latin version gives the " blood of Christ God."

[5] The Greek words, *to syngenikon ergon* (τὸ συγγενικὸν ἔργον), are otherwise translated : by Horneman, " work worthy of Christian brothers ; " by Hefele, " the work of brotherhood."

[6] *Paedagogus*, II., 5.   [7] *Ibid.*, II., 2.

partaker of the Lord's immortality." Later on, Julius Firmicus says :[1] "We drink the immortal blood of Christ. Christ's blood is joined to our blood. This is the salutary remedy for your offenses."

A similar idea of the covenanting force of blood in the symbolism of the Old Testament and of the New, is again indicated in the fact that so many of the Christian Fathers saw a token of the blood-covenant in the scarlet cord which Joshua commanded Rahab to let down from her window as the token of the covenant whereby she was made one with the people of God.[2] Thus Clement of Rome[3] and Justin Martyr[4] counted this token a symbol of the blood of Christ, while Irenæus[5] deemed it a symbol of the original passover blood ; all alike seeming to look upon it as a covenant-token ; as, indeed, the scarlet cord has been thus recognized in many parts of the world down to the present day.[6] Justin Martyr is yet more explicit in his recognition of the blood-covenant idea in the earlier and the later conjoining of God's people with Himself. Referring to the old covenant-token of circumcision, whereby the descendants of Abraham became partakers of God's covenant with Abraham, he says :[7] "The blood of that circumcision is obsolete, and we trust in the blood of salvation ; there is now another covenant."

Under the old covenant and under the new, as likewise in all the ethnic religions as well as in the Jewish ritual, covenant-union in sacrifice is represented by blood as its nexus, and by flesh, or bread, as its exhibit. Only through blood—through the proffer of flowing blood— can man be brought into that covenant at-one-ment with God, or with the gods, which justifies the exhibit of that covenant at-one-ment or union between the two parties, in mutual food-sharing.

---

[1] *De Errore*, 22 ; cited in Wilberforce's *Doctrine of the Holy Eucharist*, p. 225.

[2] Josh. 2 : 1–21 ; 6 : 16–25.   [3] *Ad Corinth.*, 22.

[4] *Dial. Cont. Tryph.*, cap. 111.   [5] *Opera*, IV., 20, 12.

[6] See p. 236 f., *supra*.   [7] *Dial. Cont. Tryph.*, cap. 24.

ETHNIC REACHINGS AFTER UNION WITH THE DIVINE.

Among all peoples, from the beginning, sacrifice has been a means of seeking union with the divine—with God or with the gods. And through sacrifice this divine-human inter-union has been deemed a possibility, in all lands and always. The idea of such a union between the human nature and the divine has inevitably come to partake of the grossness of the religious conceptions of the different peoples holding it; but even in its grossest form it has remained a witness to the primal truth which prompted it.

The ancient kings of Assyria and cf Egypt were accustomed to claim a common nature with the chief divinities which they worshiped; and this divine kinship was both secured and confirmed to them through their sacrifices in their royal-priestly character.[1] Renouf shows that this belief in the divine nature of the Egyptian sovereigns existed from " the earliest times of which we possess monumental evidence; " moreover, that these kings both sought and claimed a union with the divine by their multiplied sacrifices, and that " they are also represented as worshiping and propitiating their own genius; " since they were both god and man through their inter-union with the divine. It has already been shown that this outreaching for union with the divine was at the basis of sacrifice in India,[2] in China,[3] in Persia,[4] in Peru,[5] in Tahiti.[6] Bähr[7] and Réville[8] find this as the truth of truths in every cult; and there would seem to be gleams of this truth in the well-nigh universal habit, on the part of worshipers, of taking the name of a divinity as a portion of one's own name; thereby claiming a right to be counted as in family oneness with the object of one's sacrificial worship.

[1] Renouf's *Religion of Ancient Egypt*, pp. 167–172; and pp. 79–83, 165–169, 170–173, *supra.*

[2] See pp. 155–164, *supra.* [3] See pp. 148–154, *supra.* [4] See p. 169 f., *supra.*

[5] See pp. 175–178, *supra.* [6] See p. 328 f., *supra.* [7] Cited at p. 297, *supra.*

[8] Cited at p. 183, *supra.*

In fact, the very meaning of the primitive Chinese word, or character, for " sacrifice,"—a word which claims to show its use at least forty-five centuries ago,—gives a gleam of this universal heart yearning after divine-human inter-union as surely as the definition of " sacrifice." Dr. Legge says[1] of the Chinese term for "sacrifice " (*tsî*): " The most general idea symbolized by it is—an offering whereby communication and communion with spiritual beings is effected." Says St. Augustine:[2] " A true sacrifice is every work which is done that we may be united to God in holy fellowship, and which has a reference to that supreme good and end in which alone we can be truly blessed." So it is that all sacrifice—whether under ethnic longings or under Bible teachings— was a reaching out after at-one-ment between the human and the divine ; and this apart from any question as to the speculative philosophy of the at-one-ment.

Concerning the traditional view, in Arabia, of blood as a means of fellowship with divinities, Maimonides says:[3] " Although blood was very unclean in the eyes of the Sabeans, they nevertheless partook of it because they thought it was the food of the spirits ; by eating it man has *something in common* with the spirits, which join him and tell him future events, according to the notion which people generally have of spirits. There were, however, people who objected to eating blood, as a thing naturally disliked by man ; they killed a beast, received the blood in a vessel or in a pot, and ate of the flesh of that beast, whilst sitting around the blood. They imagined that in this manner the spirits would come to partake of the blood which was their food, whilst the idolaters were eating the flesh ; that love, brotherhood and friendship with the spirits was established, because they dined with the latter at one place and at the same time ; that the spirits would appear to them in dreams, inform them of coming events, and be favorable to them. Such ideas people liked and accepted in those days ; they were general,

---

[1] *The Religions of China*, p. 66. [2] *The City of God*, X., 6.
[3] *Guide of the Perplexed*, Friedländer's Translation, III., 232.

and their correctness was not doubted by any one of the common people. The Law, which is perfect in the eyes of those who know it, and seeks to cure mankind of these lasting diseases, forbade the eating of blood, and emphasized the prohibition exactly in the same terms as it emphasized idolatry: 'I will set my face against that soul that eateth blood' (Lev. 17 : 10). The same language is employed in reference to him, 'who giveth of his seed unto Molech;' 'then I will set my face against that man' (Lev. 20 : 5). There is besides idolatry and eating blood no other sin in reference to which these words are used. For the eating of blood leads to a kind of idolatry, to the worship of spirits. . . . The commandment was therefore given that whenever a beast or a bird that may be eaten is killed, the blood thereof must be covered with earth (Lev. 17 : 13) in order that the people should not assemble round the blood for the purpose of eating there. The object was thus fully gained to break the connection between these fools and their spirits. This belief flourished about the time of our teacher Moses. People were attracted and misled by it. We find it in the Song of Moses (Deut. 32 : 17): 'They sacrificed unto spirits, not to God.'"

On the same point Rabbi Moses bar Nachman says[1] of the ancient "heathens in their worship of their idol gods:" "They gathered together blood for the devils their idol gods, and then they came themselves and did eat of that blood with them, as being the devils' guests, and invited to eat at the table of devils; and so were *joined in federal society* with them."

Strabo says,[2] that the Persians reserved for the use of the offerers all the "flesh" of their sacrifices; "for they say that God requires the soul [ψυχή, *psyche*—the blood] and nothing else." And this idea, that the divinities were fed and nourished by the blood of sacrifices, while the worshipers were brought into communion and union with the divinities through this offering, seems to have prevailed among the Greeks and

---

[1] Cited in Cudworth's *Intellectual System of the Universe*, Andover ed., II., 542.

[2] *Geographica*, XVII., 13 (732).

Romans; and even many of the Christian fathers accepted its truth as applicable to the demons.[1] For example, St. Basil says:[2] " Sacrifices are things of no small pleasure and advantage to demons; because the blood, being evaporated by fire, is taken into the compages and substances of their bodies: the whole of which [bodily substance] is throughout nourished with vapors."

THE VOICE OF OUTPOURED BLOOD.

It has already been shown, in this volume, that in all ages blood unjustly spilled has been supposed to have the power of making its voice heard against him who poured it out by violence. This is the Bible representation of the first blood which stained the hands of a murderer. " The voice of thy brother's blood crieth unto me from the ground,"[3] was the Lord's declaration to Cain. And down to the latest times, and in all lands, there have been vestiges of this primitive belief of mankind—as thus sanctioned in the inspired revelation of God.[4] Yet, because of the sophisticated and conventional idea which has gradually come to possess the Occidental mind that in some way blood stands for *death* and not for *life*, the Oriental and Biblical idea of blood as in some sense voiceful even when separated from the body, has been so lost sight of as to be a means of shadowing and perverting various Bible texts and teachings.

A chief prominence attaches to Abel, even in the New Testament record, from the fact that his blood was voiceful after its spilling by his brother Cain. Where he appears, at the head of the martyr roll of the heroes of faith, in the eleventh chapter of Hebrews, this it is which is named as a crowning consequence of his spirit of faith. " By faith

[1] See citations from Porphyry and Origen, and references to many other writers in Harrison's Cudworth's *Intellectual System of the Universe*, with Mosheim's Notes, III., 350–352.

[2] In Commentary on Isaiah, cited in Harrison's Cudworth, as above.

[3] Gen. 4: 10.   [4] See pp. 143–147, *supra*.

Abel offered unto God a more excellent sacrifice than Cain, through which he had witness borne to him that he was righteous, God bearing witness in respect of [or over] his gifts; and through it [through this faith which gave him acceptance with God] *he being dead yet speaketh*" [1]—even after he is dead his voice is heard as before his death. It is not Abel's *memory* but Abel's *self*—his soul, his life, his blood—which is here represented as speaking; and a reference to the Old Testament record shows how it was that Abel being dead yet spoke. So again, the contrast between the blood of Jesus and the blood of Abel [2] in the potency of their voices [3] gives emphasis to the fact that it was the speaking of Abel's spilled blood that marks Abel's place in the sacred record.

That this voicefulness of the outpoured blood of the proto-martyr Abel was, in the days of the New Testament writing, understood in a peculiar literalness on the part of the Jews, is evidenced not only in this reference to it in the Epistle to the Hebrews, but in a Talmudic reference to the traditional voicefulness of a later martyr's blood, and in a coupled reference by our Lord to the two martyrdoms—in the light of their traditional outspeaking. Both the Jerusalem Talmud and the Babylonian tell of the irrepressible voice of Zechariah the son of Jehoiada, who was slain by King Joash [4] in the court of the priests of

[1] Heb. 11 : 4.   [2] Heb. 12 : 24.

[3] It is said that the blood of Jesus speaks better—not "better things" as our old version had it—than the blood of Abel. The Greek word here rendered "better" is *kreittona* (κρείττονα) "more mightily," "more surpassingly," "more excellently" (comp. Heb. 1 : 4; 7 : 7), "*not* more satisfactorily," nor yet "more lovingly." The voice of Abel (for the voice of Abel's blood is Abel's voice) was heard and heeded in its day. The voice of Jesus (for the voice of the blood of Jesus is the voice of Jesus (comp. Heb. 10 : 29) is a voice more worthy than Abel's of being heard. Therefore—"see that ye refuse not him that speaketh" (see Heb. 12 : 25). Not the memory but the very self of the martyr, in every instance, gives the voice which is to be heard and heeded as a witness to the truth.

[4] 2 Chron. 24 : 17-25.

the first temple. His blood which was left there would not be quiet. "When therefore Nebuzar-adan [the captain of the Babylonian guard put in charge of Jerusalem by Nebuchadrezzar [1]] went up thither, he saw the blood [still] bubbling; so he said to them, 'What meaneth this?' 'It is the blood,' say they, 'of calves, lambs and rams, which we have offered on the altar.' 'Bring then,' said he, 'calves, lambs and rams, that I may try whether this be their blood.' They brought them and slew them, and *that* blood still bubbled, but *their* blood did not bubble. [The one had a voice, the other had not.] 'Discover the matter to me,' said he, 'or I will tear your flesh with iron rakes.' Then they said to him, 'This was a priest, a prophet, and a judge, who foretold to Israel all these evils which we have suffered from you, and we rose up against him, and slew him.' 'But I,' saith he, 'will appease him.' [His voice shall not be unheeded.] He brought the rabbins and slew them upon that blood, and yet it was not pacified : he brought the children out of the school, and slew them upon it, and yet it was not quiet; he brought the young priests, and slew them upon it, and yet it was not quiet. So that he slew upon in it [in all] ninety-four thousand,[2] and yet it was not quiet. He drew near to it himself, and said, 'O Zacharias, Zacharias! thou hast destroyed the best of thy people' [that is, they have been killed for your sake] ; 'would you have me destroy all?' Then it was quiet, and did not bubble any more."[3]

The question is not as to the truthfulness of this narration, but as to its existence as a Jewish tradition in the days of our Lord. Putting it, therefore, alongside of the Bible record of Abel's voiceful blood, as explained in the Epistle to the Hebrews, and what fresh force it gives to the declaration of Jesus concerning the reproachful outcry of the blood of all the martyrs, against those who in his day represented the spirit

---

[1] Anachronisms of this sort are not uncommon in the Talmud.

[2] These figures are quite in accordance with the exaggerations of the Talmud.

[3] Citations from Jerusalem Talmud, *Taaneeth*, fol. 69 : 1, 2 ; and Babylonian Talmud, *Sanhedreen*, fol. 96 : 2 ; in Lightfoot's *Horæ Hebraicæ*, II., 303–308.

which caused their martyrdom : " That upon you may come all the righteous blood shed on the earth, from the blood of Abel, the righteous, unto the blood of Zachariah, son of Barachiah,[1] whom ye slew between the sanctuary and the altar." [2]

The blood is the life, and when the life is united to God by faith the death of the body cannot silence the voice of him who is in covenant oneness with God.

GLEANINGS FROM THE GENERAL FIELD.

In the study of this entire subject, of the relation of blood and of blood-covenanting to the primitive religious conceptions of the race, fresh material out of the rites and customs of different peoples in various ages is constantly presenting itself on every side. A few illustrations of this truth are added herewith, without regard to their special and separate classification.

The idea that transferred blood was transferred life, and that the receiving of the blood of a sacred substitute victim was the receiving of the very life of the being represented by that substitute, showed itself in the worship of Cybele, in the ancient East, in a most impressive ceremony. " The Taurobolium of the ancients was," as we are told, " a ceremony in which the high-priest of Cybele was consecrated; and might be called a baptism of blood, which they conceived imparted a spiritual new birth to the liberated spirit. . . . The high-priest about to be inaugurated was introduced into a dark excavated apartment, adorned with a long silken robe, and a crown of gold. Above this apartment [which would seem to have represented a place of burial] was a floor perforated in a thousand places with holes like a sieve, through which the blood of a sacred bull, slaughtered for the purpose, descended in a copious torrent upon the inclosed priest, who received

---

[1] As to the question concerning the identity of this martyr with the son of Jehoiada, see Lightfoot, as above.

[2] Matt. 23 : 35; Luke 11 : 51.

the purifying [or re-vivifying] stream on every part of his dress, rejoicing to bathe with the bloody shower his hands, his cheeks, and even to bedew his lips and his tongue with it [thereby tasting it and so securing the assimilation of its imparted life]. When all the blood had run from the throat of the immolated bull, the carcass of the victim was removed, and the priest issued forth from the cavity, a spectacle ghastly and horrible, his head and vestments being covered with blood, and clotted drops of it adhering to his venerable beard. As soon as the pontifex appeared before the assembled multitude the air was rent with congratulatory shouts; so pure and so sanctified, however, was he now esteemed that they dared not approach his person, but beheld him at a distance with awe and veneration." [1]

Here seems to be the idea of a burial of the old life, and of a new birth into the higher nature represented by the substitute blood; as that idea appears in the Norseland method, of entering into the blood-covenant under the lifted sod. [2] It also appears to represent the receiving of new life by the bath of blood. [3]

Even down to our own time in such a land as China, where the symbolism of blood seems to have as small prominence as in any portion of the world, there are vestiges of the primitive custom of partaking of the blood, and eating of the heart as the blood-fountain, in order to absorb the life of the victim; a custom which, as has been already noted, has prevailed in the primitive East and in the primitive West. [4] Thus it is recorded that, as late as 1869, one Aching and his brother, of Sinchew, in the province of which Canton is the capital, were engaged in various local conflicts and finally sought refuge in Fukien Province. There they were killed and mutilated, and " Aching's heart was cut out, boiled, and eaten by his savage captors, under the notion that they would

[1] This is cited as from a classical authority, through Maurice's Indian *Antiquities* (v. 196), in a note to Burder's Whiston's Josephus (*Antiq.* III., 9).

[2] See p. 41 f., *supra.*   [3] See pp. 116–126; 324, *supra.*   [4] See pp. 99–110; 126–133

become more daring and bloodthirsty in consequence." [1] And a Canton letter in a recent issue of the North China Mail says, that " no Chinese soldier in Tonquin during the late war lost an opportunity to eat the flesh of a fallen French foe, believing that human flesh, especially that of foreign warriors, is the best possible stimulant for a man's courage; " this being clearly a vestige of the primitive belief that the transference of the material life by absorption, is a transference of spiritual identity.

Additional testimony to the vestiges of the blood-covenant as a primitive rite in China, is given in the following letter on the subject from the Rev. Dr. A. P. Happer, who was for many years a missionary in that country :—

" In reference to the form of solemn covenant as it was made anciently among the Chinese. It is expressed as a Mêng Yeuh. The last word is a covenant-agreement treaty. It is the word used in designating the treaties between nations. 'Mêng' is the word which has the use of blood in giving sanctity to the agreement. It is composed of the characters for sun, moon, and a basin. Whether the sun and moon were the objects before which the oath was taken, and the basin was that in which the blood was held, I will not affirm. It is defined : 'An oath anciently taken by smearing one's self with the blood of the victim;' then, secondarily, 'a contract, an agreement, alliance compact.' Here is almost precisely the form of covenant, as to the mode of ratifying it, as was used by Abraham.

"As to the oath which is taken by those who enter the Triad Society in China I would remark : The name 'Triad' is given because the society is bound by solemn covenant to the great powers in the world as held by the Chinese : namely, heaven, earth, and man ; the literal translation of the Chinese name 'San hop wei,'—' Three United Association.'

" This society was organized soon after the present dynasty obtained, which was in 1644. The society is said to have been formed about

---

[1] Thomson's *The Straits of Malacca, Indo-China, and China*, p. 259.

1670, for the purpose of driving out the Tatars and restoring the previous dynasty, which was a Chinese dynasty. As the founder of the previous dynasty had been a Buddhist priest, this society was composed, at first, largely of priests, and had their meetings in Buddhist temples. Hence it has always been regarded as a traitorous association and proscribed by the laws. The Taiping rebellion in 1850 to 1865 was an outcome of it. The chief of that rebellion was the head of the Triad Society, and proclaimed himself the emperor of the Great Peace Heavenly Kingdom. One of their vagaries was this, in order to conceal their Triad connection: The chief, in reading Christian books, found that the Christian God is regarded as a Trinity. Taking the word used by part of the missionary body to designate God, namely, Shangti, they designated themselves as the Shangti Association; that is, The Triune God Association.

"The initiation into this society is with the most solemn rites and binding oath. It is done in secret meeting, in a secret place, generally at night. Swords are crossed so as to form an arch, under which the new member passes, to imply that a sword is over the neck of any one who violates the covenant. Blood is drawn from his finger, and mixed with water, which he drinks. The members are called *brethren*, and the relation is more sacred and inviolable than that of brothers by birth. Any one who violates this covenant of brotherhood made with blood *must be killed* by the brotherhood. No one may protect, screen, or assist, in any way, such a delinquent, or, rather, *false* brother, one who had *falsified* such a solemn oath.

"From this narrative we see that this manner of adding sanctity to an oath in making an agreement or covenant by blood comes down from the earliest history of the Chinese people. The Triad Society adopted *this* manner of taking an oath to fulfil all the agreements and obligations of their covenant, written in thirty-six clauses, because it was the most solemn and obligatory of any known to them."

This blood-drinking as a means of courage inspiring is also linked

31*

with the idea of blood-covenanting, in an illustration given by Herodotus[1] out of the times of the Persian invasion of Egypt under Cambyses. One Phanes was blamed by the Greek and Carian allies of the Egyptians " for having [treacherously] led a foreign army into Egypt." His sons were taken by the allies, and in the sight of both armies their throats were cut, one by one, the blood being received into goblets and mingled with wine and water; " all the allies drinking of the blood " as preliminary to a united onset against the enemy thus vicariously absorbed into the being of the allied forces.

" There is no doubt," says President Washburn, of Robert College, Constantinople," [2] that among the Sclavic races the blood-covenant [as described in this volume] still exists; especially in Montenegro and Servia." A recent German writer[3] cites a Sclavic song which gives an illustration of this custom; the full meaning of which song he quite fails to comprehend, through his unfamiliarity with the rite itself. The song describes the slaughter on a battle-field at Mohaas, in Hungary, where the outpoured blood of the combatants was intercommingled in their death :

> " There as well as here was lamentation ;
> Flooded o'er with blood the field of slaughter.
> Dark alike was blood of Turk and Christian—
> Turk and Christian here by blood made brothers."

This tender reference to blood-brotherhood in death is supposed by the German writer to be made in keen irony, although he cites it from a people who are, in his opinion, less bigoted and fanatical than Muhammadans generally.

It has been already shown [4] that Poseidonios tells of the custom,

---

[1] *Hist.* III., 11.   [2] In a private letter to the author.

[3] Dr. Friedrich S. Krauss, in a paper read before the American Philosophical Society, Oct. 2, 1885; in *Proceedings of the Am. Phil. Soc.*, for January, 1886, pp. 87–94.

[4] Page 320, *supra.*

among the primitive German peoples, of opening " the veins upon their foreheads, and mixing the flowing blood with their drink," as their method of entering into the blood-covenant. A trace of this primitive custom would seem to be found in a still extant method of making brotherhood among the students in German universities. Bayard Taylor describes this ceremony as he observed it at Heidelberg, in 1846.[1] When new students are to be made "*Burschen*" (or fellows), while at the same time the bands of brotherhood are to be kept fresh and sacred among those who are already banded together in their student life, the " consecration song" of the *Landesvater* is sung with mutual beer-drinking and cap-piercing. The ceremony includes the striking of glasses together, as held in the right hand—before drinking; the crossing of swords, as held in the left hand; the piercing of each one's cap with a sword (the caps of all who take part in the ceremony being successively strung upon the two swords of those who conduct it); the exchanging of the cap-laden swords between those leaders; the return of each pierced cap to its owner; the resting of the ends of the crossed swords on the heads, covered by the pierced caps, of each pair participating in turn in the ceremony; with the singing in concert of the song of consecration, of which these two verses are an illustration :

> " Take the beaker, pleasure seeker,
>   With thy country's drink brimmed o'er!
> In thy left the sword is blinking,
>   Pierce it through the cap, while drinking
>   To thy Fatherland once more !
>
> " In left hand gleaming, thou art beaming,
>   Sword from all dishonor free !
> Thus I pierce the cap, while swearing,
>   It in honor ever wearing,
>   I a valiant Bursch will be ! "

In this rite the cap instead of the head is punctured, and the beer

[1] In *Views Afoot,* cited in Chambers's *Cyclo. of Eng. Lit.*

alone (beer as the popular substitute for wine) instead of the old-time draught of blood and wine is shared, in symbol of the cutting of the covenant of blood.

This cutting of the head, or of some other portion of the body, in order to let the blood flow out toward another as a symbol of life-giving, is a primitive custom which shows itself in many parts of the world. Bruce says:[1] "As soon as a near relation dies in Abyssinia, a brother or parent, cousin-german or lover, every woman in that relation, with the nail of her little finger, which she leaves long on purpose, cuts the skin of both her temples, about the size of a sixpence; and therefore you see either a wound or a scar in every fair face in Abyssinia." Pitts tells [2] of a practice in Algiers of cutting the arms in testimony of love showing toward the living, somewhat like that already referred to as prevalent in Turkey.[3] Letting the blood flow over the dead, or for the dead, from gashes on the head or the breast or the limbs, is a custom among various tribes of North American Indians,[4] and in different islands of the sea.[5] This would seem to be one of the primitive customs forbidden in the Mosaic law: "Ye shall not make any cuttings in your flesh for the dead."[6]

The primitive rite of blood-covenanting by the inter-transfusion of blood through the cutting of the clasped hands of the parties to the covenant, would seem to impart a new meaning to a divine assurance, in the words of the Evangelical Prophet, which has been deemed of peculiar tenderness and force—without its symbolism being fairly

---

[1] *Travels*, III., 680.

[2] *A Faithful Account of the Religions and Manners of the Mahometans*, Chap. 3.

[3] See p. 85, *supra*. See also La Roque, cited in Harmer's *Observations*, V., 435.

[4] See article on "Mortuary Customs of North American Indians," in *First Ann. Rep. of Bureau of Ethnol.*, pp. 112, 159, 164, 183, 190.

[5] See Angas's *Sav. Scenes*, I., 96, 315, 331 ; II., 84, 89 f., 212.

[6] Lev. 19: 28; 21: 5; Deut. 14: 1.

understood. Herodotus tells of the rite of blood-covenanting among the Arabians, by cutting into the palms of the hands, in order that the blood of the two may be unalterably interchanged.[1]   Isaiah, writing not far from the time of Herodotus, uses this illustration of Jehovah's unfailing fidelity to his people : " Can a woman forget her sucking child, that she should not have compassion on the son of her womb ? yea, these may forget, yet will not I forget thee.   Behold, I have graven thee upon [I have cut thee into] the palms of my hands." [2]   A mother and a child were for a time as one ; but they may be separated and become mutually forgetful.   They, however, who have become as one personality, through an intermingling of their life-blood at the palm of the hand, cannot be wholly separated.   Jehovah has covenanted with his people in a covenant that will never be forgotten by him.[3]   The covenant relation which thus makes a friend nearer and dearer than brother, or son, or daughter, or wife, it is which is referred to in the climax of human relationships in the law of Moses, as " thy friend which is as thine own soul ; " [4]   such a friend, made by the covenant of the pierced hands, will never be forgotten by his other self.

It has been already mentioned that there were indications of the blood-covenant and its involvings in the sacred writing of the Zoroastrians,[5] and in the writings of Herodotus with reference to the Persian invasion of Egypt,[6] and now, as the last pages of this volume go to press, there comes an illustration of the existence of this rite in Persia in its primitive form at the present time.

Mr. J. H. McCormick, now of Schenectady, New York, was, for

See p. 62 f.   [2] Isa. 49 : 15, 16.

[3] The attempts to explain this figure of speech (see Rosenmüller, Stolberg, Burder, Roberts, etc.) by a reference to the custom of tattooing pictures of sacred shrines on the arms and breasts of pilgrims, gives no such idea as this of loving unity between God and his people, as more enduring than that of mother and child.

[4] Deut. 13 : 6.   [5] See p. 169.   [6] See p. 365 f.

a number of years, connected with the Royal Engineers' British Service, in India and Persia. It was while he was at Dehbeed, in Persia, in the early part of 1871 that he witnessed the consummation of this rite, and he gives this description of it: "Near Dehbeed there is a large cave where jackals frequent. On the 2d of February, 1871, a boy nine years old, who was the son of Alee Muhammad, wandered into this cave, and his cries attracted the notice of Jaffar Begg (one of my ghootans, or line policemen, who was in charge of the caravansary), who immediately armed himself, and, with two powerful dogs, entered the cave, and there in a far-away corner he found young Alee Muhammad crouched. He brought him out in safety, and handed him over to his father, who lived about half a mile away. The father's joy was so great, and he was so grateful to his son's deliverer, that he, being a Persian gentleman, proposed their entering into life-brotherhood, and Jaffar Begg joyfully accepted the proposition.

"Having procured two new pocket-knives, they both, that is, Jaffar Begg and Alee Muhammad, appeared at the place appointed, about three hundred yards from my office,—Jaffar having invited me to witness the ceremony. At 10 A. M., February 4, 1871, a large Persian carpet was spread out on the sand. The two men knelt down on it, placing a small stone in front of each. These stones were brought from the centre of Muhammadan worship at Mecca. Both men prayed to God. Each man touched his sacred stone with his forehead, his mouth, and his heart three times. Then they had a pipe together; then a cup of coffee without milk or sugar; then a second prayer; then a second pipe and a second cup of coffee; then a third prayer.

"After this Jaffar took out his pocket-knife and cut Alee Muhammad's right wrist on the inside, sucking the blood from the cut. Alee Muhammad drew his pocket-knife and cut Jaffar's right wrist on the inside, sucking the blood from the cut. Both wounds bleeding freely, the wrists were brought together, wound to wound, and the two men repeated together an invocation, calling God to witness that these two persons were now made one by blood until death. Then the hakeem, or doctor, dressed their wounds. They had a final prayer together, in which all present, except myself, joined. They had another pipe, and another cup of coffee, after which they separated. The sacredness of this bond is greater than language can express."

In the modern observance of this rite in Persia, it will be seen that the main features of the rite in all the ages are preserved. The mutual tasting of the blood, the inter-transfusion of the blood, the stones of witness, the invoking of God's approval, the mutual smoking of the pipe, the drinking together, and the communion feast, all are here. The old rite and the new are one in the blending of two lives into one in God's sight.

In Gibbon's *Decline and Fall of the Roman Empire* there is an incidental suggestion of the survival of this rite along the passing centuries in Western Asia. During the struggle of Baldwin II. to preserve the waning power of the Latin Empire of Constantinople, about the middle of the thirteenth century, "the throne of the Latin emperor was protected by a dishonorable alliance with the Turks and Comans. To secure the former, he consented to bestow his niece on the unbelieving sultan of Cogni; to please the latter, he complied with their pagan rites; a dog was sacrificed between the two armies; and the contracting parties tasted each other's blood, as a pledge of their fidelity."[1]

Several Japanese students have informed me that there are survivals of the blood-covenant in Japan, in the custom of the signing of mutual covenants in the blood of the parties to the covenant.

The Rev. Dr. John G. Paton, the veteran Scotch missionary among the cannibals of the New Hebrides, testifies to the sacred character of cannibalism among that people. He informs me that they evidently seek inter-communion with the gods by partaking of the blood and the flesh of their victims. This testimony corresponds with that of other

[1] Milman's *Gibbon*, Am. ed., Vol. VI., p. 121.

missionaries as to the basis of cannibalism in the root idea of divine-human inter-communion in the blood and the flesh of substitute sacrifice.

And so all the gleanings from the world's field tend to show the unique importance of the idea of blood as the life, the offering of blood as the offering of life, the divine acceptance of blood as the divine acceptance of life, and the sharing of blood as the sharing of life. Here is the basal thought of sacrifice, in its true meaning in the sight of God and man.

INDEXES.

TOPICAL INDEX.

SCRIPTURAL INDEX.

CRITICAL ESTIMATES

OF

THE BLOOD COVENANT.

FROM *The Old Testament Student* (PROFESSOR W. R. HARPER, PH.D., EDITOR).

The volume is a marvel of research, considering that the field it covers is hitherto unexplored. The author seems to have ransacked all literature, ancient and modern, archæology, medical science, travels, poetry, and folk-lore; Egyptian, Assyrian, Greek, and Roman antiquities, Chinese and Indian lore, Scandinavian sagas, and patristic literature, have yielded their contributions of illustrative facts. This material is handled with consummate scientific skill. There is no flight of imagination, no tumid rhetoric. Everything is subordinated to a presentation of facts, and such inductions as may be derived from them by no undue pressure. We do not see, therefore, how the main principle of the book can be successfully controverted. The facts are indisputable, and they tell their own story. Nor can we refrain from commending the volume as a most striking and valuable contribution to the religious thought of the world. It is emphatically one of the few books that no religious thinker can afford to be without. We doubt if any man can rise from its perusal without feeling that his grasp of saving truth is stronger, clearer, and more comprehensive than ever before.

PROFESSOR WILLIAM HENRY GREEN, D. D., LL. D., OF PRINCETON THEOLOGICAL SEMINARY, IN *The Presbyterian Review*.

The ingenuity with which this multitude of seemingly heterogeneous details are brought into mutual relation, and the fresh and often unexpected light thrown upon them by the connection in which they are here placed, or the aspect under which they are viewed, keeps the reader constantly on the alert, and makes the volume as suggestive and instructive as it is entertaining. The enthusiasm and earnestness of the author manifest on every page cannot fail to secure attention, even from those who hesitate at some of his conclusions. . . . The most interesting chapter to a majority of readers will doubtless be that in which application is made of the principles of the volume to passages and institutions of the Bible. The illustration thus afforded of the meaning of circumcision (p. 215) is very happy; so are the remarks on the sacrifice of Isaac (p. 224), and on our Lord's words : " He that drinketh my blood hath eternal life " (p. 276).

PROFESSOR CHARLES A. BRIGGS, D. D., OF UNION THEOLOGICAL SEMINARY, IN *The New York Evangelist*.

Dr. Trumbull rightly sees that the essential thing in sacrifice is not the *death* of the victim, as is commonly supposed, but the *life* of the victim, which is secured in the blood for the purposes of the sacrifice. It is the use that is made of this blood which is the most important feature of sacrifice. . . . We thank the author for this fruit of vast labor and persevering research. It is worthy of the study of all students of religion.

PROFESSOR GEORGE E. DAY, D. D., OF YALE THEOLOGICAL SEMINARY, IN *The New Englander and Yale Review*.

By a wide induction of particulars, which exhibit favorably the learning and reading of the author, he has shown the existence, in different ages and countries, of a form of blood-covenanting in which two persons, through the intermingling of each other's blood, or by mutually tasting or drinking of it, or by its transfusion into each other's veins, establish an eternal friendship, on the basis, thus conceived to be gained, of a common life, soul, or nature. This the author presents as the true key to the symbolism of blood in sacrifice, both in the heathen world and in the Scriptures of the Old and New Testament. . . . It is no objection to this theory that it is new. If the respected author has not established on a satisfactory foundation the theory he propounds, he has been successful in bringing together an amount and variety of interesting facts bearing upon it which make his volume entirely unique.

DANIEL CURRY, D. D., LL. D., IN *The Methodist Review.*

This is a curious, a remarkable, and a very valuable book. The author in his reading having detected, as many others have done, the occurrence among widely separated races of men of the practice of making use of blood in covenant-making, set himself at work to find out the *nexus* by which this common practice among different peoples is connected together. . . . The book is well written, the subject ably thought out, and the conclusions stated in a manner wholly unobjectionable. It is well that such a book has been written, and its intelligent and discriminating reading will do good.

PROFESSOR SAMUEL IVES CURTISS, D. D., IN *The* [LONDON] *Expositor.*

"The Blood Covenant," by H. Clay Trumbull, D.D., author of "Kadesh-Barnea," and editor of *The Sunday School Times*, is a marked book. The author seems to prove beyond a doubt that the blood covenant is one of the most ancient and universal institutions. This idea is founded on the representation familiar to Old Testament scholars, that the blood stands for the life. Those who enter into the blood covenant pledge their life-blood in each other's defense, and form a more solemn bond than any which can be established by marriage or the closest natural relationships. Dr. Trumbull shows that substitute blood was the basis of inter-union between God and man, and that the shedding of blood, not the death of the victim, was the important element in sacrifice.

PROFESSOR F. GODET, D. D., NEUCHATEL, SWITZERLAND.

I have been astonished at the mass of facts which you have been able to bring together and to group around this central idea. It is a study completely new, and one which I hope will bring forth fruit.

CUNNINGHAM GEIKIE, D. D., LL. D., BOURNEMOUTH, ENGLAND.

Allow me to express my admiration at the research you display on every page; at the wide induction on which you rest your conclusions; and on the most striking results to which these conclusions point. I think it a most admirable book; intensely interesting and of the highest moment in the light it throws on things most sacred.

FROM *The Churchman.*

We hardly know which has struck us most strongly—the varied and curious learning so copiously displayed in this book, or the keen and convincing reasoning by which it is applied. It is not easy to get away from Dr. Trumbull's conclusions, or to overlook the fact that he never begs the question or forces unduly the manifold citations he uses in support of his theory. . . . In the bearing of this topic on Scripture, especially as elucidating the general idea of sacrificial covenant, and also as illuminating a host of minor passages, otherwise obscure, we acknowledge the great value of this work. It seems to us to throw a true and important light upon the sacrament of the Holy Communion, and to rescue it alike from Roman perversion and Zwinglian degradation. Throughout we have been impressed by its reserve of power, its care not to press unduly any analogy. It seems to us a model of what biblical study should be, at once removed from the indiscriminate catching at every straw of resemblance which floats on the surface, under the plea of pious opinion, and from the skeptical rationalism which would reduce everything to its lowest terms of bald and meagre interpretation.

FROM *The Examiner.*

To say that the book is interesting, fascinating, instructive, suggestive, is only to say what every intelligent reader will admit after reading a dozen pages. . . . A flood of light is poured on the Incarnation, the Atonement, the Lord's Supper. Dr. Trumbull believes his thesis. He argues for it strongly, with wide and accurate learning and with reverent faith. He has written a book that every Christian student ought to read and to re-read. You may not agree with it, but you will find it bristling with facts, and remarkably suggestive. If the author is right in his positions, then both exegesis and theology, as human sciences of divine things, are improvable sciences.

FROM *The* [GERMAN] *Reformed Quarterly Review.*

Whoever has read Dr. Trumbull's "Kadesh-Barnea" will have formed large expectations of any new book from his pen. He will expect the fruits of broad scholarship, of wide reading, of patient research, of an earnest purpose, and of a noble enthusiasm. Nor will he be disappointed in the present work, which, written in a clear, nervous, and beautiful style, fascinates the reader by its freshness and novelty. . . . The theme is new, and the treatment of it interesting and fresh. . . . The book is a marvelous array of facts gathered from every quarter under heaven. The collection of them must have involved a wide range of reading. Nor are they facts that are simply curious, or of interest to the student of myth and folk-lore, of primitive ideas and customs, and of man's origin and history. They are facts that are of the highest value, especially to the theologian, on account of the bright light they cast on many pages of the Bible. Beliefs so deeply rooted in the human mind that they find expression in forms of blood-covenanting everywhere and at all times, cannot be devoid of truth, and must be taken into account, if only for their illustrative power, when we come to the interpretation of the Scripture. Indeed, they have an important bearing on biblical doctrine, particularly on that of the Incarnation, the Atonement, and the Lord's Supper.

FROM *The American Hebrew.*

This is a most important study in biblical archæology, and manifests a spirit of research which was once distinctively German, but which has within recent years found domicile in America. Dr. Trumbull had manifested in his " Kadesh-Barnea " an industrious and patient studiousness, which, coupled with intelligence and culture, may be relied on for inviting scientific results. In the present work, however, he exhibits in a still higher degree these rare qualities. There is something veritably portentous in the thorough manner in which he masses the widely scattered facts concerning the significance of blood-covenanting among various peoples.

FROM *The Moravian.*

We consider this remarkable and original work the most important and highly significant contribution to biblical theology that has been made within recent years. . . . The book will be a revelation to many, not altogether agreeable, perhaps, to those whom it will necessitate to modify or surrender dogmas long held on the authority of speculative reason and traditional interpretations of Scripture, but heartily welcome to all who really want to know the truth, and care for it more than for mere opinions, however old and humanly authoritative. As a positive scientific commentary on all Bible teachings and references to the symbolism of sacrifice, the Atonement, and the Lord's Supper, it must take the place of every other commentary, and is absolutely essential to every open-minded student of Scripture.

Impac Chris Tian Books

FOR THOSE SEEKING MORE INFORMATION ABOUT THE BLOOD/COVENANTS

TRUMBULL, H. Clay
_____**THE SALT COVENANT**...................................12.95
_____**THE THRESHOLD COVENANT**....................12.95

Murray, Andrew
_____THE BLOOD OF THE CROSS............................6.95
_____THE TWO COVENANTS...................................6.95
_____WITH CHRIST IN THE SCHOOL OF PRAYER..6.95
Nee, Watchman
_____NORMAL CHRISTIAN LIFE...............................6.95
Price, Charles
_____THE REAL FAITH...6.95
Kenyon, E.W.
_____BLOOD COVENANT...5.75
Whyte, Maxwell
_____POWER OF THE BLOOD......................................5.99

CASSETTES

Prince, Derek
_____THE EXCHANGE MADE AT THE CROSS...........5.95
_____THE BLOOD, THE WORD, OUR TESTIMONY..5.95
_____GOD'S ATOMIC WEAPON,
            THE BLOOD OF JESUS...........................5.95

SAVE $18.24
     Entire Above Set of Books & Tapes Only $72.00

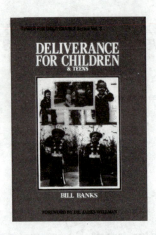

DELIVERANCE FOR CHILDREN & TEENS

The first practical handbook for ministering deliverance to children.

The material in this book is arranged to help parents in diagnosing their children's problems and in finding solutions for destructive behavior patterns.

The **Doorways** section of this book illustrates how demons enter, and how they take advantage of innocent, vulnerable children. More than a dozen categories of routes of entry are identified, and examples given!

The section on **Discipline** will be especially helpful to parents who wish to avoid problems, or remove them before they can become entrenched.

The **Mechanics of Ministry** section will help you, step by step, in ministering to a child needing help.

You will learn simple, surprising truths. For example...
* Easiest of all ministry is to small children! * Discipline is the most basic form of spiritual warfare and can bring deliverance!
* A child can acquire demonic problems through heredity or personal experience! * Deliverance need not be frightening if properly presented!

The
Acts
of
Pilate

ANCIENT RECORDS RECORDED BY
CONTEMPORARIES OF JESUS CHRIST
REGARDING THE FACTS CONCERNING
HIS BIRTH, DEATH, RESURRECTION

♦

TRANSLATED FROM THE ORIGINAL LANGUAGES
BY DRS. MCINTOSH and TWYMAN

♦

EDITED BY REV. W.D. MAHAN

This book was a favorite of the late Kathryn Kuhlman who often read from it on her radio show.

Early Church Writers such as Justin refer to the existence of these records, and Tertullian specifically mentions the report made by Pilate to the Emperor of Rome, Tiberius Caesar.

Chapters Include:
- *How These Records Were Discovered,*
- *A Short Sketch of the Talmuds,*
- *Constantine's Letter in Regard to Having Fifty Copies of the Scriptures Written and Bound,*
- *Jonathan's Interview with the Bethlehem Shepherds   Letter of Melker, Priest of the Synagogue at Bethlehem,*
- *Gamaliel's Interview with Joseph and Mary and Others Concerning Jesus,*
- *Report of Caiaphas to the Sanhedrim Concerning the Resurrection of Jesus,*
- *Valleus's Notes — "Acta Pilati," or Pilate's Report to Caesar of the Arrest, Trial, and Crucifixion of Jesus,*
- *Herod Antipater's Defense Before the Roman Senate in Regard to His Conduct At Bethlehem,*
- *Herod Antipas's Defense Before the Roman Senate in Regard to the Execution of John the Baptist,*
- *The Hillel Letters Regarding God's Providence to the Jews, by Hillel the Third*

THE ACTS OF PILATE $9.95, plus $2.00 Shipping

IMPACT CHRISTIAN BOOKS, INC.
332 Leffingwell Ave., Suite 101, Kirkwood, MO 63122

Impact Christian Books

332 Leffingwell Ave., Suite 101
Kirkwood, MO 63122

AVAILABLE AT YOUR LOCAL BOOKSTORE, OR YOU MAY
ORDER DIRECTLY. Toll-Free, order-line only M/C, DISC,
or VISA 1-800-451-2708.

Visit our Website at *www. impactchristianbooks.com*

Write for *FREE* Catalog.